D1252315

HEARTSOULDETROIT

HEARTSOUL DETROIT

CONVERSATIONS ON THE MOTOR CITY

PHOTOGRAPHS BY JENNY RISHER | EDITED BY MATT LEE

FOREWORDS BY LEE IACOCCA & LILY TOMLIN
AFTERWORD BY VERONICA WEBB

CONTENTS

OUR COUNTRY WAS BUILT BY PEOPLE
—LARGELY IMMIGRANTS—
WHO WERE HARDWORKING,

DEDICATED

AND

DETERMINED

TO MAKE A LIFE THAT WAS BETTER
FOR THEMSELVES AND THEIR FAMILIES.

FOREWORD

MY OWN IMMIGRANT PARENTS sacrificed a lot for me so that I could get a good education and make something of myself. Detroit, the city where I spent almost 60 years of my life, is my adopted hometown. And maybe only there, because of the inventiveness of Detroiters, could I have worked my way up at Ford Motor Company from student engineer to salesman to president of the company. What I was able to accomplish could only have happened in America.

I was obsessed with cars, even as a boy, but it's never been just about cars. It's about doing the right thing in whatever path you choose. The automobile industry dramatically changed Detroit in just four decades—from a frontier town in the late 1800s to one of the greatest industrial cities in the world. But more importantly, the auto industry changed the entire U.S. economy. (It also satisfied a lot of young people who fell in love with fast cars, like the Mustang, as I did.)

Look at Detroiters and you'll see that many have families who are linked in some way to the auto industry. And not just Ford, but also Olds, Dodge, Chrysler, Cadillac. They were all based in Detroit. What is it about the Motor City that made it so special? Detroit has had a knack for attracting creative people, inventors, people who are excited by a challenge. So much culture has come out of Detroit. Some of the things we take for granted in our homes or offices, like a refrigerator or an automatic coffee maker, were all invented by Detroiters.

People came to Detroit with dreams. They also worked hard and they had a purpose, whether they were following a path in the arts, music, film, sports, business or the auto industry. *Heart Soul Detroit* is a snapshot of all that's good about America. It recognizes Detroiters who, despite having humble backgrounds, were able to make significant contributions that go far beyond the borders of this city.

Because I remember my roots—as I'm sure so do many of the people in this book who were born to immigrant families, had relatives who worked in the auto industry or were born in Detroit—I believe you can never stop dreaming. And not just dreaming, but being diligent and purposeful to make your dreams a reality, no matter how much hard work that takes. That's what made America great. That's what made Detroit great.

— LEE IACOCCA

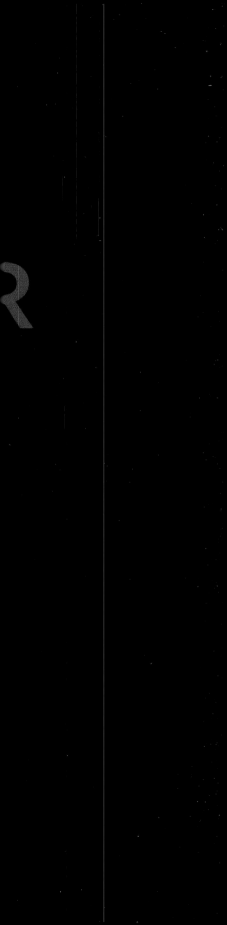

FOREWORD

WE LIVED IN AN INNER CITY, blue-collar neighborhood where I was surrounded by many different types of people—people I loved and people I loved to imitate. It was a culturally diverse city, just like the old apartment house where we lived, populated by a real cast of characters—my parents and even my kid brother Richard included. If you conjure up just about any kind of people, you'd probably find them in this apartment house. Like Detroit itself, it was a real cross section of America.

As a kid, I'd wander from apartment to apartment, just hanging out, 'playing the room' and doing whatever the folks did who lived there: If they played Rook, danced The Chicken and drank Dr. Pepper, that's what I did. If they were very old, and went to bed at 9, I made sure I showed up early. Some couldn't get or hold a job, and some were retired professionals who lived on fixed incomes and couldn't move away: Mrs. Clancy who had taught for years in a private girl's school, who wore filmy kimonos and whose lover (she'd confided) had been killed in the Spanish Civil War. Mrs. Rupert, a botanist, whose furniture was covered with camouflage silk and apartment was as green with plants as a jungle. The paperweight on her desk read 'Don't Go Away Mad—Just Go Away.' It was Mrs. Rupert who was determined to teach me to be a lady and to marry well.

Thankfully, those two lessons never took.

In my spare time, I spent a lot of time in the building's shared backyard, where I'd mingle with pensioners and young people, conservatives and communists, educated professionals, hospital workers like my mom, and factory workers like my dad. We had socialists, too, passing out their literature, and people from all kinds of different ethnic groups. I'd listen to their accents and watch their gestures, their actions—how they put on their coats or wore their hair, how they talked on the phone, you name it. How and why they laughed or cried or went crazy with rage. How they behaved when they felt rejected or accepted. I'd see the same neighbor playful one day and miserable the next. I think Ernestine and Edith Ann found their beginnings in that old building—which was razed after being burned and gutted in the 1967 riots—now a simple field waiting to flower new dreams.

This Detroit neighborhood imprinted on me the desire and inspiration to create and inhabit characters that moved, mystified or delighted me. And Detroit didn't just make an impression on me. Some people think there's a showbiz bug in the water because this city has produced so much talent. Jenny Risher and Matt Lee's book, *Heart Soul Detroit*, celebrates all the energy, creativity, and eccentricities that came out of this city, and it's this same energy and creativity that is once again moving Detroit back to the vibrant, gritty, dynamic city with all its diversity in which I grew up.

— LILY TOMLIN

DURING THE YEARS
I LIVED OFF WOODWARD AND KIRBY,

I FELL IN LOVE WITH DETROIT
AND ALL ITS

BEAUTY.

PREFACE

FOR A YOUNG PHOTOGRAPHER, it was impossible to pass up exploring the abandoned buildings that defined a decaying cityscape—Chin Tiki, the Packard plant, Michigan Central Station—they all captured my imagination. I would wonder what each building—what the entire city—had looked like in its prime. I imagined bustling streets with shiny new cars and people hurrying to and fro, the entire city moving to a Motown soundtrack. The boom of the automobile industry and Ford's $5 workday. Della Reese and the Detroit jazz scene. Hudson's department store during the holidays. The Grande Ballroom. Cars lined up on West Grand Boulevard with star-struck passengers hoping to glimpse Smokey Robinson or The Supremes coming out of Hitsville USA.

A conversation with my friend Veronica Webb about all of the amazing people, past and present, who hail from Detroit, led me to launch this project in May 2010. Along with photographing some of the most notable people who have called Detroit home, my intent was to ask them to describe the city through their experiences. My co-author Matt Lee and I began compiling a wish list of potential participants that would, hopefully, create a multidimensional portrait of the city. Of those we asked, some accepted; some declined. I personally contacted everyone who participated, communicated extensively with PR agents, managers, and personal assistants, and scheduled the sessions.

When we did get time with a participant we had an hour, if we were lucky, but often far less. *Heart Soul Detroit* took three years to complete, and the sittings occurred in many locations throughout the country, in many different environments: photo studios, tiny hotel conference rooms, backstage after concerts, office hallways, a back porch by the pool, a living room. I took great care to ensure all of the portraits appear to be shot in one location, in one room, in one day, to foster an aesthetic of collective reflection on Detroit: what the city means to the participants, how it inspired them, and where they are now because of the time they spent here. Gradually, I began to fully realize the importance of recording these stories—especially those of the older generations, of our parents and grandparents—that, layer after layer, reveal how Detroiters have been shaped by what came before.

Throughout *Heart Soul Detroit* we've adopted a unique format designed to draw you into the dialogue and make you a participant in the conversation. Each interview has been printed as a Q&A—but without the Q. This style choice allows you to be the person with whom these extraordinary individuals are directly sharing their stories—portraits both of themselves and of Detroit. Our goal has not been to remove the context in which their thoughts were shared, but rather to create as authentic a narrative as possible. Through each profile, I'm hoping you will see how the Motor City has intimately touched everyone who has set foot on her streets, and through them, all of us. There truly is 'no town like Motown.'

— JENNY RISHER

WHAT CAN ONE SAY ABOUT A CITY
THAT GAVE THE WORLD

SMOKEY ROBINSON AND IGGY POP?
BERRY GORDY AND BILL FORD JR.?
LILY TOMLIN AND LEE IACOCCA?

IS IT JUST A COINCIDENCE THAT SO MANY

VISIONARIES

HAVE CALLED DETROIT HOME?

INTRODUCTION

SOME WOULD SAY, YES—that the remarkable Detroiters we feature in this book are simply an interesting, but essentially random, collection of successful and imaginative people who might have emerged from any big city.

We doubt it. We think the answer is much more substantial: That the city of Detroit, past and present, is a unique place where dreamers have room to breathe, their visions are allowed to unfold organically and, most importantly, where the tough, spirited people possess a rare individuality and work ethic that allows them to create remarkable things.

After all, Vienna may have produced some of the world's greatest classical composers, but Detroit gave it Motown. New York in the '70s was an undeniable hotbed for rock 'n' roll—but it would never have happened without the MC5 and The Stooges. That's right, all of those über-hip New York and London rockers were taking their cues from a handful of kids from Detroit who were just doing their thing.

And Detroit is a place where a former amateur boxing star working a day job at Detroit Edison can set up shop in an anonymous rec center and turn dozens of kids into world boxing champions. That's precisely what boxing trainer Emanuel Steward, who, tragically, passed away shortly after we completed this book, did at the Kronk Gym in the '70s and '80s. Steward, like so many of the other people we feature in *Heart Soul Detroit*, had no real reason to think he would succeed, aside from his innate self-belief.

Such stories are nothing if not inspiring, and we hope that hearing all the subjects in this book tell their own stories in their own words inspires readers. One lesson to be gleaned from these pages is that the real action in life—the trenches where culture, business, and social mores are truly evolving—is rarely where the brightest spotlight is. That's a fact we learned when a skinny white rapper calling himself Eminem, from a now famously challenged background, went on to become the most successful musical act of the 2000s. Or when sports writer Mitch Albom turned a heartfelt remembrance of conversations with a sage professor into the most successful memoir ever published.

Clearly, Detroit is much more than a geographic designation. In addition to being an authentic, big-hearted place where artists and entrepreneurs have been largely unimpeded to pursue their visions, resulting in the seeds of everything from the auto industry to alternative rock, Detroiters have also, hailing back to their tough roots, always had the courage and determination to pursue their dreams. A black record mogul in 1959? A white rap star? Thirty-some world boxing champions? Who would believe that?

As you'll see in these expressive photos and insightful interviews, wonderful things happen when you combine authenticity with freedom and backbone. The men and women featured in this book accomplished amazing things as a result of their talent, determination, and vision. And they all have one more thing in common: They are all from Detroit.

— MATT LEE

BERRY GORDY

GROWING UP HERE, I always felt the warmth of the people of Detroit and heard that no one would ever starve here. Detroit was called 'The Motor City.' But it always felt more like a town to me. So I named my company Motown.

MOTOWN HAD A SIMPLE PHILOSOPHY: that all people have the same kind of feelings about love and life. And we wrote songs that reflected those feelings.

My criteria for artists was simple: They had to be talented, to work hard, and to have integrity.

WE CREATED MUSIC FOR ALL PEOPLE, black and white, Jew and Gentile, cops and robbers. Our music was a combination of everything we knew, from gospel to jazz to blues to funk. Motown could never have been what it is without the unsung heroes of the Motown family who believed in my vision, and the artists who spread their love, even after they were shot at in the South while on the Motor Town Revue tour. They and their music brought emotional integration to this country long before intellectual integration happened.

THE THEN-MAYOR OF DETROIT, Coleman A. Young, called me one day and asked me to put my feelings about Detroit into a song for the city. I responded with 'Hello Detroit.' Sammy Davis Jr. loved the song and did a marvelous recording of it. He performed it in Detroit and elsewhere, and because of that, lots of other people learned why Detroit is so special.

WHEN PEOPLE WOULD ASK ME TO DEFINE THE MOTOWN SOUND, I WOULD ALWAYS SAY,

'RATS, ROACHES, SOUL, GUTS, AND LOVE.'

Later, it became the sound of young America. Later still, it became the sound of the world.

MOTOWN MUSIC is as real and true today as it was when we made it. It will live forever. ★

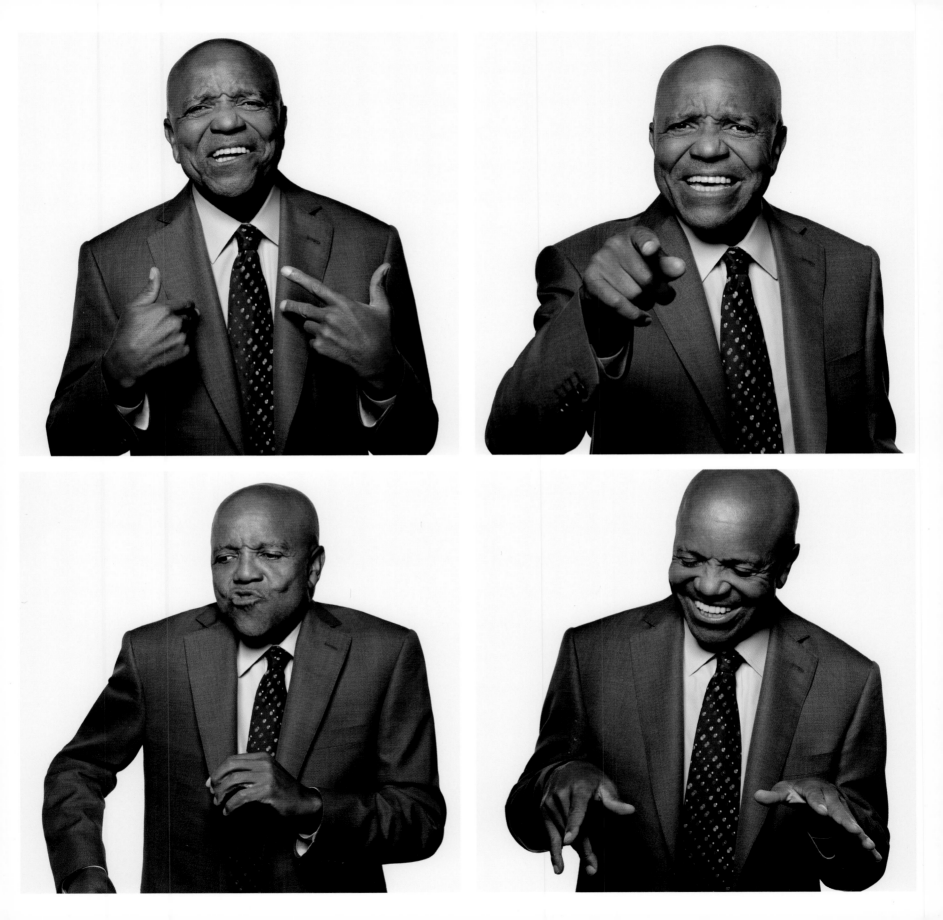

MARTHA REEVES

I FELL IN LOVE WITH MUSIC at the age of 3. My mom, when she was dressing my hair, would hold me close and teach me songs. She had a beautiful voice, and I wanted to sound like my mom. My dad played guitar and sang the blues. Being an evangelist minister's child, he didn't go worldly, but he could play the blues. He'd learned the blues by listening to records. Gave me a bit of the blues.

My biggest influence was the church, though—singing in church. I sang in church from the age of 3 on. I was always into church. That's all we had. I couldn't listen to secular music until I was 11 years old. That was the rule in our house.

DELLA REESE? I fell in love with Della at church. We were at New Liberty Baptist. And I'd go in there with a friend, because our church was becoming defunct. When granddaddy died, the church just fell apart.

We were sitting there, my first time at New Liberty Baptist, and the pastor said, 'Ah, Della's in the house; give us a song.' I didn't know who Della was. But this beautiful lady stood up, and she started singing 'Amazing Grace,' and the rafters seemed to shake and the spirit was all over that place. I was in awe of how beautiful her voice was.

The next morning I was preparing to go to my little nine-to-five at the dry cleaner's. I look at the TV, and there's Della Reese singing one of her hits. 'Don't you know, I fall in love with you...' I said, 'That's the Della that was at church yesterday! Della Reese.' So my dream activated. I said, 'She's from Detroit, maybe I can be famous, too.'

I WAS DISCOVERED when William Stevenson, better known as Mickey, came to the Twenty Grand. I'd been awarded a few nights in the club for winning an amateur contest. William Stevenson walked up to me on my third night, after I did my last song. It was 'Canadian Sunset.' I also sang 'Fly Me to the Moon' and 'Gin House Blues' that night. I wanted a variety of songs.

HE GAVE ME A CARD AND SAID, 'COME TO HITSVILLE USA; YOU HAVE TALENT.'

I went the next morning and he said, 'What are you doing here?' I said, 'Don't you remember giving me a card?' He said, 'Yeah but you're supposed to call for an audition and you didn't. I'm doing something right now. Answer this phone; I'll be right back.'

He was gone for three hours... I took over. I started answering the phone. 'A&R Department (artists and repertoire), may I help you?' By the time he got back, I was indispensable. He said, 'Can you stay the rest of the day?' I said 'OK.'

That night I had to go home and tell my parents where I was. I was 21, but I was living in my dad's house. So the A&R director's assistant took me to my house. Both he and my mom were from the South, and they had an immediate rapport. And it was all right with my dad that I go back the next day.

That went on for about five weeks. I was singing backup, doing demo records, holding auditions, helping to write songs, making up backgrounds, calling in people to do sessions. Then, at one point, it was time to find a backup group for an artist named Marvin Gaye. He was a drummer on 'the list.' There were four drummers on the Funk Brothers list: There was Benny Benjamin, Richard 'Pistol' Allen, Uriel Jones, and Marvin Gaye.

The Andantes, the girls who usually did the backup singing, weren't available. So I called in the girls I had sang with after high school, The Delfonics, and asked them to come in and do the backup work. Berry Gordy liked their sound. So we did 'I Have to Let Him Go' and 'Stubborn Kind of Fellow.'

I remember, Marvin took those glasses off his eyes, and that pipe out of his mouth, and that hat off that he wore down to cover his face, and when we looked at him we went crazy, seeing just how fine he was. He was as good-looking as Sam Cooke. I was amazed at all of that talent. Before that he'd been playing drums for Smokey Robinson on the road, very low-profile.

We were the first girls to sing behind Marvin Gaye, on 'Stubborn Kind of Fellow,' 'Hitchhike,' and 'Pride and Joy.' All of the other girls were jealous. I can say that we brought Marvin Gaye into the soul of Hitsville's music.

HOW DID WE GET OUR NAME? Berry said, 'They can't use the name Delfies for contractual reasons. If they don't come up with a name in 15 minutes we'll call them The Pansies or The Tillies.' We didn't want to be either of those. So I sat down with a pen and paper. I thought, 'Van Dyke is on the East Side; Motown's on the West Side.' There's always been an East Side-West Side war. And I wanted everybody to know I was from the East Side, because it was scary!

SO WE PUT DELLA REESE AND VAN DYKE STREET TOGETHER, AND THAT'S HOW WE GOT VANDELLA.

I'M VERY PROUD to have sang 'Dancing in the Street.' When I first heard it, Marvin Gaye was singing it. It was like a love song to a girl. It was soft and melancholy and very low-keyed. I said, 'Well, I've been in the street, dancing.' I remembered, as children, we'd block the street off, put our little record players on the porches, feed everybody on the block and we'd dance. We'd dance in the street.

I'd also been to Rio de Janeiro and carnival in New Orleans. I wanted it to seem a little more exciting, so when we recorded, I went, 'Calling out around the world…' They said, 'Oh, it's a hit!'

The music stopped, and the guys were in there saying, 'We've got it now; she did a good job.' Then the engineer said, 'I didn't have the machine on.' I wanted to kill. Anyway, I sang it again, without any stops or mistakes. That's why it has a live sound, and that's why it's so exciting. I put everything I had into it the second time.

MY LAST DAY OF CITY COUNCIL was Dec. 9, 2009. It was a thrill and a joy to serve.

I'd rather be around musicians than politicians, because they're of a different mindset. I sort of took my religion into the city council. I abstained from everything, drinking and smoking, to serve with a clear mind, and I voted the way the people who elected me wanted me to. I feel I did a real good job.

I wanted to run because, as a performer, and one of those who did not leave Detroit, I represent Motown Records. And the children look up to the Motown artists; we inspire them.

I put my hat in the ring, I won my primary, and then I won my general. Next thing you know, I'm sitting at the table, beating on the gavel, bringing the meetings to order! I'm going, 'Woo, look where I am! What did I do?'

It was a good experience. I think I did a lot of good. I passed a few ordinances. I helped get a tax break for small businesses. You don't see a lot of evicted furniture out on the streets anymore, because I suggested that we take it off to the dump after three days of sitting there. If the people whose stuff it was couldn't come back and get it, then throw it away. Don't let the kids play with it.

It was good that I did the four years, and I think I was successful, but I'm very happy to say I won't have anything else to do with politics for the rest of my life, except to vote. I'll do that.

IN TERMS OF HONORING MOTOWN, I did my best. I had a few dozen blocks of Grand Boulevard secondarily named 'Berry Gordy Boulevard.' I'm still working on getting a corporation so that I might get some statues made.

It's a dream of mine, to have a statue of Stevie Wonder sitting on some books, playing his harmonica, because Stevie got his degree in music. He went right on to college. He should be the inspiration of anyone in show business. And although she wasn't with Motown, there should be a statue of the Queen of Soul in Detroit, where she's sitting on a crown, because she has proven herself to be the undisputed Queen of Soul. ★

SMOKEY ROBINSON

BERRY GORDY IS MY BEST FRIEND. I met him quite by accident. Well, I thought it was by accident at first, but I think it was fate, because when I look back on it there was no reason for him to be where he was when I met him.

Berry was the main songwriter for Jackie Wilson, and Jackie Wilson was my idol when I was a kid growing up in Detroit. And we went to an audition for Jackie Wilson's managers, who rejected us. But Berry happened to be there. We sang five songs that I had written, two of which Berry liked. He followed us outside after they rejected us and he asked me where we got the songs. I told him I had written them, and he introduced himself.

That's how we met, and the rest is history.

When we went for that audition, we were calling ourselves The Matadors. Claudette's brother used to sing with us. But when he turned 17, he had his mother sign for him to go to the Army because he wanted to travel. We were just singing locally then, and it didn't look like we were going to get a break.

At that time, there were a lot of groups and groupettes in Detroit: The Temptations were The Primes; The Supremes were The Primettes. We were The Matadors and Claudette sang in a sister group called The Matadorettes. We used to rehearse at her house, and she knew our songs. So we called her the day of the Jackie Wilson audition and said, 'Will you go down and do this with us?' She did. Berry liked two of our songs, and he liked Claudette.

We had to change our name to a group that fit some guys with a girl, so we put a bunch of names into a hat. I happened to put 'The Miracles' in there. We shook the hat up, pulled out a name, and it was The Miracles.

So, it was a miracle!

THE REASON THAT MOTOWN only happened in Detroit? I have a belief. I was going to say a philosophy, but it's a belief. I believe that in every town, every village, every city, every suburb in the world, ratio-wise, there's the same amount of talent that was there in Detroit.

Our edge, the reason that we became what we became, was because we had Berry Gordy. He had a dream. His dream made so many dreams come true.

So, if every town and every city had a man like him, perhaps that would have happened somewhere else. But it happened on that scale because of him.

WE WERE JUST KIDS; KIDS WHO LOVED TO SING.

Diana Ross grew up four doors down from me; she was Diane then. Aretha grew up around the corner. The Temptations lived right across Woodward. One of the guys in The Miracles was Pete, and The Four Tops lived on his block.

WELL, I HAD THE FIRST HIT with The Temptations. Berry recorded some songs with them, I recorded some songs, but nobody could get a hit.

The Miracles and I had been on tour and we were heading back to Detroit. It was my turn to drive. Everybody else was asleep, and I started to hum 'The Way You Do the Things You Do.' It was just in my mind. And that was their first really big hit.

After that, all of the producers and writers jumped on The Temptations. They recorded them using Eddie Kendricks to sing lead, because he sang 'The Way You Do the Things You Do.' But David Ruffin and Paul Williams were in that group, and I knew that they were awesome singers. I figured if I could get a song David Ruffin sang sweet on and record it, I'd have a hit. And 'My Girl' was that song.

AS A SONGWRITER, 'My Girl' has become my international anthem. When I do concerts, I do a tribute to The Temptations and we end with 'My Girl.' All over the world, as soon as people hear the opening notes, they start singing.

It's way beyond anything I can explain. It's my wildest dream come true.

DIANA ROSS? We were just kids growing up on the same block. I have a niece, Sharon, and she and Diana were close friends, and Diana used to spend the night at our house.

My oldest sister raised me after my mom passed. My oldest sister had 10 kids. With me, 11. But it would be nothing for 30 kids to be at our house; it was the gathering place. And Diana was one of those kids.

After a while, she and her family moved to the Brewster projects. And the next time I heard from her she was about 16. She called and said, 'Smoke, I've got a group and I want you to hear us sing. Maybe you can sign us up with Motown.' I said, 'OK, come on down, baby!' So they came down. They were great; I loved them. Diana always had this unique voice, and I knew she had a great chance of being a terrific artist.

MOTOWN, I'M VERY PROUD TO SAY, broke down not only racial barriers, but international ones.

The first year or so that we were in business, if you were black and you were in Dearborn or Grosse Pointe, you'd better be working for somebody, and you better be able to prove it. That's how it was. But when we started to get popular, we started to get letters from white kids in those areas. 'We love your music, but our parents don't know that we have it.' Then, after a while, we'd get letters from parents! 'Hey man, we heard our kids playing your music, we love your music!'

When we first started to take the Motor Town Revue to the Deep South, we would go to an arena and one side would be white and the other side would be black. They didn't even look at each other. But when we went back a year or so later, they were dancing together; there were white boys with black girlfriends, black boys with white girlfriends, like that. We gave them something that they could share, something that they had a common love for.

Not only that, we were in the Cold War with Russia, and a couple of our acts, like The Temptations, went to Russia. They said that when they got there, it was like the King of Russia had come, with people meeting them at the airport. I'm very proud of that.

OH, I REMEMBER MY FIRST CAR distinctly. My dad was a master mechanic, so my first car, my dad went to the junkyard and got parts from about five different cars and he made me a car.

Then, he had a 1958 Pontiac. He bought himself another car and gave me the Pontiac. It was one of those cars that would go when it wanted to and stop when it wanted to. One day I had a recording session at Hitsville and I was about two blocks away from the studio and it stopped. I had to get out and leave it sitting there, people blowing their horns. I was so mad when I got to the studio. Berry's office was in the next building; I went in and said, 'Man, I have to get a car!' But I wasn't old enough. I was ranting and raving. He said, 'Calm down; when you finish your session, I'll go down and co-sign for you.'

General Motors was right down the street. I stopped at the bank on the way, got some money, and I went in and drove off in a 1962 Cadillac convertible. It was candy apple with a shiny coat on it, beige leather interior. It had everything a car could have on it in those days. They opened up the big showroom doors, and I drove it out of there for $4,800. And that was the first new car I'd ever had in my life.

FAVORITE MEMORIES? I'll do two. The Miracles and I were performing at the Michigan State Fair when 'Shop Around' was out. It had gone to No. 1. They interrupted the show and stopped us right before we sang 'Shop Around,' and Berry came up and presented us with a Gold Record. It was just awesome. 'Shop Around' was the first million-seller for Motown. What a moment.

My second one is right now. This moment, right here, because I've been doing this since way before you were born. You're here, and you're asking me about my life, what I'm doing. So I'm blessed. This is the other moment. ★

MARY WILSON

MY MEMORIES of the Brewster projects are actually quite wonderful. People think, 'Oh, you were poor, you lived in the ghetto.' But these were new buildings, so it was like living in a new apartment.

My favorite memory was singing on the streets and hanging around with all of the different people. I grew up in southwest Detroit, right on the edge of the city. And I remember when we first moved into the Brewster projects, I think it was in 1956, I was blown away, because where I'd grown up, in the neighborhoods, there weren't a lot of people. I found it very exciting. We lived in a 14-story building. Some of the projects were pretty old in the area surrounding us, but the building we moved into, the six buildings in the center, were new. So it was like moving into a new condo.

In fact, I went back a while ago and some of the same people were living there. 'Hey, Mary, how you doing? Remember me?' It was a wonderful time, the Brewster projects.

I HAVE MANY GREAT MEMORIES of Detroit, but one of them was going to Hudson's at Christmastime. It was wonderful because they would have the whole 12th floor decorated like a fantasy Christmas. Santa Claus was there, with the trees and gifts everywhere. Hudson's was the bomb!

I'll tell you, Halloween used to be such a great time. We would line up and walk all over. There would be lines of kids up and down the street, everywhere, and we would get candy. That was one of my favorite things. It was safe to run around; you'd go into all kinds of neighborhoods. Halloween was really, really fun. The children today are missing out on what we enjoyed, just being able to go any- and everywhere, and have a great time.

WELL, WHEN I STARTED SINGING, I was in kindergarten. I remember being in the glee club in the second or third grade. Our first trip was to the Ford Rotunda, where our school was chosen to sing. So that was one of the first times I sang. Then, from the third grade on, I was in every choir, glee club, ensemble. And in high school I became a soloist for our choir.

THE SUPREMES FIRST STARTED SINGING IN 1959, BUT WE WERE CALLED THE PRIMETTES.

FLORENCE BALLARD AND I attended the same school, and we entered this talent show in the eighth grade. I had just seen Frankie Lymon and The Teenagers on television, and I loved them, so I decided to pantomime to one of their records. I got my brother's do-rag, because in those days the black guys wore processes, so they would put this rag around their forehead so the grease wouldn't roll down. I brought my brother's, and then I also used his black leather jacket. I had on some jeans and a comb in my back pocket.

I was pantomiming 'I'm Not a Juvenile Delinquent.' Florence Ballard was at the same show but I didn't know her at the time. She came and she sang, 'Ave Maria,' and boy, I was mesmerized, because her voice was so big and beautiful. We were only 13 years old, maybe 12.

After the show, she and I got together and we were talking. She said, 'You had the crowd going,' and I said, 'Your voice is really beautiful; we should become friends.' And we walked home from school that day and we became best friends. Then we said, 'You know, everyone's starting these little groups and they're singing, so we should, too. If anyone asks us, let's remember each other.'

Sure enough, some months later, some guys approached her about being in a group. It just so happened that her sister was

dating their manager, Milton Jenkins. And he said he wanted to put a girl's group together to match the boy's group. They were called The Primes. Two of them, Paul Williams and Eddie Kendricks, went on to become two of The Temptations.

So Florence asked me if I would want to be part of it, and I said, 'Yeah, but I've got to ask my mom.' One of the guys, Paul Williams, went over and asked Diane if she wanted to be a member. We didn't really know each other very well; we just lived in the same area. There was one other girl, Betty McGlown, and she was actually, probably, the first one in the group.

That's how we came together as The Primettes. And, of course, everybody knows, years later, we became The Supremes. That's how we started.

WE WERE THE PRIMETTES from 1959 until 1961. Then we went to Motown Records to audition, and after Berry Gordy finally signed us, or said he would sign us, he said he didn't like our name and that we should change it. We didn't really want to change it; we liked it. But in order to sign the contracts, we had to change it. We each went out to neighbors, friends, anyone we knew, and we asked them, 'What do you think we should change our name to?'

So then it was time to sign the contracts. No one had brought in their little slip of paper with all the names we had collected except Florence. So Berry said, 'You've got to have a new name.' Florence said, 'I know. Out of all of the names I collected, I'm going to choose The Supremes,' which was on her list.

WE THOUGHT, 'SUPREMES?
THAT SOUNDS LIKE A BUILDING OR SOMETHING.' WE DIDN'T LIKE IT AT ALL.

But we had to take it because we had to sign the contracts then and there. We were just teenagers, which was really cool.

THE FIRST TIME WE MET BERRY GORDY? Probably in 1960 or 1961. We got an audition with Motown. I remember how excited we were. We said, 'We've got to make sure we're dressed right,' and we picked our favorite songs, and we went to the studio and auditioned for Mr. Gordy.

We thought they liked us, but then, at the end of the audition, Mr. Gordy said, 'You girls are really good, but maybe you should come back and see me after you graduate from high school.' Talk about a downer. It was a real downer.

That was our first encounter with Mr. Gordy. But pretty soon we convinced him that he should sign us, and he did. And that's the story.

BEST CONCERT? Oh gosh. Florence, Diane and I doing 'The Ed Sullivan Show' was perhaps the best time in my life. Because, first of all, we didn't have any recordings that were big prior to that. We had about seven recordings that were local hits.

Then, another one of the best memories is when we were doing Dick Clark's Caravan of Stars. We were on that with The Drifters, The Shirelles, and I met all kinds of people. Our record 'Where Did Our Love Go' was released at the same time we were on tour. In the middle of the tour, our record went to No. 1. So we became stars while we were on tour. I remember how very happy we were, because our dream had come true.

WITH 'WHERE DID OUR LOVE GO,' we had recorded maybe six, seven, eight songs that did not become hit records. So when Berry Gordy put us with Holland-Dozier-Holland they brought us a number of songs, and one of them was 'Where Did Our Love Go.' And we didn't necessarily like the song. It's very simple.

They said, 'No, trust us, it's going to be a hit.' So we had to record it. And we did, and it became a hit. So, we were wrong, they were right.

FLORENCE BALLARD, unfortunately, died at a very young age, so it's hard for me to summarize what she would say today. She didn't have a chance to live the full range of her life. She was so young. But if she were still here today, and God, I wish she were, I think she would still want to be remembered as a singer, because she was such a great singer.

For me, though, she had the best humor in the world. Florence was so funny. Most of the world has no clue about her personality. But whenever she laughed it was like hearing Santa Claus laugh. It was infectious. Everybody would laugh. She was bubbling, bubbling up. ★

HOLLAND-DOZIER-HOLLAND

EDWARD HOLLAND JR., LAMONT DOZIER, BRIAN HOLLAND

LAMONT: We were all at Motown. They were there before I got there.

BRIAN: We were all Motown kids; that's how we got together.

EDDIE: But the chemistry... well, let me explain it my way.

See, the situation is, once in a while you run into two people who are talented, both together and apart. Together and separate they have a unique way of approaching songwriting. Follow what I'm saying? But when they're together, that's when you come up with something really unique. And as for me, fortunately, I was able to develop as a lyric writer.

The beauty of it, what would really fuse the thing together, was that Lamont and Brian were brought up similarly. They had similar backgrounds, similar personalities. They're not impatient, they're not short-tempered. At least back then they weren't!

So you take personalities that are very similar, and they were able to develop things. If their personalities would have been miles apart it would have never developed. One would say, 'No, I want it my way,' and another one would say, 'No, I want it my way,' because that's what happens. But for whatever reason, they instinctively would hear what the other suggested, and they would try, wholeheartedly, with all the power in them, to make the song the best they could. There was no ego, they were just saying, 'We want this to be the best it can be.'

One would come up with something and the other would say, 'Well, let's try it this way.' There was never conflict, and that's highly unusual. That's really what created the whole chemistry.

LAMONT: Accomplishments? Some of the awards overseas, like the Ivor Novello Award in London, stand out. The Ivor Novello is a very distinguished award that was given to us. Being that we're not British citizens, it was very special, because it's England's most prestigious songwriting award. And the Grammys, of course.

EDDIE: Also, we'd already been inducted into the Songwriter's Hall of Fame, but a couple of years ago they gave us the highest award that they can give, the Johnny Mercer Award. And that was very exciting.

LAMONT: That was the pinnacle, in terms of what we've achieved so far.

EDDIE: Did you mention the Rock and Roll Hall of Fame? The Rock and Roll Hall of Fame was the most exciting to me, because those awards are not given out to songwriters. They're generally for the artists.

LAMONT: It's rare for a songwriter to get one.

EDDIE: That was crazy because it meant, 'Although you're not performers, your contribution was so great that we have to acknowledge it.' It really hit me when I walked into the Rock and Roll Hall of Fame in Cleveland. Nothing really excites me, by the way, but this excited me. It stopped me in my tracks. Because when I walked in there and saw all of these idols of mine, all of these people that I was so excited about growing up, I said, 'Wow! I'm in here with these guys!' That was the most exciting thing, to me, in my life, ever.

LAMONT: You Know, we really didn't, at the time, think about how long these songs would last. We were just working to come up with the best song we could write. We had no inkling that those songs would still be around today. It was wishful thinking to be a Johnny Mercer, or Rodgers and Hart, or Rodgers and Hammerstein.

BRIAN: Irving Berlin, those people.

EDDIE: Not based on style, but based on effectiveness and longevity.

LAMONT: Yeah, longevity. Right. Who knew?

EDDIE: The biggest thing on my mind at the time was that I would just try to write what other people would want to record. That's about it.

I remember, years ago, I used, 'baby, baby,' for The Supremes. And I said, 'I should change that. If I change those words, it would be more adult,' but I never got around to it and—

LAMONT: It became a signature sound of ours, that 'baby, baby,' and a certain type of rhythm. It was about the feelings we injected. Ultimately, it became the Motown sound.

EDDIE: It's not about how interesting the idea is. It's how appealing the song is, the melody and the title. Because often you'd come up with very sophisticated titles that are not appealing, they just sound intellectual.

LAMONT: You don't want to go over peoples' heads. I may write all kind of poignant things, but at the end of the day you want to have commercial hits, and you have to stay within the level of the average listener's mind.

EDDIE: Another one I went through the same struggle with was

'Baby I Need Your Loving.' It was hard for us... but for some reason it felt right.

LAMONT: The Supremes? They had a top 20 hit before 'Where Did Our Love Go,' but, yes, that was the monster hit that catapulted them into stardom.

EDDIE: I remember Diana Ross coming off the Dick Clark Caravan of Stars tour. She came off for a break. She was in the office and said, 'Do you think I'll ever be really big, really successful?' I said, 'Yeah, I think so.'

The great thing about it was that when they went back on the tour they weren't aware of what this record had done. This record had exploded all over the country. They didn't know that because they were busy doing these shows.

So when they went out there again they were amazed. The crowds went crazy. They thought they were screaming over something else; then they realized it was them. They didn't realize the impact it would have with this record. 'Where Did Our Love Go' had exploded while they were out there with the Dick Clark tour.

LAMONT: Not really, no. I don't think there was more pressure on us the more success we had.

EDDIE: For me there was.

LAMONT: I think between the first big hit in '63, up until '68, thereabouts, we hit a stride.

EVERYTHING WE TOUCHED SEEMED TO HIT THE MARK, HIT THE BULL'S-EYE. WE KEPT **OUR EYES ON THE PRIZE.**

Not so much on the prize, but the material, the work and being true to the work as songwriters.

We got so used to No. 1 records that when we went to a No. 5 we felt like failures. It just felt like we had fallen short in our quest.

As for some of the songs that I really like that we did together, I would say 'Reach Out I'll Be There' and 'Baby I Need Your Loving' by the Four Tops; 'How Sweet It Is (to be Loved By You)' by Marvin Gaye; '(Love is Like a) Heat Wave' by Martha and the Vandellas, and 'Stop! In the Name Of Love,' 'I Hear a Symphony,' and 'You Can't Hurry Love' by The Supremes. Those are some that stick out in my mind.

EDDIE: Well, there are a lot of special memories from Detroit. The main thing, I think, is the relationship with the company, our relationships with the people there.

It was a very easy environment. You asked earlier, 'Was there any pressure?' There was never any pressure. The only pressure was what we created for ourselves, the competition. The competition there was fierce: 'If you don't get the record, then Smokey will get it, Norman Whitfield will get it, Ivy Hunter will get it.'

LAMONT: It was healthy competition.

EDDIE: We just kept pushing, pushing the competition.

LAMONT: With some of the songs we might have been talking a little bit about what was happening in Detroit, with the riots and things. We were writing songs about 'Nowhere to Run'; people were going off to Vietnam. I remember I had a party for one of the kids who was going to Vietnam. Unfortunately, he got killed over there. He had a feeling he wouldn't return from Vietnam and he didn't. But I remember once he was talking about the songs we wrote, how they kept him going when he was over there, the memories of home.

All of that stuff brings back memories of what was going on at the time, the assassinations of Kennedy and Martin Luther King, the wars, everything. A lot of the songs that those soldiers were playing in Vietnam were the songs we wrote, and they kept the morale up.

EDDIE: Basically it was referred to as 'feel-good music.' I was surprised; I heard a lot of comments like that from soldiers, and people struggling through tests in college. Students would tell me, 'That's how we got through these courses in college.' I don't know how they could listen to the music and get through the books, too, but a lot of them did.

LAMONT: And then there was a time a guy told me how he had a girl, and he didn't know what to say to her. They had this little Nash Rambler. It was an old car that you could lay down in the backseat. Then he put on 'Baby I Need Your Loving,' and...

EDDIE: I love those stories.

LAMONT: 'Baby I Need Your Loving' was responsible for a lot of kids. ★

CLAUDETTE ROBINSON

THE FIRST LADY OF MOTOWN? Mr. Gordy gave me that title. He called me that because I was the first female artist signed to Motown Records, and also to Mr. Gordy, under his personal management. We, The Miracles, met Mr. Gordy in 1957. Our first record came out in 1958, but at that time, there was no Motown. Motown didn't begin until 1959. So when we became a part of Mr. Gordy's family, in terms of artists, there weren't any others. The only other artist that Mr. Gordy had at that time was Eddie Holland, and he was a singer; he would do demos for Jackie Wilson.

So when we met Mr. Gordy we were his first group. There were no others. I know that many claimed to be, but if you can find the original contract you'll see that it was The Miracles. And Claudette Robinson, at that time Rogers, was the first female signed to Motown, as part of The Miracles.

Actually we didn't have an official name at that time, because the guys had been called The Matadors. But Mr. Gordy gave me that name because I was the first female there. There weren't any other females for several years.

BEING THE ONLY WOMAN in The Miracles was absolutely fantastic! I'm saying that because, at all times, I had what I felt were my full-protection bodyguards. It was an amazing experience because they were such true gentlemen, and I have to use that word, and raise it up in really large letters. They were so very nice, always, in terms of being gentlemen with me, around me, taking care of me, making sure I was safe, secure, and all of the wonderful things that most women would love to have. It was like having your brother, your cousins, your friends, all in one. Of course, one, Bobby Rogers, was my cousin, and Smokey became my husband!

THE NAME THE MIRACLES has an interesting story. We had just recorded our first record, 'Got A Job.' And we realized that the name 'The Matadors' just didn't work for our group; we wanted to make sure that the name would reflect having a girl in the group. So we all put names on pieces of paper inside a hat and pulled out 'The Miracles.' The rest is history; we became The Miracles.

Some of the other names in the hat? Well, there were many choices... Four Gladiolas and a Rose, The Miracle Tones, others.

YES, 'MY GIRL' still makes me smile. It's absolutely a wonderful song written by both Smokey and Ronnie White. Ronnie passed away about 12 years ago, of leukemia.

Well, I don't think Smokey ever really wrote a song and said, 'This is specifically for you, Claudette,' except for 'More Love.' However, many times the lyrics he wrote would have something to do with our lives. Like 'Since I Lost My Baby,' that was actually written as a result of me having several miscarriages. Smokey was expressing his feelings of loss for my miscarriages. However, when you hear the song, you don't think of that, because you're thinking of it as a love song.

A FAVORITE MIRACLES CONCERT? There were many. But one that made a great impression on me was the very first time we performed at the Apollo Theater in New York. The promoter wanted to send us home. He said, 'This group is horrible.' It wasn't that we couldn't sing, but we didn't have great choreography, just our own. There were so many seasoned artists on the bill with us; we were so green and so young. I think we were probably the youngest on the show. So Ray Charles had someone write a full arrangement for us. His gesture meant a great deal to me, and to the group as well. The fact that someone took time out to do something like that for us, to get us going...

The Apollo audience is a very, very tough audience, but they were kind to us from the beginning. I don't know if it was because we were young and so green that they said, 'Let's give them another chance.' And as I look back at it, we needed that chance.

Another really big 'Miracles' day for me was when we received our gold record at the Michigan State Fair in Detroit. While we were performing Berry Gordy came up onstage with this big plaque. Mr. Gordy announced that we had just sold 1 million records for 'Shop Around.' That was a real surprise to us. We could not believe it and were taken aback.

I WOULD SAY MY ULTIMATE memory was receiving a star on the Hollywood Walk of Fame, on March 20, 2009. Who would have thought that five young black kids from the ghetto would have been honored and blessed to achieve a place in history and be cemented forever on the Walk of Fame?

MOTOWN BECAME the soundtrack of America, and that extends to the world. We can all be so very proud of that.

WE ARE SO BLESSED AND HONORED
THAT MOTOWN BECAME AND STILL IS THE
SOUNDTRACK OF AMERICA.★

GEORGE CLINTON

I WAS A STAFF WRITER AT MOTOWN. One of the songs I'm most proud of was the one we did for The Jackson 5. It was called 'I'll Bet You.' Funkadelic did it first, but then The Jackson 5 did it. I guess Michael was about 11 or 12. It was on the back of a Kellogg's Corn Flakes box. You could cut it out. Another one was 'Can't Shake it Loose' with The Supremes. Diana Ross did it, 'I'm into something and I can't shake it loose!'

It was nice, writing. Competition is why you learned so much, just all of the different people you had to write for. Whoever got a hot song got to cut the next record on The Temptations, Supremes, Marvin, whoever. Or you got the B-side of it, which was just as good. If you were good enough, you'd make it to A-side sooner or later. But just working around Holland-Dozier-Holland. Fuqua and Bristol, Stevenson and Hunter, Ashford and Simpson. Norman Whitfield. There were so many greats. Berry, whenever he felt like coming in and showing everybody that they still was chumps. He did it whenever he felt like it—just come in and do it, a shotgun, every little bit hurt. It made you feel like, wow, you're still in grade school.

Smokey was my idol. I learned a lot from how he played with puns. Funkadelic, we got ridiculous with it. We just made fun of the whole concept of puns and writing songs with hooks, all kinds of hooks. We had so many hooks, it was ridiculous. I think that's why we got a lot of samples from artists later on, because we had so much silliness in the songs, readily available for somebody to take one piece of it and make a whole other song out of it.

WE GOT OUR FIRST HIT record with '(I Wanna) Testify.' That was Parliament. We did a few songs as Parliament, then we did one as Funkadelic, for my mother. Because we saw Motown was peaking and the English groups was coming over, playing rock 'n' roll and blues. Motown was headed toward Las Vegas, that's where black music was headed, where rock 'n' roll bands were coming over here and playing old blues music that my mother listened to, rock 'n' roll I'd heard in school.

We saw that it was changing. So we turned around midstream and named the band Funkadelic. And we had Parliament and Funkadelic, just to make sure we didn't miss the boat, all because the new thing the kids was into now was rock 'n' roll, psychedelic. So just to be safe, we named the band Funkadelic. Sly Stone and us was pretty much thinking the same thing: psychedelic black group playing rock 'n' roll.

MOTOWN WAS A REALLY FUNKY LABEL; the first label actually to have electric bass on records. Most records up until then had upright bass and jazz bass, or organ bass. Until James Jamerson came along, and he started playing 'Shop Around' and 'Postman.' That was really funky. And that was their signature. And then they started putting the violins on it, which made it mostly crossover music, which we call 'pop records.'

A lot of people don't realize how funky Motown records were. They were really funky. But it was so sophisticated in the production that it got by without a lot of people noticing. We, on another hand, took that same theory and just turned the guitars loud as ever, on Funkadelic. It still was Motown, still the same patterns, but we made the guitar solos loud, and made long, long records. That's basically what Funkadelic became. Not only that,

FUNKADELIC DID ANYTHING IT WANTED TO DO.
WE DECIDED WE'D NEVER GET CAUGHT IN A PARTICULAR BAG AGAIN.

AFTER 'TESTIFY,' with Parliament, it was hard to get another single, because we hadn't been going that Motown route. So we said, 'Forget even chasing after the chart.' We went with the underground rock 'n' roll. You didn't have to be on the chart.

You'd never hear Jimi Hendrix with a No. 1 single. And that's when we did 'Free Your Mind... and Your Ass Will Follow,' just psychedelic to no end.

And that way, it lasted forever. Like today, you see the Red Hot Chili Peppers and groups like that, and they'll swear 'Free Your Mind... and Your Ass Will Follow' was Funkadelic's greatest record.

WE ACTUALLY GOT NO. 1 with 'Tear the Roof Off,' which is still one of the hottest songs around. 'Tear the Roof Off' is probably in a commercial every year. And 'Flash Light.' Most of those songs, 'Needy,' 'One Nation Under a Groove,' they're strange songs, different types of songs, but they were like the hottest records for disco. And it was all basically louder than anything else. Handclaps made you want to flinch on 'Flash Light.' The bass was on a Moog, as opposed to a Fender bass.

OUR RECORDS LAST FOREVER. You can go back 20 years later and they still work.

THE MOTHERSHIP? It's in Tallahassee, in my studio, lit up, operative and everything. I'm getting ready to put it in the Smithsonian.

The idea came from watching The Who, 'Tommy,' the rock opera, Pink Floyd doing 'The Wall.' And then 'Hair.' We knew everybody in 'Hair' when it came out. We said, 'We want to do something with funk, a funk opera.' And instead of taking the royalties from the 'Mothership' album, they got us a line of credit for a million dollars, and I bought the spaceship and all the props around it, costumes. Everything had to be expensive, because I was going to do it, for the first time, for a black group. It had to be bigger and more expensive than anything else. And when we did the 'Mothership,' we got Rogers & Cowan as publicists. *Newsweek*, *People*, everybody came to see it. And it's lasted to this day. We still get a lot of attention because of that.

WE'RE STILL HERE. I don't think nobody ever survived like we've survived, and still doing it.

To me, we never succeeded. I don't ever want to succeed. I always want to be right behind it, just behind success. I'm always chasing happy. In the pursuit of happiness, I like to be right behind it. And we're still right there.

THE BEST SHOW IN DETROIT? Wow, hard. We did shows at the Twenty Grand. For the band, the shows at the Twenty Grand, people still talk about how we used to strip, get naked, and run up and down the tables in the club. It was an exclusive club in Motown. People would be there with minks on, and we were running around with sheets and diapers.

The Grande Ballroom shows, they'd never seen nothing like it. That was during the days of the psychedelic in Ann Arbor, Ted Nugent, Iggy Pop, and all of that stuff. Those were hot. We were pretty much out of our mind. Everybody was. It was turn on, tune in, drop out. We was already out of school, so we tuned in and was high as hell. We was a little older than everybody else. We got out there with all of those hippies, and the next thing you know, we were old hippies.

There was so much fun between Detroit, everywhere, the East Side, which was rock 'n' roll, psychedelic, then you come over to the ghetto, or the Twenty Grand, which was sophisticated. It was hard to say which was the best show.

ANYTIME YOU HEAR somebody's music, and their parents say, 'That ain't music,' or you hear older musicians say, 'That ain't music,' that's your new funk.

It's got to turn you on in four bars, eight bars. If people start moving their head and saying, 'What's that?' you've got some good funk.

I'M AN ALIEN. I know that. I know I'm from the Dog Star, planet Sirius. The Dogons tribe from Africa. Crazy is a prerequisite in the music business, period. But in funk, you've really got to be crazy. And pretty much everybody around us is that way. They're dedicated to it. Oh yeah, we're definitely not from here. There's no doubt of that.

RUFF! I'VE BEEN DEFLEAED, DETICKED, AND I GOT MY RABIES SHOT, AND

I'M READY TO BURY THE BONE. RUFF!★

MEL FARR

I THINK I SHOULD GO back before then.

YES, I WAS ROOKIE OF THE YEAR, All-Pro for the Detroit Lions. But my story, really, is that I came here to play football for the Lions in 1967. And in 1967, when I was driving down 94, I saw smoke. Detroit was on fire because of the riots.

So I came here in the midst of that real moment that was very depressing for our city. I immediately said, 'Hey, I'm going to go out here and make a difference on the football field.' But while doing that I was reading the paper, and Henry Ford II said that he was going to make car dealerships available for African-Americans.

I've always been the kind of guy who sets goals. When I was 12 years old, I set a goal to be a professional football player. And the closer that I came to accomplishing those goals, the happier I was. I think that's happiness. And I think that's man's main purpose on earth, to be happy. Who wants to be sad?

When I heard Henry Ford II was going to open up Ford dealerships to African-Americans, I said, 'You know, I've accomplished the goal of being a professional football player. So what I'm going to do now is, I'm going to be a Ford dealer. African-Americans can be a Ford dealer, because my father was a used car dealer back in Texas, where I was born and raised. That's something I should really look into.'

So I went out there and got a job, in the offseason, working at Ford Motor Company. I worked for Ford Motor Company for several years in the offseason. So it wasn't by accident that Mel Farr went out and took a dealership that had gone bankrupt twice, on 10 Mile Road at Greenfield in Oak Park, and made it the largest African-American business in the country. I went out and I learned how to be a successful auto dealer.

I PLAYED FOOTBALL FOR THE LIONS for seven years and worked at Ford Motor Company for six years in the offseason. And I was very instrumental in Ford Motor Company developing a dealer training program for African-Americans.

Not only was I playing football and working for Ford Motor Company, but I was going to the University of Detroit at night, working on my degree. So I really felt that I prepared myself for the day that I couldn't run the football anymore.

At 29 years old, I retired from the Detroit Lions and I bought the dealership in Oak Park with a partner. He and I didn't see eye to eye about how to run it. And the two guys that were there before me went bankrupt. And we were going bankrupt for a third time. I told my partner, 'Hey, let me buy you out.' So I bought him out in November of 1979.

Then, in 1979, 1980, prime interest rates went up to 18, 19 percent. It was a real struggle for us. So I said, 'If I'm going to go out, I'm going to go out with a bang.'

I THOUGHT I SHOULD MARKET Mel Farr for two reasons. No. 1 is that I was a professional football player. No other dealer in Detroit was a professional football player. And the second thing was that I was an African-American.

So, I said, 'Well let me see. I'm at 10 Mile at Greenfield. Right across 8 Mile there's a whole lot of black folks. I'm going to get their attention.' I said, 'What makes Mel Farr different than any other dealer? Well, I'm an ex-football player, I'm a superstar.' I said, 'I'm going to call the dealership 'Mel Farr Superstar, your superstar dealer.'' Then I said,

'ALL SUPERHEROES, THEY FLY.

I'M GOING TO PUT A CAPE ON AND I'M GOING TO FLY ACROSS THE SCREEN.

And if I go out of business, I'm going to go out of business with a big bang.' I got my cape and got some cameramen, and we started doing these commercials on television, 'Mel Farr Superstar, for a Farr better deal.'

Man, we got a lot of buyers in there. But in 1980, '81, when interest rates were at 19 percent, credit was very tight. I couldn't get people financed. So I went to the chairman of the board of Ford Motor Credit, and I said 'I've got all these people who were laid off because of the economy, but they're back to work now.

Their credit is bad, but they want to buy automobiles. I'd like to start a plan where I put X dollars in reserve for all of those customers who have problems with financing so that my Loss Liquidation Rate is equal to branch average.'

He said yes. And those were the decisions that allowed me to take that dealership from zero sales in 1975 to more than a half a billion dollars in 1997, '98, and the No. 1 African-American business in the country. It was my marketing strategy and the idea of getting a financing program for these customers. I became the guy who sold cars to customers who had challenged credit.

LET ME TELL YOU HOW THAT HAPPENED, how I ended up singing background on 'What's Going On?'

I can't sing. Marvin Gaye and Lem Barney, who played football here with me, we played golf every weekend and became very good friends. So we were playing golf at Palmer Park, and we left and went to Marvin's house, which was on Outer Drive.

Marvin started banging on the piano, singing 'What's going on?' Then he says, 'Hey, we'll do a song.' He was not singing at that time because his partner Tammi Terrell had died, and he was in a kind of depression. He was going to give the song to another group, the Dramatics. But he said, 'I'll tell you what. I'll sing this song if you guys sing background,' Lem and I. So we went into a studio and we cut the record, and it was a lot of fun. We were just having fun.

Then the song stayed on the shelf for about a year, because Berry Gordy said, 'We want some professionals to do the background.' And boy, I'll tell you, they had professionals come in there to try to do it, but they couldn't get the kind of sound we had. So he finally released it with us singing in the background and *Rolling Stone* said it was one of best songs ever written.

So, I'm kind of excited by the fact that I had the pleasure of singing with Marvin and Lem. We did it from friendship. But then Marvin said, 'I'll tell you what—you guys are singing background, so I want to play football.'

He was serious! Marvin went from 165, 170 pounds to about 190 pounds; he lifted weights and ran; he did all those kind of things. He wanted to be a running back. He didn't have the ability, but he really, really wanted to try it.

So we took him out and met the coach and told him Marvin wanted to try out. The coach said, 'OK, Marvin, let me see.' But then the team finally called back and said, 'We don't think so, because we don't want the liability of somebody hitting you in the throat and messing up that beautiful voice you have.'

So, that's how it happened. We were having fun, and came up with one of the greatest songs ever written.

No, no, we did it on Davison. Berry had a studio on Davison, right off of the expressway.

YOU KNOW WHAT MY FAVORITE CAR was, and probably still is today? They don't make it anymore. The Escort. Because we didn't have any product in 1979, '80. We had the gas-guzzlers, we had the Granadas. They were not good-looking automobiles, and they broke down every time you turned around.

Then Ford came out with their first front-wheel-drive car, and that was the Escort. And boy, I sold all the Escorts in the world. I was the No. 1 dealer in the country in selling Escorts for 10, 15 years.

To drive, I would say the Thunderbird. But I had a Toyota dealership, Lincoln dealerships; I sold Mazdas, VWs, Hondas, Kias, so I had my pick.

I THINK THAT IF THE CITY'S going to come back, it's going to be done by businessmen, the Dan Gilberts and Dave Bings of the world. You need businesses to create jobs. I think that some innovative things are going to have to happen. And we can do it, but it's going to take thinking outside of the box. And hopefully, I'm going to be one of the individuals who are going to be thinking outside of the box to get jobs back here in Detroit.

That's one of the reasons I decided to move back to Detroit.

SO I'M KIND OF A COMPLEX PERSON. I say, 'When I die, I want my tombstone to say, 'Here lies nothing,' because I want to use all of my energy and my effort and my knowledge while I'm on this earth. No one knows what you can do with it 6 feet in the ground. ★

BILL FORD JR.

THAT GETS HARD TO SUMMARIZE. Obviously, there were a lot of things that he did that were unique. He had the $5-a-day wage. He insisted on profit sharing before anybody had thought of that; in fact they branded him as a communist for doing that.

Probably, in the end, though, it was the whole idea of bringing freedom and mobility to the average American that was his greatest accomplishment. Prior to the Model T—this is incredible—most people never traveled more than 20 miles from home in their entire lifetime. You think of that, and then you think of what the Model T brought to people, it really changed where they worked, where they lived, and where they played. They could choose to live in the suburbs, they could go away for the weekend, they could do things that they could never have done before.

THERE ARE A LOT OF GREAT STORIES. Probably the one that's the best metaphor for today is when he built his first car. He built it in his garage, and when he finished building it, he realized that the garage opening wasn't big enough for him to drive out. So he took a sledgehammer and beat down the garage wall so he could drive the car out.

That's a good metaphor for pounding down anything that stands in your way. And that continues to drive our company today.

We've gotten through the toughest of times, we did it on our own, and we did it the old-fashioned way. We pulled ourselves up by our bootstraps and not only survived, but set the stage to thrive. I think he would have loved that.

He also would have loved the fact that we're pushing the envelope on technology. He would have loved to have seen this new technology that's being developed, things like Sync and My Ford Touch, or safety technology that's unprecedented, not just for the driver, but for pedestrians outside of the car.

Most importantly, I think he would have loved all of the new technology going into the engine itself, whether it's electrification, hybrids, plug-in hybrids, biofuels, or making his internal combustion engine even better, which we're still doing.

WHY IS IT IMPORTANT to have the family involved? First of all, it does not allow us to become a nameless, faceless corporation. There's a sense of accountability here. People know that I'm here and I'm not going anywhere. A lot of executives bail when the going gets tough, get a big payout and walk away. That won't happen here. I think it's reassuring to both our employees and the public to know that there's somebody they recognize, and they know is accountable.

If you think about what we've been through in the last seven or eight years, I don't think it's coincidental that Ford, with our family ownership, navigated through a very difficult time where

I THINK MY GREAT-GRANDFATHER
WOULD BE VERY PROUD OF THE COMPANY TODAY. WE HAVE A FIGHTING SPIRIT I THINK HE'D REALLY ADMIRE.

others could not. Because the family was completely behind the company in the plan to turn this place around. And that freed up the management to not worry about any extraneous stuff and to just get to work and get the plan executed.

ONE OF THE THINGS that's unique about Ford, not only in my fourth-generation family—in fact, we have the fifth generation working here as well—is that so many of our employees are multigenerational, and so many of our dealers are multigenerational. That really humanizes the company. Many of our employees and our dealers tell me stories about how their father or their grandmother worked at Ford, or their aunt or their uncle got to know Henry Ford II, or their grandfather knew Henry Ford I. That creates a tie and emotional bond to the company that other companies can't replicate.

I'm very proud of it. It's something that I wake up every morning thinking about: 'How can I not only preserve it, but make it better?'

It's very rare to have a family at the head of a company more than 100 years after it was founded, particularly a company of this size. I think it does make us a uniquely American story.

THE LOGO? I'm not a great historian on this, but apparently they fooled around with several logos back near the founding of the company, and ultimately came up with what we know now as the Ford blue oval.

I don't think it's his script. But it's close to what I've seen of his signature.

THAT'S EASY. IT'S A MUSTANG.
I LOVE ALL OF THE MUSTANGS,
FROM THE '64 THROUGH THE PRESENT.

Some are better than others. I wouldn't say that the early '70s were my favorite, but I do think, by and large, that the Mustangs we've had over the years have been terrific. I've had way too many of them. I particularly like the convertibles. I just love, on a day like today, putting the top down. It's got a great sound system, and it's a blast to drive.

I DO COLLECT CARS, but I like to collect cars that mean something to me personally. I tend to collect cars that were important during my career.

My favorite was probably our GT, which was the car that we came out with for our 100th anniversary. It's a replica, in many ways, of a race car that we had in the '60s, the GT40. It's immediately recognizable; we didn't make very many of them.

People love them. Everywhere I drive, people stop me. If I have one car in my collection that stands out, it's probably that car. But it's not a car you would drive every day.

GROWING UP, I was in Detroit a ton. I would go to Hudson's all the time, particularly at Christmas. They had the 'For Children Only Shop,' where you could go in. Your parents weren't allowed in, and you could go in and do your Christmas shopping. It was very neat, and I loved that place when I was a kid. I'd go with my sisters.

I went to every Lions game at Tiger Stadium when I was a child. I used the city for everything. My dentist was there, my barber was there. Everything I did was in the city of Detroit. This was all pre-riot. After the riots, a lot of that changed, unfortunately.

I still went down for sporting events, though. Even today, we built Ford Field down there. I'm in the city a lot. We go to the Red Wings games, Tigers games, Lions games. I never miss a Lions game. We go to concerts. I'm really excited that there are signs of rebirth.

I literally grew up with the Lions. It was something that was part of my life since I was a little boy. We'd go to every training camp when I was a kid. I went through a phase where the players were my heroes, and then all of a sudden a few years passed and they were my peers. Now they call me 'Mr. Ford,' which makes me realize that I'm getting a lot older.

I've always loved football, and I love the Lions, so, Sunday, for me, in the fall, has always been about the Detroit Lions, and always will be.

I WAS GREEN LONG BEFORE green was in. In fact, I took a lot of heat over the years for having environmental views on the industry. A lot of our competitors thought it was ridiculous.

I knew that this day would come, though. And despite it being a very unpopular stance through the years, I feel like I was able to move the needle in a way that I'm very proud of. We had the first sustainability report of any major corporation. We completely redid the world's largest brownfield site, the Rouge, and made it the greenest and most interesting auto plant anywhere in the world. We had the first hybrid SUV on the market, and we're leading the charge, no pun intended, on electric vehicles and plug-in electric vehicles.

WE'VE COME A LONG WAY, and I love where we are. We're a leader now, and it's something that was a long haul to get to. For me, personally, it was, at times, a very difficult journey because, as I said, it wasn't always very popular. But it was absolutely the right thing to do then, and it's even more the right thing to do today. ★

LEE IACOCCA

I'VE ALWAYS LOVED CARS. I hung out at a Ford dealership back when I was young. And then later, I took automobile engineering at Lehigh, which is a great engineering school. I've just always been in love with cars.

I wanted to be where the action was. I loved starting from scratch and then building a car that was really great—I never got tired of that. Between Ford and Chrysler, I spent 58 years building cars, which you can only do if you really love it.

MY FAVORITE CAR, by a million, is the Mustang. It's a classic—I spent most of my life on that car. And then there was the Jeep line, which I bought and which turned out to be highly successful. The minivan, though, that was probably the biggest coup of all. To me, my greatest successes were the Mustang, the Jeep line, and the minivan.

YOU ASKED HOW WE NAMED the Mustang. Well, each prototype had a name. One was called 'Allegra,' one was called 'Stiletto,' and another was the 'Cougar.' The 'Cougar' is the one that became the Mustang. You know, when you're trying to decide on a car name, everybody wants to get in on the act, and everybody has his own ideas. A lot of people would write in and say, 'What do you think of this?' And then a man named John Najjar named the car 'Mustang' after the World War II airplane, and I don't know, it just had a really all-American feel to it. In the end, that's what we wanted, so it stuck. And it became a legend.

It was unveiled at the World's Fair in 1964. On my right side was Henry Ford, and on my left side was Walt Disney. The timing was just lucky, but it got a huge send-off.

We ended up selling 417,000 cars in the Mustang's first year, by April 17. No one ever thought it would be that kind of a success. No one. Ever.

But it was a beautiful car—and a great buy at $2,368. It was fully equipped, too, so they beat the doors down for that price. I ran into a guy recently who said to me, 'You're the guy who did the Mustang. Well I just spent $2,368 on the sound system on the new one.' Back then, see, that was the price for the whole car: carpets, hubcaps, wheel covers, all the standard equipment. So we had an equipped car at a great price, and it had a terrific look.

When you're doing a project like the Mustang, you have to surround yourself with great designers and engineers. That's what I did. We had such a great team. Nobody ever thought it was going to sell that much, but we sold a million cars in the first two years, and we proved everyone wrong.

WHAT'S INTERESTING is that the minivan crowd was actually the Mustang crowd. The people who bought the Mustang grew up, got married, had two kids, and then they needed something. The minivan. I always have one, they're just practical. I think they're

still selling 20,000 or 25,000 minivans a month, 24 years later. So you could say we hit the marketplace right.

WHEN PEOPLE ASK ME the secret to my success, I tell them to work hard and love what you do. I say that to everybody. If you don't love what you do and you don't like going to work in the morning, you'd better get out.

When I wrote *Iacocca: An Autobiography*, I didn't know if it was going to sell, but it ended up selling 2.7 million hardcover copies. All of that money from the book proceeds went to charity, to help start my foundation, which gives almost all of its money to the fight against diabetes.

WHAT DID I DO TO RELAX? When I lived in Detroit, I went to every Tigers game and every Lions game I could. We had a box in the name of the company, so we went to every event. And of course, hockey, the Red Wings were big-time, so I became a hockey guy. In fact, Gordie Howe and Al Kaline were two of my neighbors. Detroit is a great sports town.

I ENDED UP DOING 65 TV COMMERCIALS. I did so many I'm a member of the Screen Actors Guild—and I still have my card.

I can't say why the commercials worked so well. I had a very good advertising agency. Leo Kelmenson had good, creative people in styling and in marketing. If you can get that kind of team, you usually have a winner.

THEY CAME UP WITH THE LINE:
'IF YOU CAN FIND A BETTER CAR, BUY IT.'
THAT BECAME FAMOUS.

DETROIT, TO ME, was a highly creative place with a lot of guts. It had great employers. A lot of jobs were created in Michigan, thanks to the auto industry. There have been a bunch of bad times recently, but the Big Three are coming back strong and doing very well. They're building more of the kinds of cars people want. Hybrids are big, and full electric will see their day soon. That's probably the future: a plug-in hybrid.

MY FIRST CAR WAS A '38 FORD. The war had just ended, so I got a used one from my father. It was a beat-up old thing. But then I traded up. ★

TIM ALLEN

I WOULDN'T CALL IT being a 'performer.' I just like being the center of attention. I liked disrupting class, which goes back to being the center of attention. Same in the family. But I had a sense of humor like my father... and I like using it to get my way. It's really manipulation. All of this sounds pretty negative. But I give money to the church.

I WENT TO ERNEST W. SEAHOLM. That's the Swedish word for white people. It's all white people. Anglos, I think they're called now.

SPORTS? ARE YOU KIDDING? That would require me listening to people. I don't like taking orders. I've been in trouble all my life because I don't like listening to people. Well, I actually hung out with the sports guys, because the better-looking girls with the nice legs were always with them. So I would go work out in the gym with the football players, hoping that the cheerleaders would notice. Didn't work out that way. But, no, I didn't play any sports. Not that I couldn't. I did try out in college for football and actually got very close to making the team. Then I got hit by a real football player and said, 'I don't know about this.' Really. Seriously.

YES, I DID ACT in high school, every single day, baby! Every day. That's improv. 'How quickly can I get kicked out of this class?' I got kicked out of a lot of classes for acting. I never thought that was fair, because on your report card it said, 'Does not socialize well with others.' That always got marked on mine. But I got kicked out of class for socializing too well with others. I said, 'How could that be? Because the whole class was laughing.' So, obviously, I got along well with everybody but the teacher. But, no, I didn't get into a lot of theater. To me, life is theater.

THAT'S TRUE, MY CAREER was started on a dare. It was a lovely man whose dad was a radio announcer with WJR. He used to come into the store I worked at in Birmingham called the Sportsman.

And every day we'd talk about how we were going to get into radio and showbiz. And one day he says, 'Well, why don't you do it at Mark Ridley's Comedy Castle? They have open mic night.' And it was just like that. 'What are you, chicken?' Who would have thought I'd respond to that?

A FAVORITE VENUE? I did Meadow Brook when I started getting big. That was nice, to do an outdoor arena and have people eating fried chicken right while you're doing your gig.

I remember I did a show down on Telegraph, around 6 Mile, during the World Series. I was supposed to go on between innings. That was the gig. I made $70. People were throwing beer cans at me because they didn't want me up there. Yes, the memorable ones, to me, are the ones where I just barely escaped with my life. Those were the early, early clubs along Telegraph, way down by 6 and 7 Mile. I think they're probably strip clubs now. They probably were strip clubs then, but I was so busy trying to get my job done... Ridley's has always been a great place to perform. The Holly Hotel was fun.

I CAME UP WITH THE IDEA FOR
'HOME IMPROVEMENT'
SITTING IN MY HOUSE IN BEVERLY HILLS, MICHIGAN, IN THE BACKYARD.

For years, I'd said, 'This is a real sitcom here.' There are acre lots there; I still don't know what my neighbor looks like. When I go home to see my parents, he's still there. I thought, 'There's a show here.'

CAR GUY? Huge.

I've loved cars all my life. My dad, before he passed away, was a big car nut in Colorado. And then we moved to Michigan, and

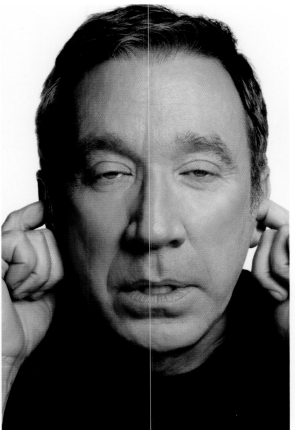

the coolest thing about it was that it was where they made cars. It was the coolest thing in the world.

I WORKED FOR GM FOR A WHILE, AT THE TECH CENTER. YOU'D SEE PROTOTYPES. IT WAS THE MOST EXCITING THING IN THE WORLD.

I saw the '71 Camaro, way before it came out. You'd see it cruising around Telegraph and Woodward. For a guy like me, it was too cool. It's still too cool to be from the Motor City.

I was at GM Photographic. I was there as a summer intern, then I got a job for a while, but I don't think they would have kept me around. I was caught in the bathroom, twice, opening up blueprints. My boss said, 'Do you think that's OK? Didn't it say 'Secret'?' I said, 'Yeah, but I work here.' 'You're an intern, you're not supposed to be opening up those tubes and reading.' So I saw the new Camaro. It's not like I was going to run over to Ford and tell them. But it was really cool to see what they were like four to five years out. My job was nothing, but I made sure they remembered me.

BUILDING STUFF? I've just always liked it. My dad liked it. I like tearing stuff apart, shocking myself, then paying someone to put it back together.

WELL, PRIOR TO THE PRESS getting ahold of it, we used to actually race down Woodward. It was the most fun ever.

We lived around the car companies and some of the parents would bring home cars. 'Try this one out! It's got a new 440 in it.' 'Try this!' 'And we'd race. It was safe—I mean, as safe as it can be when you've got 16-year-olds going 100 mph. And then they did a '60 Minutes' piece, and it became against the law. Now the Dream Cruise has turned into a huge thing. But those days, before it got popular, were the coolest to me, because it was organic.

NO, I DIDN'T HAVE A HOT CAR growing up. I was from a family of 11. I was lucky to get out of the house, because we had to rake leaves and do laundry... well, actually, I never did laundry in my life. I don't know why I said that. My sisters were stuck in the laundry room. We were out raking leaves. I had rich friends, and everyone I knew had a car but me.

MY FIRST CAR was my brother's Corvair, which was a great car. But I had some incredible ones. I had a Volkswagen Baja Bug. For my summer job, in lieu of payment, they gave me that car.

That was at Munk's Motors in Pontiac. It's still there. He built me a Volkswagen. I took it to college in Mount Pleasant. And the car would freeze. Literally, the car would freeze, and I thought maybe putting a plastic bag over the exposed engine would help. I thought that would keep the engine warm.

I'm not a real bright guy, so my roommate took the car to get a 12-pack of beer, and, later, I said, 'Boy, there's a real smell back there.' I said, 'Did you take the plastic bag off the engine when you took it to the store?' 'No.' So it heat-sealed the plastic bag. I don't know why I bring that up.

Yeah, that was my first car, Baja Bug, VW with a big motor in it, flared fenders and all. The first real collectible car I had, much later, was a Ferrari 330 GTC, which I still own. Bought it back in Chicago, when I lived in Michigan. Silver.

THAT'S RIGHT, I RACED with Steve Saleen and Bob Bondurant. That was a dream come true. I couldn't believe I was allowed in a race car. Disney sponsored it. I have no idea what they were thinking. 'Home Improvement' sponsored a race car with their No. 1 TV star in the car. I had a job so I never got to practice. I'd show up at the race and I'd always be at the back because I never qualified. But every now and then I'd get up to third, fourth, fifth place, even though I started in the back.

The team captain said, 'If you ever did this seriously, you might be pretty good at it.' I had another job. But it's the best experience I've ever had. That and sport biking. I always wanted to take a super bike and lay it on its side, and I did just that. It's wonderful. ★

SYD MEAD

ALL KIDS MAKE MARKS, because it's an immediate satisfaction. You move your hand with a crayon and there it is. And kids like instant gratification.

By the time I was 3, I was drawing a car with people waving out the windows. Then, in grade school, I was cutting out stencils and spraying the paper with paint to make a scene. By the time I was 6, I was drawing trucks, fairly well-drawn representations. And by the time I was 10, I was doing portraits of people—my Uncle Henry, for instance. This is all going to be in the autobiography.

HOW DID I END UP STUDYING at Art Center? John Reinhart was the head of automotive styling at Ford, particularly the Advanced Studio. When I was in the Army in Okinawa during the Korean War I sent him some car drawings, because an article appeared on the new Continental. He designed that, the Mark II.

He sent back his comments with a very nice letter saying, 'If you like this sort of thing you should go to Art Center in Los Angeles.' So that was the link. When I got out of the Army at Fort Lewis, Washington, in '56, I flew down to Los Angeles, visited the school, and there were fiberglass and chrome models of cars. I thought, 'This is a good choice.'

I ENDED UP IN DETROIT because Ford hired me. So I drove here in my '52 Oldsmobile and went to work at Ford, at the Advanced Studio. This is 1959. Really, you were supposed to drive the car that the company you were working for made. So I have this '52 Oldsmobile, which was a luxury car back then. I got comments from people at Ford styling. 'Why are you driving a GM product?' 'It's none of your business! I bought this before Ford hired me.'

I lived in Royal Oak first, because my roommate didn't have a car and had to catch rides going across the northern tier of the cities to GM's Tech Center in Warren. Then, when he got married and left, I moved out to Lahser Road, then to Indian Village.

YES, IT WAS AN ALBERT KAHN home, done early in his career. I had a lot of friends. We had parties. I had a lot of fun in Detroit. You're younger, and you're driving through frozen ruts with these big 2-ton cars, but you don't care. It's just the way life is.

THE DESIGN CULTURE IN 1959? When I graduated, when anybody graduated, from a technical school like Art Center, which was top-tier, you were paid $4,000 a year. Now that sounds like not very much, but that was the price of a new Cadillac. I use the Cadillac standard. Now, should you graduate and make about $85,000 a year, that's comparable.

My favorite comment on the car culture was from Joe Oros, who was head of Ford styling. The joke was that his two best friends were 'Max Width' and 'Max Length,' because cars were wide and like rectangles. They were oblong, rectilinear solids, with deck raisers on the side, deck raisers on the back, a lot of glass. Cars were about 16, 17, 18, 19 feet long, and weighed 2 tons or more. The car culture was celebrating an exuberance of design expression for make recognition, because you really could tell whether it was a Dodge or a Ford or a Chevy or an Oldsmobile or a Pontiac.

Well, at the Advanced Studio we didn't do production cars. Mostly we were doing experimental body shells and concept cars. So on the Falcon Futura I did the taillight vessel. That's the only production part I ever designed that went into production. That's my contribution to American automobilia.

WHEN I STARTED MY OWN CORPORATION in 1970 I had already turned down Chrysler. They wanted to send me to South America, to be their idea person for their studio in Sao Paulo. And I had already turned down General Motors. So I started my company with no clients—but my first account was Philips of Holland, which is a global, multinational company.

So I started off quite well. But it was pure, naïve luck. I've never had a business plan, for more than 40 years. Some of my clients have had business plans and they were out of business in three years.

Then finally, in 1975, I thought, 'If I move to California...' My clients were not in Detroit anymore. They were out in New York, Chicago and overseas, with Philips.

MY CONCEPT OF 'SCENARIOS'? Scenario is story, and nothing exists as a single entity. It's always embedded into social or other environments, either visual or in actual use.

When I was doing a lot of work for Philips, from 1970 to '82, I was visualizing future trends in product. And they make everything—refrigerators, cameras, radios. I always thought of a scenario. 'How is this going to be used? Who's holding it?' I've been doing that ever since I learned how to draw, to fulfill my fantasies of the world that I was in, in my mind.

THE TRANSITION TO FILM wasn't a transition, really. If you have a design ability you apply that ability to whatever design task is at hand. My work in film is pretty much like anything else I've done. I make sure I understand the problem, make sure I understand what the client wants to have happen as a solution, and I'm off on another creative adventure. The process is exactly the same.

'VISUAL FUTURIST?' The term came from when I got a call from my entertainment lawyer in regard to my work on 'Blade Runner.' She said, 'They're doing the titles; what do you want to call yourself?' And I thought, 'It has to be a bumper sticker,' so 'visual futurist.'

I'M VISUAL. I CAN PAINT, DRAW. SO I THOUGHT,
'VISUAL FUTURIST'
WAS SORT OF A SUBJECTIVE, ILL-DEFINED TERM THAT SOUNDED GOOD.

I've never done anything for the past. If it's happened, you can get it in a book somewhere. People hire me to invent what something should look like that doesn't exist, and to show why it should look that way.

WELL, WITH 'TRON' I was already working on 'Blade Runner,' and then 'Blade Runner' went into post-production after final photography. I got a call from Don Kushner, who was the producer on 'Tron.' I had lunch with him at Disney's campus in Burbank. So my lawyer started negotiations with Disney. I'd already done 'Star Trek: The Motion Picture.'

In 'Blade Runner,' I sort of inched my way into the full breadth of what had to be visualized for the film—street sets, vehicles, props, interior sets. 'Tron,' I designed all the vehicles, except for the butterfly thing at the end, some of the sets, and did the logo.

You can't imagine two more different films than 'Blade Runner' and 'Tron.'

I WOULD SAY MY FAVORITE PROJECTS to date have been designing the interiors of four large private aircraft. The first was a 727 for the Sultan of Brunei, completed and delivered. The next two were both Boeing 747s, one for His Majesty King Fahd of Saudi Arabia and the other one for the Sheik of Oman. These were finished and delivered.

I did a third 747 for the Sultan of Brunei. That job became the victim of palace intrigue; it was accepted by the sultan but never built. These jobs were favorites because they demanded original design invention matched to extremely stringent fabrication and installation parameters, all of which I had to learn about rapidly.

WHAT DO I THINK THE FUTURE will look like? I'm giving a plug to this guy, Mark Stevenson. He wrote *An Optimist's Tour of the Future*. He went all around the world, contacted people who were working on technologies that are either in the experimental stage or could be applied now if you got rid of government regulations in that particular slot. It's a very encouraging book. We have more people working now on solutions on everything than we ever did before.

Contrary, I think, to what the media concentrates on, how bad things are and how much worse they're going to get, technology can solve all its own problems and always has, and I think will. ★

SELMA BLAIR

I WAS BORN IN DETROIT Sinai Hospital, in June of 1972. Sinai is now no more, but I am.

ATTENDING CRANBROOK was probably the best time of my life, until now, because hopefully now is always going to be the best time in my life. But I loved Cranbrook. I didn't start going there until ninth grade, and it was the most beautiful place in the world to me. I thought I'd be a writer or a photographer. Then, senior year, I was doing a play, and my English teacher, who knew I wanted to be a writer, said I should be an actress. I wasn't that great of a writer. My mentor is telling me to be an actress, but it was very kind of him, because I wasn't any good in that play at all. At intermission nobody came back. But I came back and finished the play. It got me into a love of all things beautiful and creating beautiful things for people, or attempting to.

I GOT INTO PHOTOGRAPHY at Cranbrook. My parents bought me my first Nikon, a very standard, wonderful camera that I still shoot with to this day. Every other camera of mine was stolen—not in Detroit, by the way, in Italy.

My inspiration, when I was young, were really offbeat photographers like Joel-Peter Witken, Cindy Sherman. I think that's what got me into acting, was Cindy Sherman and her stills. I would photograph myself in different guises. I thought, 'Wow, this is amazing, I'd love to be an actress.' I don't know if I had my own voice as a photographer so much as I admired and loved the photographers I studied. I can have my own voice more in acting.

There's a guy named Todd Kessler who was my dearest guy friend at Cranbrook, and he's now gone on to be a hugely successful writer in Hollywood and television. He writes the show 'Damages'; he created that and wrote for 'The Sopranos.' So we would do plays together. He was Benjamin to my Mrs. Robinson at Cranbrook. He's someone I've stayed in touch with. He has yet to hire me, but he's a dear friend.

COMING TO LOS ANGELES after I had grown up in Detroit, it was a fairy tale. It just seemed like vacation all the time, and just so surreal. They're opposite poles.

THERE'S A
CREATIVITY AND A LIFE FORCE
IN DETROIT THAT'S UNSHAKABLE.

When I meet people from Michigan, I can tell right away that they're from there. They have such drive. I think the cold winters and the character of Detroit really shapes people in an amazing way.

HOPEFULLY, I CAN LAST A LONG TIME and work with more of my favorites, like Lily Tomlin.

BEING A PART OF the 'Hellboy' franchise was a blessing, to be a superhero. I have my own action figure. And to work with Guillermo del Toro was an unparalleled experience.

I LOVE MAKING MOVIES.
HOPEFULLY, I'LL ALWAYS HAVE THE GIFTS TO BE ABLE TO DO STUDIO FILMS—IT'S A NECESSITY, TO MAKE A LIVING. BUT I LOVE THE CREATIVITY THAT CAN GO INTO INDEPENDENT FILMS.

I still feel like a new actress who hasn't hit her stride. So I feel a sense of adventure when working with other people who are just starting out. That's the kind of giving back I do. I do shorts for people. Kids at NYU, I'll still do their films for them, if they contact me. I love the studio films, too, because there are amazing things that can go on with bigger budgets and a wider range of people seeing it. You need that. I've done a lot of independents, maybe too many, but I can't see stopping it.

MY FIRST CAR? Ha. It was a beat-up Dodge Charger, which was a real 'shit-shaker,' my mom called it. It was intensely ugly. Sorry, Detroit. My mom, though, drove a 1979 Corvette Stingray. It was navy blue with a white interior, and it was a really cool car. I thought I was a really big deal at Cranbrook, because I drove a white Jeep Cherokee Limited. I had the gold pinstriping. I felt really, really cool in it. I was happy just to have any car.

OTHER THAN MY HOUSE, the first thing I bought—I'm not a huge spender, but after 'Cruel Intentions,' I bought a Rolex that my mom had had growing up, that I always envied. When I was growing up, she wore a really simple black-faced Rolex, stainless steel. That was my first purchase for myself, and I still wear it every day.

I USED TO LOVE, for my birthday, going to The Whitney. There'd be some great jazz singer, and I'd get to have mimosas. It was beautiful. And I loved going to the Detroit Grand Prix. One year, I rode in the pace car with my friends, and we didn't get off the track in time, so the cars were released and our pace car was still driving around the track with the Grand Prix cars on it. We had a real adrenaline rush. Then we all had dinner at The Whitney afterward. I loved it. ★

JERRY BRUCKHEIMER

I ALWAYS DREAMED about making movies when I was young.

I loved going to the movies. My mother used to drop me off on Saturdays to watch matinees.

That was from the time I was old enough to be alone—10, 11. I wanted to be a part of it. I didn't think I could be an actor; that wasn't my skill. But I thought maybe I could do something behind the scenes. I was always good at organizing things. I organized a baseball team when I was like 10 or 11 years old, and a hockey team when I was 12.

No, I don't remember which theater. It was downtown. That's too far back.

I'm a big fan of David Lean, so I loved his movies—'The Bridge on the River Kwai,' 'Lawrence of Arabia,' 'Doctor Zhivago.' Those were the early films I loved.

BEING A PRODUCER is no different than being the manager of a ball team. You don't own the team; the studio owns the movies. But our responsibilities are to hire the coach, which would be the director or the writer, hire the players, which would be the actors, and make sure that they perform to their ultimate abilities. There are very similar parallels. You have to hire everybody. Creatively, you have to work on the stories with the writers and make sure you get something you feel would make a terrific film. That's your job.

I GREW UP NEAR Northland, between 7 and 8 Mile.

MY DAD WAS BROUGHT from Germany to Detroit by a cousin of his who had a very exclusive women's store downtown. My dad worked as a salesman for his cousin. That's how he got in.

Then my mom was brought here by her brother. My mother is one of 14. My one uncle came over here with a pregnant German

Shepherd—that's all he had—sold the puppies, bought a hind of beef, and became one of the biggest restaurant suppliers in Detroit. And he ended up bringing quite a few of the 14 over.

MUMFORD? The majority of the students were very bright. Ninety percent of them wanted to go to college. It was a community that valued education a lot; there was a lot of competition for good grades. The families put so much importance on education that the children were motivated to do well. Once the kids were done with high school, they really wanted to go on to college. A lot of them are doctors, lawyers, engineers. They were very motivated students.

DETROIT WAS VERY INDUSTRIOUS. It was the automobile capital of the world. There were hardworking people; there were immigrants from all over the world. I remember the Polish section; all of these different sections. It was a very industrious city, and yet it was artistic because the cars had such interesting designs. So there was a lot of creativity. It was a nice community.

REALLY, I DIDN'T KNOW EDDIE MURPHY'S **MUMFORD SHIRT FROM 'BEVERLY HILLS COP'** WAS GOING TO BECOME SO FAMOUS.

You don't know a movie's going to be a success. You just don't know. Yes, the shirt was my idea—but no, it wasn't my shirt. We had one made. I don't think they had Mumford sweatshirts in those days.

That picture was originally going to take place in Pittsburgh. But since I'd already made a picture there, I thought it would be fun to go back to my hometown and do it, because it's a great place to film. Then, once we were in Detroit, I figured it'd be great to give Eddie Murphy some character. Since it was an ethnically diverse neighborhood, I thought it would be interesting to have him wear his high school alma mater T-shirt. Why not Mumford?

I PLAYED A LITTLE HOCKEY when I was younger, and I still play today. That's because my dad used to take me to hockey games in the old Olympia, downtown, when I was 7, 8 years old, to see the Red Wings.

THAT'S TRUE. I tried to build a hockey rink in our backyard, but it was too sloped. I couldn't do it.

GORDIE HOWE, TED LINDSAY. Those were my favorites.

WELL, AFTER COLLEGE, I got a job in a mailroom of an ad agency in Bloomfield Hills. After I got out of the mailroom, I worked on Pontiac and Cadillac. I think we did some Dow Chemical, too. But mostly Pontiac and Cadillac.

No, not California. From Detroit I went to New York. I did a Pontiac commercial on Bonnie and Clyde that was written up in *Time* magazine. And from that commercial I got hired by a big New York agency to do Pepsi-Cola.

I got to New York, worked on a bunch of campaigns for Pepsi, won a lot of awards, and then was brought to California by a director who I'd worked with in commercials who was going to make a movie at Fox.

I GUESS 'AMERICAN GIGOLO' was the one that started it. It was a big success at the time. And 'Flashdance.' Those were the two early ones.

I'm proud of all of my movies. I can't single one out. They're all your children. You can't point to one and say, 'This is the one.'

With 'Pirates of the Caribbean,' I think, first of all, it's a unique way of telling the story, because pirate films have been a disaster for 40 years. Our writers came up with the idea that you have to return a treasure rather than steal a treasure; there was this supernatural twist where it turns them into skeletons in the moonlight. It was a different twist on pirate movies. So it was very inventive, how we approached it.

Before we did 'Pirates,' Johnny Depp was basically known for very artistic films, and kind of stayed away from big Hollywood movies. He did very wonderful, smaller movies. So this kind of broadened his audience.

NOT REALLY. I DON'T PREFER one medium over another. Television is very fast. Movies take a long time to get made. A film can take years to get made. Television—9, 10 minutes, you know if you're a success or not.

They're both the same medium though. They're both about storytelling. They tell interesting stories, and they captivate audiences with those stories. It doesn't matter if it's on a big screen or a small screen.

YOU LEARN, YOU PICK IT UP. I've been here a long time. The more you do it, hopefully, the better you get at it.

TELL A GOOD STORY.
HAVE GREAT CHARACTERS, GOOD THEMES.
THAT'S ALL IT IS.

Just try to find intriguing subjects, intriguing venues or genres that haven't been looked at for a while. I always try to find something fresh. 'Pirates' was fresh. We're going to do a Western next, which is new. Not many people go to Westerns anymore.

MY HAND AND FOOTPRINTS in front of Mann's Chinese Theatre? It's pretty cool. It's very exciting; it really is.

'PIRATES OF THE CARIBBEAN: On Stranger Tides' just crossed a billion dollars. So we have three movies in the top 10 movies of all time—'Pirates' two, three and four.

The highest-grossing R-rated comedy was 'Beverly Hills Cop.' It might still be, if you go by those dollars when we made it.

STAY IN SCHOOL, get a good education, work hard. The harder you work, the luckier you get. ★

SUTTON FOSTER

MY FONDEST MEMORY OF DETROIT IS GOING TO SEE 'ME AND MY GIRL' AT **THE FISHER THEATRE DOWNTOWN.**

I was 14, and it was the first time I'd ever seen a professional, live performance, and it changed my life. There was an understudy in the lead role, and at the end of the show the curtain fell, and we heard the entire cast burst into applause for the guy who had gone on. Ever since then, I knew that I wanted to be a performer on the stage, and I am.

WHEN I WAS 13, my father relocated to Detroit. He worked for General Motors. We moved to Troy the summer before my seventh grade. He was a district sales manager, which means he sold cars to dealerships. We'd moved from a small town in Georgia. I was involved in dance and theater, and being in a subdivision of a major metropolitan city like Detroit, there were so many more opportunities than there were in Georgia.

FAVORITE THINGS TO DO? I was so busy, because I was always in dance classes, or in my high school drama program, or working at community theaters like Stagecrafters in Royal Oak. Detroit really opened up new doors for me. We would go down to the Fisher Theatre and the Masonic Temple, and the Fox—that was something we did for fun. We went to the touring shows when they came into town.

I remember I would watch the Tony Awards every year and think, 'Oh, I can do that; I want to be a part of that.' And I still pinch myself, that I'm doing what I dreamed of doing when I was on the couch when I was 15. It's incredible.

THAT'S TRUE, MY BROTHER Hunter and I discovered acting around the same time. That was in Georgia. I was 10 and he was 16. We both realized we could sing; nobody in our family had any background in theater or singing or performing.

When we moved to Michigan, my brother went to the University of Michigan and studied acting and theater. I was in high school. We kept encouraging each other, and we still do. It was like, 'If she can do it, I can do it,' and vice versa. And we've kept that going. We did a show together in Michigan, over the summer. We did a production of 'Evita.' I was 16, and he was in college. And we've been in two Broadway shows at the same time. We were in the revival of 'Grease,' back in the '90s, and then 'Les Miserables.' We overlapped for a couple of weeks in those productions.

WELL, I STARTED OFF DANCING. That was really where I began. The singing and the acting came after. I don't know if I ever set out with a game plan. I just kept going and learning and challenging myself. I loved it so much. And to have an opportunity like 'Anything Goes,' the show I'm in now, where I get to do everything that I spent my whole adolescence practicing, it's incredible.

I WENT TO TROY HIGH SCHOOL. Mr. Bodick was my teacher. He still works there, and we're still very close. He came to the opening of 'Anything Goes.' He's one of those teachers who totally believed in you. He's a special man, and we always had a special relationship. I was so grateful. He believed in me and encouraged me and pushed me. He created a very warm, safe environment, and that's what I like to have with students when I teach. It's amazing, to be able to share with him what I've accomplished. It's so important to me. He will always be a major part of my life.

The fondest memory I have from high school drama is that it was a place where I fit in and belonged. I was kind of a nerdy kid who fell between the cracks, and the theater department was where I had friends and fit in. I'm so grateful for that. If I didn't have that, I think I would have been lost.

THAT'S TRUE; I DID. There was an ad in the Detroit newspaper for a national tour of the 'Will Rogers Follies.' I was 17. I auditioned on the stage of the Fisher Theatre, and they flew me to New York for a callback and I got the job. So I was on tour when I was 17. That was how I got my break.

Tommy Tune was the director, and a man named Jeff Calhoun, who is a very famous director here in New York, was in Detroit and basically discovered me. He found this scrawny 17-year-old and gave her a shot. Every time I see him, I think, 'Thank you for that!' It was amazing. Incredible.

THEN, LATER, GETTING CAST IN
'THOROUGHLY MODERN MILLIE' CHANGED MY LIFE.

It was one of those things where it just sort of happened, and the next thing you know, I was thrust into this position, and it changed my career. It was a huge break. I cried for hours and freaked out. But, again, people took a risk on me and believed in me, and I went for it.

SOME OF THE HIGHLIGHTS? Well, every Tony night is a thrill. When Liza Minnelli came and saw a show, it was a highlight. And Carol Burnett has seen me perform. I've admired her my whole life, and she came to see 'Anything Goes.' Your mind kind of explodes, because you grew up admiring these women, and now they're watching you. It's intense.

Then, things like the Kennedy Center Awards are thrilling—to be able to meet the president and be in a room full of all of these incredible people. Your mind goes, 'Wow, how did I get here?' My brother and I went to the Kennedy Center Honors together this year. We were sitting in the White House. 'How did this happen? I guess I'm just going to take this in.'

Unbelievable.

I REMEMBER, IN MY 20S, I was performing at a show in California and having a moment, thinking, 'This is what I've always wanted to do, and I'm doing it.' I was 25. I still pinch myself. I'm still trying to figure everything out, figure out what makes me happy and how to sustain this. It is amazing to be able to do what I love and get paid for it. I never want to take that for granted.

'ANYTHING GOES' is going so great. It's an amazing year, and I feel lucky. It's been a dream come true. ★

LILY TOMLIN

I WAS BORN IN '39; my family moved here in '35 or '37. My mother and dad moved to Detroit from Kentucky so my dad could get a job as a factory worker. A lot of people came up and migrated from the South to the big industrial cities so that they could work. My dad was more of a city dude; he liked to be in the city.

I visited him at work a couple of times. I was well into my teens or early 20s. I was dumbfounded to see how noisy it was, how awful, how unbearably oppressive the sound was, the machinery. Everything. And I thought of my dad working there for 35 or 40 years, however long it was. I had empathy for my dad anyway, but I really felt more sympathetic about the fact that he went to work there every day for all of those years and it was so noisy.

He was what they called a job-setter. He wasn't educated at all. He was a country boy. But he had an intuitive intelligence and understood how to put a machine together. A job-setter gets blueprints and figures out how to set up a machine to create a certain kind of part. In fact, my dad would often come home from work and he'd bring me some complex part that he'd made and say, 'This is what I did today, babe.' And I sensed his great pride in it. He worked for a brass parts factory, Commonwealth Brass.

THE DETROIT NEIGHBORHOOD I grew up in, we lived in an old apartment house called the D'Elce. It was named for the man and his wife, for whom he built the building. His name was supposedly D, and her name was Elce. It was on the corner of Byron and Hazelwood, across from Herman Kiefer Hospital on the Byron side, and across from Hutchins Intermediate School and Cobb Field on the Hazelwood side.

Now, Hutchins was way down at the edge of the street, near Woodrow Wilson, and that's where I went to junior high. I went to Crossman Elementary, which was pretty much a block in the other direction, toward Hamilton—or what later became the John C. Lodge, where the freeway was built.

That was my neighborhood and I really made use of it. I was a kid who loved my neighborhood—especially living in an old apartment house with 40 apartments. I would go to each apartment and hang out; I kind of played the rooms. I'd go to one apartment and we'd do a certain kind of thing, then we'd go to another apartment and it'd be older, more conservative people. If they were Southerners, like my mother and dad, we would dance—dance the chicken, play canasta or rook, drink Pepsi, things like that.

I SPENT A LOT OF EVENINGS with Mrs. Rupert, who was a botanist. She was in her 50s. She was determined to make me a lady. She thought I was the kid in the building that had the most potential to rise above my station.

Every Saturday I would go shopping with her. We'd go to Hudson's downtown and she'd teach me how to select fabrics and linens. I was delighted by her. I was tall and lanky, and she was short and *zaftig*, and she seemed like a girlfriend to me even though she was in her 50s.

GROWING UP in that old building with all of those different kinds of people really influenced me. The building was probably more middle-class at one time, and then people like my mother and dad, who were working-class Southerners, came in.

It was largely a black neighborhood, and most of my friends were black. In the summers I would go to Kentucky, where my parents were born, and I would stay on the farm with my aunts and uncles and my grandmother, and I would just be appalled at how they knew nothing about black people. They didn't understand anything.

SO I HAD ONE FOOT IN THAT **RURAL KENTUCKY CULTURE** AND ONE FOOT IN **INNER-CITY DETROIT,** LIVING IN THE BUILDING WITH SO MANY DIFFERENT KINDS OF PEOPLE.

As a result, I understood how different people were in the world. They would have these outward opinions and points of view—but underneath they were all so similar. I think that's what caused me to have such affection for the species and not to be so judgmental of a person.

WHEN I WENT TO CASS TECH they didn't have a performing arts curriculum.

IN FACT, I GRADUATED IN '57, AND IT WAS REALLY OUT OF STYLE TO BE THEATRICAL.

I used to sublimate my performing by being a cheerleader. That was another kind of performance, but it was a socially acceptable performance. There was a drama club, but the kids were kind of on the outside. They weren't embraced by the school. And I was much more popular, a cheerleader.

I WENT TO WAYNE STATE for a while, and I got into a variety show that they put on annually for scholarship money. They were doing all of these sketches, which would be a takeoff on 'Gunsmoke', or the Academy Awards. All parody, no real content. And I thought, 'Gee, I do stuff like this, but it's much better.'

DETROIT WAS ONE of the preeminent jazz cities. When I was a teenager, and I thought I was so hip anyway, many a night I sat in the Minor Key or any number of the clubs, wearing sunglasses all night and being cool. Everybody came to Detroit. It was just the hippest. It was totally great. I've seen Miles Davis, I saw Carmen McRae, I can't imagine who wasn't there, that I missed at the time. This is all in the '50s.

THE AVALON, it was on Linwood and Davison. It's probably not there anymore. It was a Wisper and Wetsman theater. I was 14 and my girlfriend was on the candy counter. I was on the aisle with a flashlight, as an usher, and we would take one candy out of every box and make a little stash, and then close the box back up. When our friends came to the movie house we would give them popcorn, because it was all inventoried by container. And then we'd wash the container out and resell it.

DETROIT WAS SUCH A GREAT CITY. It was just one of those great, working-class cities. Vibrant people who were smart and tough and political. They're gutsy. I wouldn't have traded it for anything.

But then there was all of that white flight from the city, and going to the suburbs, and they just left the city flat, in that horribly bad time. From the mid to late '60s onward, the city was decimated. It was so tragic. My old apartment house burned down in the '67 riots. Later, I'd go back, and a lot of the houses on our street had collapsed, caved in from neglect.

IF I PLAY AROUND DETROIT or anyplace nearby, I always go into the city and spend a couple of nights, and go down to Greektown, which I always loved. And then, I always go to the Art Institute, which I was mad for. My favorite painting is Bruegel's 'Wedding Dance,' which I used to see on field trips from grade school. First of all, it's a beautiful painting. But the peasants are dancing in white aprons and caps, and the men all look like they have erections! They probably do. Of course, this was about as exciting as anything I had any chance to see, outside of a *True Confessions* magazine.

I would drag everybody over to see that painting. So whenever I go back, I always sneak into the room where the Bruegel is, and if I can, have somebody with me take a quick snapshot. You're not supposed to do that, with a flash. I have a couple of pictures like that, looking back at Bruegel. If only I had a picture of when I was about 7, it would be divine. ★

ALLEE WILLIS

OK. I GREW UP IN NORTHWEST DETROIT. Well, I was actually born on Monterey and Linwood, which is in the Davison area. But then, when I was 5, we moved to northwest Detroit, on Sorrento. I went to Mumford High, and I went to Schulze Elementary.

MY DAD OWNED the second-largest scrapyard in the city. This was in the 1950s and '60s, with the booming automobile industry. I would spend every Saturday down at the scrapyard, which was on Mt. Elliott. The building is still there. The scrapyard isn't.

One of the 'almost biggest thrills' of my life was that they were going to film 'Goldfinger' at my father's scrapyard. Because in one of the scenes the villains actually get crushed in that compactor. And at the last minute it didn't happen. I literally have never been able to see 'Goldfinger.' I don't want anyone talking about 'Goldfinger.'

A very bizarre thing happened. I co-wrote the musical 'The Color Purple.' And when it was on Broadway, a girl came up to me and she said, 'Oh, I heard your dad is in the scrap business.' And I said, 'Yeah,' and I told her the 'Goldfinger' story. And she said, 'They shot 'Goldfinger' in *my* father's scrapyard.' I couldn't believe it. It took me 40 years to figure out what happened.

DETROIT WAS INCREDIBLY exciting in those years. It was the city of the future. Everyone had a new car every year. The cars were spectacular. It was considered a completely cosmopolitan city. I thought it was much hipper living there than in New York or Los Angeles, or certainly Chicago, because it was funky, too. There was a groove to the city.

Once I got too old to go to the scrapyard every Saturday, I would go and sit in front of the little Motown house and I would sit on the lawn. You could watch everyone walk in. You could hear the bass through the walls. You could hear the background vocals. So I knew half those records before they came out. That was incredible.

TO THIS DAY, I HAVE NEVER LEARNED HOW TO PLAY AN INSTRUMENT, **DESPITE SELLING MORE THAN 50 MILLION RECORDS.** AND MOTOWN WAS REALLY MY EDUCATION.

WHAT MADE ME SWITCH from performing to writing? The album didn't sell. So that kind of took care of that.

The writing just seemed to work. So I got a few songs cut a year. And then in 1978, Patti LaBelle heard some of my songs and she started regularly cutting them. She turned me onto Herbie Hancock, and in pretty quick order that led to Earth, Wind & Fire. Then it exploded.

At one point I was getting more than 100 songs cut a year, but was very bored, because I felt like people wanted the same song over and over again. That's when it expanded into 'I'm going to paint, I'm going to collect, I'm going to do video sets.' Basically whatever anyone asked me to do.

'What Have I Done to Deserve This,' I think, is one of the most prototypical songs of my style, because it's comprised of five separate parts that most people would have turned into five separate songs.

NO. 'LEAN ON ME' was Bill Withers. I wrote 'Lead Me On.' That was a Maxine Nightingale hit. I had the No. 2 and 3 songs at the same time, with 'Boogie Wonderland' and 'Lead Me On.'

'Lead Me On,' actually, that was the biggest domestic song I ever had. But it hasn't lived on the way that something like 'Boogie Wonderland' has. I mean, 'September' I still hear every day. I always say that's a song that wouldn't die.

HOW DOES A WHITE GIRL HAVE SO MUCH SOUL?
IT'S MY FAVORITE QUESTION AND MY FAVORITE QUALITY IN THE WORLD TO HAVE.

Detroit. It's Detroit. That's what I heard growing up. That's what I love. Music made me feel so good. When my parents were out, I would go in their room and listen to their radio. I would turn that thing on and dance from 8 at night to 1 in the morning. Nothing made me happier.

I WAS LUCKY ENOUGH to have several key hookups in my life, one of which was Patti LaBelle, and one of which was Earth, Wind & Fire. I learned more from them rhythmically than I ever could have any other way, other than playing myself.

I've had songs on almost every singles chart that there is. I still think, other than the theme from 'Friends,' you can usually feel the funk in my stuff.

WELL, I KNEW NO ONE coming up in Detroit, especially because I wasn't actually doing music when I was there.

Lily Tomlin and I were introduced by Pee-wee Herman. She was doing a workshop in Santa Barbara for the show she eventually took to Broadway, 'The Search for Signs of Intelligent Life in the Universe.' She liked me and said, 'Could I fly you to New York to critique the show?' Unbeknownst to me there was a character who physically was based on me, because I've had this hair forever. So it's a character that bitches through the whole show; her name is Kate. And her hairdresser gets so mad at her for having to listen to her bitch all the time he whacks her hair off on one side.

We just have always done things together, and have been very united in our love of Detroit. And while doing her website, which includes a Detroit section—both of our sites have Detroit sections—she told me that her very first job was at the Avalon theater, which was the local theater near the house I was born in,

and where I saw my very first movie, which was 'Creature From the Black Lagoon.'

I have a very distinct memory, not of the movie, but of this usher who did this outrageous routine with a flashlight walking us to the seats. It was like this figure eight. So as we're doing the site, Lily tells me her first job was as an usher at the Avalon, and she had a flashlight routine. And I died, because obviously, it was Lily Tomlin who sat me when I was 10 years old.

JERRY BRUCKHEIMER, I had no idea, went to Mumford. I ended up getting a Grammy for 'Beverly Hills Cop.' My song 'Neutron Dance' was used in the film. It was never supposed to stay in the film. They had it in as a temp track, which they then sent to other songwriters and said, 'Copy this song; this is the feel we want.' And they had the nerve to send it to me, which was outrageous.

So with Danny Sembello, who I wrote 'Neutron Dance' with, we decided to rip ourselves off, and we stripped all of the instruments off. We wrote a parallel lyric, like if there was a bill collector in one song, there was a landlord in the other. We used pretty much the same drum track, new instruments, a different melody. Sent that song in. Never heard back from them. So I figured I got screwed, because everyone is copying my song and that's it.

About three weeks before that song was released, I got a call that Jerry Bruckheimer had heard the second song we had written. He'd grabbed the tape out of the garbage to record over, checked to see if anything was on it, heard it, and said, 'This has to be in the film.' So they never found anything better than 'Neutron Dance,' which ended up in the film.

I got a call to go up to his office to see a screening. This was a week before it opened. The first scene opens up and this cigarette truck is careening through a city, and I go, 'It's Detroit!' And that song, which had not been written for that movie, was so psychically tied to that film.

So I'm sitting there, tears coming down. It was at a very low point in my career; I thought I'd never have a hit again. And the second the song stops, Eddie Murphy emerges with a Mumford T-shirt. I died. And Jerry came over and asked if I was all right. I said, 'I went to Mumford.' He said, 'You're kidding; I went to Mumford.' He was four years older than me, so we didn't cross. But it's incredible.

The 'Beverly Hills Cop'-Mumford thing is so strong. It was a fluke I was even involved in it. It was good being involved in that, I'll tell you. ★

TYREE GUYTON

I HAD THE EPIPHANY for the Heidelberg Project when I was standing on the porch of the house with all of the dots on it, looking over Heidelberg Street.

It was like a vision. I saw the importance of going out there and utilizing the space. It was a way to educate people through art. I'd been talking to some of my neighbors, trying to get them to go to an exhibition. That wasn't going to happen. So I saw the importance of bringing it to them and taking my art to the street.

My studio at the time was on Heidelberg Street. The house with the dots on it was my studio, downstairs, in the basement. And right next door to the house with the dots on it, there was another house. It was abandoned. I remember looking at that house, and it was like the house was speaking to me, it was talking to me. I went out there and I made a dot on it. It just took off. The dot was red, and the project began to grow to what it is today.

THE DOT? I've been to Sydney three or four times, working with the aborigines. I was commissioned to go over and do a big project. I saw the importance of reading and studying and listening to the aborigines. And in talking with them, I began to really understand the dot, the significance of it.

The dot is life, the circle of life, and how in this life energy circles around and around, and how life repeats itself over and over, never stopping.

I STARTED OFF WORKING at Ford Motor Company back in the late '70s. I left there and went to the Detroit Fire Department. But I always had this desire to do more. Something about being an artist just wouldn't leave me alone. That's how you grow in life.

At Ford, I worked at the frame plant. I hated it; I hated that job. I was working the day shift, too, and I had to be there at 6. I worked there for almost seven years. It was dirty and greasy, but I needed to do that in order to move up. As I look back, I needed to work at the factory and the fire department. That gave me inspiration to move on, and to become an artist.

AT CCS, I started off in the industrial design department. I thought I was going to be a designer. It gave me the tools. It gave me what I needed in order to do the Heidelberg Project. It helped me to understand the importance of learning to visualize, learning to see it with your third eye. Once you see it, there's no stopping it. Once you learn the rules of the game you can kind of play with it, break them. That's what I've done with the Heidelberg Project.

CCS is a school that brings the best out of you. Last year, I received a doctorate of fine arts degree from CCS. So now it puts me in a position where I can kind of call my own shots; I can make it up now. And I tell people, 'Now that they gave me this doctorate, whatever I do is art,' from my point of view.

WELL, WHEN I WAS A KID, HEIDELBERG WAS A STREET THAT WAS FULL OF PEOPLE AND HOUSES AND BUSINESSES. IT WAS

A THRIVING NEIGHBORHOOD. I GREW UP THERE.

I witnessed the change. The 1967 riots brought about a great separation. The insurgency that took place here in the city. I was 12 at that time. It was unbelievable. I was living on Heidelberg Street. It was a beautiful day. We had a war in the city at the same time we had the situation in Vietnam. I witnessed the National Guard driving up and down the streets in tanks and Jeeps, and a helicopter that landed on the main thoroughfare, Mt. Elliott. I witnessed all of that. I heard gunshots. At nighttime, there was a curfew. You had to be inside at a certain time. I saw all that. It's something I'll never forget.

I saw the importance of doing something that was kind of radical, that would make a difference.

We can't go back in the past. The future is waiting on us. I saw the importance of tapping into those new possibilities. Looking back at being a kid on Heidelberg Street, playing there, having all kinds of people living there when I was growing up in this very mixed neighborhood, gave me the strength that I needed to create the project.

What my wife says to me quite often is, 'You still live there; you just don't sleep there anymore.' I'm there all the time when I'm not traveling. I'm there cultivating and adding to the project, overseeing different events and people who work there.

MY UPS AND DOWNS and waltz with city government over the years has had a lot to do with change—a lot to do with introducing something new, something different, something that was radical and whimsical.

You're talking about a neighborhood, how you define neighborhoods. So I had to go in there and redefine what I thought a neighborhood should be today. Government had somewhat of a problem with that.

Over the years, though, standing up and fighting with the government has brought about some great changes on both sides.

Today the government has great respect for the Heidelberg Project. They demolished the project twice. Every time they demolished the project, I built it back. I was not going to stop, because I saw the importance of it. What the government wanted to do was to argue about the aesthetics of it. I heard that, but I wanted to show them it was working. And if it's working, let's not fight against that. Let's let it do what it needs to do. Let's try to make this a win-win.

Something the government said to me that I thought was really interesting is that art belongs in an institution. Hmm. We have to talk about that.

THE PROJECT IS A SOLUTION. It's one of many solutions. It brings people from all over the world to an area that's considered to be broken down.

OVER THE 25 YEARS WE'VE BEEN THERE, WE'VE HAD PEOPLE COME VISIT US FROM 110 COUNTRIES.

THE HEIDELBERG PROJECT IS A MEDICINE.

YES, THAT WAS ESTHER GORDY EDWARDS. She was one of our honorary board members. Nobody wanted to give us any money because we were fighting the city government. All of the foundations backed away from us, all the sponsors. And Esther Gordy was the person to give us our first $1,000 to start over again.

We didn't have any cash. She said, 'I'm going to give you your first thousand.' That gave us the money to stay out there. She was the first, when everyone else wanted to stay away, because they were concerned with their own relationships with city government. She didn't care. She said, 'I'm going to help you to fight and to regroup.' We needed that.

MY GREATEST MEMORY OF DETROIT? I would say it was when I was a kid. I was 6; my Grandpa Mackey was working at a scrap yard. He came home that day and he'd found this toy car. It was big. And he gave it to me. I'll never forget that.

He was a commercial painter, and he would take me with him. He gave me a paintbrush, and he would talk to me about mixing colors and direction, balance.

As I sit here, talking with you, I can see it in my mind like it was yesterday. ★

ANNA SUI

MY PARENTS MET IN FRANCE. They were both going to school in France and they got married and lived in Europe for a while. And then my father got accepted at the University of Michigan for his master's degree. He was a structural engineer at a big architectural firm in Detroit. My mother raised us. I have two brothers.

First we lived in Dearborn Heights. Then we moved to West Bloomfield, and I went to West Bloomfield High School. In terms of extracurriculars, I was in the National Honor Society. I think that was it.

OH, YEAH. I ALREADY KNEW I was going to Parsons. I already knew I was going to be a fashion designer when I was in high school.

When I was a kid, I read an article in *Life* magazine about two young ladies who went to Parsons School for Design. And when they graduated, they went to Paris, and Elizabeth Taylor and Richard Burton opened a boutique for them. As a kid, I thought, 'OK, this is what I have to do. I have to go to Parsons.'

I remember my babysitter had *Seventeen* magazine, and in the back there was an ad for Parsons. So I got my mom to buy me *Seventeen*. And I looked at the ad in the back, and I wrote to Parsons, and I got a registration catalogue. Then I knew exactly what I needed to do to get into Parsons. I started taking art classes, because they required a portfolio. I needed a certain grade point average. And everything I did from that day on, I worked toward going to Parsons.

Many years later, I went back and reread the article, and one of the young ladies, her stepfather was a very famous photographer, Irving Penn. As a child, you don't understand those kinds of things. You just think, 'This is the secret; all you have to do is do this.' I always use that as an example of how sometimes that dream can take you further than anything.

THAT'S WHY MY MOTTO IS,
'LIVE YOUR DREAM.'

YES, I WAS IN DETROIT at the time when Alice Cooper, Iggy and the Stooges, the MC5, all of those bands were playing every weekend. Also, every English band, the British Invasion, all of those people came through. All of that really inspired me. I thought about the way those rock stars dressed, the way the groupies and the girlfriends all dressed. That was always the most exciting thing to me.

You can see that in my work.

No, I didn't see a lot of the shows. I was too young. I think you had to be 21 or 18. They served alcohol, so you couldn't get in. But there were outdoor concerts that I could go to. So I did see Iggy; I did see Alice Cooper, at Edward Hines Park.

HUDSON'S WAS A PLACE that we went to for special occasions, especially at Christmastime, because they always had incredible Christmas decorations in the toy department. They had an incredible display of train sets and miniatures and so many things.

I remember, as a kid, I loved looking at all of the miniatures, because they'd have whole towns of miniatures. I thought, 'Oh, they're the perfect size for my Barbie doll.' So I would try to buy cakes and different things that I could use when I was playing Barbie. That's what I loved the most about Hudson's, the toy department.

I guess I always liked dolls. As a child I collected them. I had Barbie dolls, I had baby dolls, I had dolls that you just put on a shelf. I've always liked those. I don't know, I think it's just that little girl in me that will always be there.

Then, when I got older, Hudson's had really great fashion, too. I remember one of the first things I bought in the fashion department: Betsey Johnson was doing a line called 'Alley Cat.' They carried it there, and that was my favorite.

As soon as I was old enough, I figured out a way to take the bus downtown. From Dearborn Heights there was a bus that went directly downtown.

I WOULD SNEAK THERE AND NOT TELL ANYBODY WHERE I WAS, AND I WOULD GO BY MYSELF AND LOOK AROUND IN HUDSON'S.

THE GENIUS FILES? As a kid, I started saving pictures that I liked, things that I thought were inspiring. I had a box under my bed. When I moved to New York, I brought that box with me. Steven Meisel used to always come over and say, 'Can we look at your genius files?' because we loved all of the photographs and pictures and things I saved. We would spend hours going through them. I still have those, but they're much bigger now. It takes up a big closet in my office. It fills a whole shelf area.

WELL, I'VE NEVER REALLY THOUGHT, 'I've made it.' It's just as hard today as it was in the beginning. Every season is a different challenge. I don't know if I think about that. Receiving the Council of Fashion Designers of America Lifetime Achievement Award, that was a marker. But it's never gotten easier.

I hope that I have a continued influence. Let's put it that way, because I'm still working. So it's kind of like you're just trying to keep your head above water every season, to maintain.

THANK YOU VERY MUCH. It was amazing to have Andrew Bolton write the new book, and Steven Meisel and Jack White do the pieces that they did for it. It was really a labor of love.

I WAS A BIG WHITE STRIPES FAN. I met Jack from his then-wife, Karen Elson. Karen modeled in my shows since she started, and I went to see him play. It was on tour when I met him. I went backstage.

It was funny, because you know how backstage there are a million people? You just don't know where you fit in. Suddenly, Jack said, 'Hey, Anna, I've got to show you something.' I just about fainted that he knew who I was. We went to a corner and he pulled out a Polaroid, and it was him with Jimmy Page. And he said, 'Look at this picture we did today.' After that, we were friends forever. It was so special, that he showed me that.

I NEVER REALLY HAD A CAR. I drove my dad's car. I remember, when I first started driving, he'd just bought a Camaro. Although that's known as a muscle car, there was no muscle in that car. It was beautiful outside, but whatever kind of engine they had in the Camaro... it was fun to drive, but people were always trying to race, and there was no power in that car. It just looked like it on the outside. ★

JOHN VARVATOS

IT'S HUGE TO ME, growing up Greek, because I grew up in a Greek community. Not the community itself; Allen Park wasn't Greek. But we spent a lot of time with our church and our cousins, and our godparents, so on weekends it was very Greek.

Culturally, it was a big thing. It was very close and humble, and family-oriented. It definitely had a long-lasting effect on the way I look at family. Everybody was very respectful, because they came from such humble beginnings. Very, very humble.

My mother was a housewife with five kids, so she was totally busy taking care of us and taking care of the house. And my dad was an accountant.

I FIRST BECAME INTERESTED in fashion because I became interested in girls in junior high, and I noticed, a few times, when I wore something, I got compliments on it from girls. So then I started to think about, every day, what could I wear, how did I look? Because up until then, you were just a kid putting on anything. And then all of a sudden you're like, 'Oh, they like that turtleneck...'

I still wear a leather jacket I bought when I was 17. Iggy and the Stooges had an album out, 'Fun House,' and inside the jacket all the guys had motorcycle jackets on. Just black leather motorcycle jackets and skinny jeans. A little bit like the Ramones, but the Ramones were many years later. There was something in my mind that clicked with it.

I LOVED THE STOOGES. My favorite band of all time. And I wanted to look like that, so I found out what kind of jacket it was and I bought it. Actually, it was made in the Downriver area. It's a very famous leather jacket company; it's called Buco. I saved up all my money from working through the summer to buy this jacket. And I've kind of traveled my life with it. It's probably the thing

I've worn the most. If you asked me what's my one possession I have that I would never get rid of, besides my family and my record collection, that would be it.

The Stooges were my icons, and I wanted to look like my icons. That had an influence on everything else I did in fashion, too.

MY FAVORITE VENUE OF ALL TIME WAS
THE GRANDE BALLROOM.
IT'S WHERE THE MC5 AND IGGY AND THE STOOGES AND PEOPLE LIKE THE WHO AND LED ZEPPELIN ALL PLAYED.

It was small. You can't even imagine that people like The Who played it. I saw the MC5 there. The electricity and the sweat and no air-conditioning, it was a whole different thing.

And then Cobo Hall was a basketball arena, and it was the bigger arena at the time. Bob Seger's biggest-selling album, his double-live album, was recorded at Cobo. The most impressive show, at that stage of my life, was when I saw Led Zeppelin there. I saw Black Sabbath, The Who. A lot of the most memorable shows I saw growing up were there.

RIGHT, THERE'S A JOHN VARVATOS store in the old CBGB. Well, when CB closed, it was very sad. But it had really deteriorated, in terms of the acts that played there over the last 10 years. At one time, it was such a historic place, but it had really become a shadow of what it was.

It closed, and I never gave it another thought, other than it's sad. And then one day somebody invited me into the Bowery to talk about doing a joint venture on a club or something. It wasn't

at the CB space; it was in the neighborhood, but they knew the landlord of the CB space, and I said, 'Is there any way to take a look at it?' And I walked in, and it was totally gutted.

There was something, though... when I went upstairs and looked around, and saw all of the posters still on the walls, it was like a lightning bolt. I thought, 'I should do something with this.'

It wasn't done from a commercial point of view. But it is, to me, the most exciting thing in my brand today. We do something called Thursday Nite Live. This Monday we have Tommy Stinson from The Replacements. I'm thrilled to have that show there. And we've had Guns N' Roses, tons of people.

It's such a good feeling, watching the crowd packed and dancing. It reminds me, a bit, of being at the Grande.

MY RADIO STATION? It's called 'Born in Detroit.' What happened was, people heard rumors about a show that we were putting together at the old CB space. We had an MC5 reunion, and we had Slash, and Tom Morello from Rage Against The Machine, Perry Farrell, Joan Jett, people who'd played there. All the money went to the VH1 Save The Music Foundation, which I'm on the board of.

Scott Greenstein, who's the president of Sirius XM, called me one day and said, 'I hear you guys are going to do this event; we'd like to broadcast it. But we'd like you to come up and do a little thing that we can play before the show.' So I went up to Sirius. I did an interview, then they said, 'OK, now go over to the studio and do your own show.' 'Do my own show?' 'Yeah, we thought you understood that? You have to do an hour show.'

I tried to think of something that I could kind of pull out of my butt. So, I said, 'We're celebrating the opening of this store in the Bowery, and celebrating the music history in the Bowery, but the roots of a lot of that come from Detroit, from the MC5 and The Stooges, and every one of those people will tell you that they've been influenced by them.'

So I started talking about Detroit, the Grande Ballroom, and then I started playing music, telling stories. When it was all said and done, Sirius heard it and they said, 'Why don't you do a regular show?' We finally agreed I'd do the show once a month. I called the show 'Born In Detroit,' because, I thought, 'This is the music that was born in Detroit, and I was born in Detroit.'

I WAS TALKING TO IGGY yesterday. Somebody sent him a book from France, all of these pictures of Detroit, that's really beautiful and sad at the same time. I said, 'I have the same book. It's kind of heartbreaking, part of it.'

You see him onstage and he's an animal. You see him offstage, he's the sweetest guy possible.

The interesting thing is that every one of those people, Wayne Kramer, Alice, Iggy, there's something about them you can't put on paper. There's an instant connection. And even other musicians who remember their time in Detroit, there's something about the crowds there. I asked Robert Plant why he liked Detroit so much, and he said that they had the best crowds anywhere in America. When they would start a tour they'd want to start someplace where people are insane into you. And L.A. or New York, it just wasn't the same.

HIGHLIGHTS? There are a couple of them. No. 1 would be winning the American Fashion Awards I've won for Menswear Designer of the Year. Not just for me, but the entire company, because everybody works so hard.

Then the other thing is, how the whole music and fashion thing got blended. It wasn't something I set out to do; it was just because of my passion for it that it organically morphed into something.

DETROIT HAS A REAL SOUL TO IT. When I was growing up, it was that soul that got us through all of the terrible other things that were going on there at the time. And somehow, there's this soul there that connects people. So even though it's super-difficult, unemployment's 30 percent or whatever, they're still held together with this deep soul.

When you think of soul, you think of Motown. It's all about passion.

DETROIT, FOR ME, HAS SURVIVED THROUGH ALL OF THESE THINGS BECAUSE OF **ALL THE SOUL AND PASSION THAT IT HAS.** ★

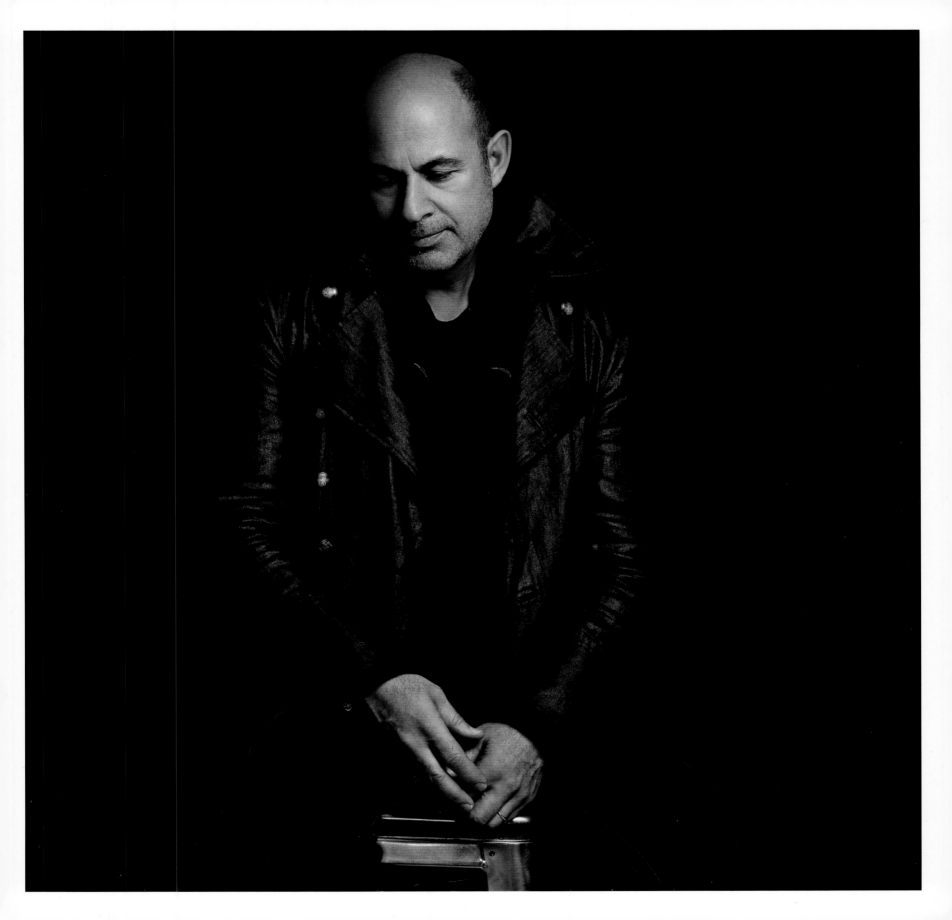

VERONICA WEBB

I WENT TO WALDORF. It's in Indian Village. It's a small high school, so a lot of people might not know it. It's very artistic.

It was always beautiful, walking those blocks to and from school, to see the architecture, these homes that said Detroit was a place where people could make a great life for themselves.

ON ONE HAND, Detroit had all these urban problems. But on the other hand, it's so beautiful. We had a small backyard where we grew everything from roses to pole beans to raspberries. The neighbors had a cherry tree that would blossom, and there would be pink blossoms and cherries in the yard. The sky is so beautiful at night, the river's right there, the lake is right there.

And then, people made cars, and they took pride in the cars that they made. Everybody had a new car every year, a factory job or a government job, and I always had the sense Detroit was a poor man's paradise. You could come from nothing and make a decent living, you could work as many hours as you wanted. People had a chance to turn their lives around. There's something particularly American and romantic about that.

WHAT DID WE DO FOR FUN? Bob-Lo, the State Fair, Skateland, Eastland Mall. I loved going to the Detroit Institute of Arts. I could never get enough of it. Belle Isle. We would canoe on Belle Isle, have picnics and go to the greenhouse. We went to church.

I ALWAYS WAS INTERESTED IN ART. I was lucky because I went to a school that really fostered that, and I had a mother who understood how much I loved it, and who encouraged me. She was very creative. My mother could make everything. She made all my clothes, knitted all my hats, scarves, socks, winter coats. The whole family loved fashion. My mother taught everybody how to make clothes.

MY SISTERS? One is a doctor, the other is a math specialist for the board of education.

I also went to the Detroit Community Music School. I was in the dance program there. And CCS was right next door, the local art college. I would always see students outside, sketching. So I was always exposed to art growing up.

WELL, WHEN I GOT TO NEW YORK I was working as a cashier in a store in SoHo, and I got discovered. On the same day there was a makeup artist, a hairdresser, and a modeling agent who all came through the store and suggested I should model.

THE MOMENT I REALLY KNEW I was on my way, though, was when I got booked for my first real fashion show.

Back then fashion shows were really mysterious. It was like nobody could see a show or get into a show or even knew anybody who was in a show. And I was in the biggest fashion show in New York. Paul Cavaco, who's now the fashion director of *Allure* magazine, booked me for a show called Fashion Group. I wore something from every major designer at the time. I had on something from Calvin Klein, something from Donna Karan, something from Ralph Lauren, something from Oscar de la Renta. I went out five times. I had one outfit from each major designer. So I knew I was on my way.

THE WORLD OF MARKETING, advertising and retail went through a really big change in the early '90s. Corporations began to respond to and court an ethnic consumer base for the first time in a somewhat equal and significant way. It was an amazing time to be there, because that's when everything changed.

That's when more and more models of color started to get covers and cosmetic contracts. So there was a feeling of being part of something bigger and more positive than just creating consumer goals. My generation of models was very vocal about equal pay for minorities, and the need for beauty from every race and creed to be showcased as ideal.

WHAT WE ALL
EMBRACE AS BEAUTIFUL AND ASPIRATIONAL
IN ADVERTISING HAS SHIFTED DRAMATICALLY IN THE LAST FEW DECADES.

I feel that I was somehow part of making that happen, and I'm proud every time I see a diverse or unconventional choice of beauty depicted in a magazine.

WITH BEING A SPOKESPERSON FOR REVLON, I think there's a reason a role like that is called a spokesperson. Visually, you have to be appealing to and represent the part of the consumer base that people are going after. You also have to be able to speak to the values of the brand, and what it can do for the customer. And you have to have an interesting enough life outside of fashion that you have something to talk about, which then helps to bring the product into reality.

SO I HAPPENED TO BE IN THE RIGHT PLACE AT THE RIGHT TIME, AND I ENDED UP WITH A
REVLON CONTRACT.

I was the first black woman to get a contract, a full cosmetic contract, which is, for models, the best thing that you can possibly get working in this industry.

The greatest thing we did there was change the industry and made it a necessary and competitive thing for businesses to give women of color contracts that were commensurate with their counterparts who weren't minorities.

OTHER HIGHLIGHTS? Magazine covers and cosmetic contracts are the pinnacle of commercial success. For me, though, it's really collaborating with other creative people—whenever I've been in the presence of greatness, with photographers like Steven Meisel or Richard Avedon, or designers like Azzedine Alaïa or Isaac Mizrahi. People who are truly creative and full of ideas. Fashion is at its best when people mix and match ideas to come up with something fresh and original.

Those are my career highlights. It's all the moments that I can't really capture in pictures. It's the thrill of seeing things made.

THERE WERE SO MANY TIMES in my career I felt like, 'What am I doing here?' Sometimes it was a legitimate question; I didn't know what to do because I'd never been in worlds like that before, where there were 14 forks on the table. Or where there were things that, growing up, I wouldn't have even dared to touch in a store that are suddenly being put into your hands: 'Here, this is yours, interpret it and make people see how they can use it in their lives.' It can be intimidating when you're young and you don't even understand whose life those clothes and jewels could possibly be for. But then you go back to what you learned from your mother growing up: Anything can be yours if you work for it.

ONE MISCONCEPTION ABOUT MODELING is that it's a job that's handed to you and it takes nothing to do it. I was a kid working for myself alone in a big city with no business experience. It's an expensive business to be in, and it takes a long time to make money in the industry, if you're lucky enough to be able to work long enough to clear a profit.

In order to make money you have to be willing to move every time you get a call from your agent. So it can be your mother's birthday, your sister's having a baby, whatever—you drop everything and go halfway around the world at a moment's notice. There were years on end when I was on the road almost 200 days a year. And you have to learn how to control every aspect of your appearance. A small change like gaining 5 pounds before fashion week can cost you hundreds of thousands of dollars in lost bookings.

The other misconception is that models actually look like models. Every great model you've ever seen had to become a model by making herself look like one. That's one of the greatest lessons I learned. I remember Azzedine said to me, 'Anyone can become beautiful at any time.' Sometimes it's just a question of a haircut, or the right dress, or believing in yourself. ★

CONGRESSMAN JOHN CONYERS JR.

I GREW UP FIRST on the East Side and then we moved to the West Side. My father was an organizer for the United Automobile Workers when they organized Chrysler.

MY BROTHER NATHAN went to Cass Technical High School, which was the premier high school. And the rest of us went to Northwestern. Judge Damon Keith went to Northwestern. He was before my time. There were some interesting people who went to Northwestern.

My dad came from Monroe, Georgia, and my mother was born outside of Jackson, Mississippi, at Pelahatchie. That's an old Indian name.

Oh, yeah. My dad gave us the motivation. All of us went to law school.

I remember the first time I read one of his books. It was on Clarence Darrow. My dad always wanted to be a lawyer, but in that part of Georgia that he came from, at that time, they didn't even have segregated schools—they didn't have any schools for people of color. He was self-educated and he was a good speaker, and that's how he became a union leader. But he always wanted to be a lawyer.

I went to law school, my brothers went to law school, everybody, we all just fell into it. It was something we all wanted to do.

I went to Wayne State University Law School. After I came out of the service, I finished up my undergrad and started law school. I got a scholarship at the end of my first year.

Then something very unusual happened that caused me to end up in Congress. The lawyer that was working for my Congressman, John Dingell, was taken by then-Governor John Swainson. So my father and his friends that were supporting Dingell said, 'Why don't you take Johnny Conyers, because he'll be graduating from law school?' And he did, amazingly. I started working in his office part time, until I finished law school. Without that, I wouldn't have been able to run for Congress, because I was just out of law school.

I BECAME ACTIVE IN CIVIL RIGHTS because my father was active for working people having the right to collective bargaining and rights at the workplace. So Julian Bond, the former state senator of Georgia, who was very active, and I became friends.

Then I began to meet Martin Luther King, who would come to Detroit, and Reverend Abernathy and others who would come in, and I got to know them.

WHEN I FINISHED SCHOOL, I STARTED GOING DOWN SOUTH TO REPRESENT PEOPLE WHO WERE ARRESTED FOR PROTESTING. THAT'S WHERE I MET ROSA PARKS.

So when she and her husband left Georgia and came to Detroit, she was in my first campaign for Congress.

WELL, THEY BLACKLISTED HER. They wouldn't let her work. She was a seamstress. Who cares about one seamstress in the state of Georgia? But they were so furious because she brought in Martin Luther King. They brought him in from Alabama. They shut down the public transportation for over a year because she wouldn't sit in the back of the bus. And she finally won. So they hated her for that, the people in the state. She and her husband finally had to leave.

Her husband knew some people in Detroit, so they said, 'Hey, let's go to Detroit.' And she was in my campaign. She'd come and sit, and people would say, 'That's Rosa Parks.' They were pointing to her. They were thunderstruck. She helped me win my election. I won by 128 votes. I was endorsed by King, and Rosa Parks was in the campaign. So if it hadn't been for her, I wouldn't have gotten elected. She and King affected everything I've done.

I said, 'She's going to be the first person I'm going to ask to work for me,' and she accepted. She worked for me for 21 years.

OFFICE MANAGER. She was very well-known, so people would come to my office all the time to meet her. They didn't care who she was working for. She was a very gracious, humble lady. Everybody liked her and she was very courageous, because in those days you could get in big trouble protesting segregation.

She was the only one who ever came to me and said she wanted a reduction in her pay. I was surprised; I said, 'What are you talking about?' She said, 'Well, you let me travel so much, and I feel so bad that I can't be here all the time, so I'd be willing to take a cut.' I said, 'Rosa, you've got to be kidding. I'm honored that you're working for me. You honor me, you can take all the time off you need.'

That's how humble she was. She had a huge memorial service here. People came from everywhere.

THE CIVIL RIGHTS MOVEMENT had a big effect on Detroit. Because Detroit was segregated, too. The housing was segregated, schools were segregated. They wanted to segregate the workplaces. The unions were fighting against segregation. There was a big fight going on, whether the unions should be segregated. Because frequently, before then, they had been. So it affected the whole country.

Then we had the Supreme Court decision of 1954, Brown vs. the Board of Education, where they said segregation was illegal and unconstitutional in the schools and everywhere else.

When I came to Congress, segregationists ran the place, because the people in the South all had the seniority and they were all the chairmen. African-Americans not only couldn't run for office, they couldn't even vote. So it was a very turbulent period.

I can understand what's happening now, though. The election of the first African-American to the White House has created a huge pushback, and that's why the president has so much difficulty getting anything done.

So it still goes on. We're not through with racism, but we've come a very long way. There's very little segregation in housing. Employment is pretty fair. But the problem still persists.

I THINK THIS IS ABOUT long enough. You get the drift.

OK, one or two more.

I FELT LIKE ANYBODY would feel about the president. Very proud. I knew him before he became president. He came by to see me, to ask me if he should run, and would I support him. I said, 'Of course.' I was the first member of Congress to come out for Obama for Congress. He lived in Chicago, so we were back and forth all the time with Reverend Jesse Jackson.

I HAVE TO SAY MY PROUDEST ACHIEVEMENT WAS FINALLY GETTING A LEGAL HOLIDAY FOR MARTIN LUTHER KING JR., BECAUSE IT TOOK 15 YEARS.

And I did that right after his assassination; I think it was the third day after.

I kept thinking about how he was the greatest person in my life, who affected my political outlook, and who I admired most, and still do. And of course, he's celebrated now around the world.

When we were fighting for the holiday, every year I would lead a march on Washington on his birthday. And ambassadors would come from other countries and join us. And they'd say, 'We don't understand what the problem is here; we celebrate his birthday in our country, and you don't.' I'd say, 'That's why we're marching.'

King and his wife, Coretta, and his kids, they created history. King never stopped. He got the Voter Rights Act passed and the Civil Rights Bill enacted into law. And he was having a march against poverty in America when he was assassinated.

So that was a great moment in my political history that I thought was very important. Because there were a lot of people who didn't want it. King was the object of death threats, his home was bombed, he was arrested repeatedly. But he was the one who galvanized the right-thinking people into doing the right thing, and gave his life for that. So he was a great American. And the monument that went up for him has just opened up. It's a fitting tribute. He's between Lincoln and Jefferson. ★

DR. JACK KEVORKIAN

THAT CAME LATER.

That became a passion when I was in Long Beach, in the hospital. I was employed there. I was sitting in the lounge watching TV and '60 Minutes' came on. And they reported that the Netherlands had legalized euthanasia. I said, 'Oh, we need that.' I'd seen the need for it in my internship and residency. I saw people who really wanted to die. But I didn't dare say anything because I'd get kicked out of school or lose my residency.

I went over there, to the Netherlands, to see if there was some way we could connect. But they weren't interested in teaching anybody who wasn't Dutch. Some of my other ideas they found a little bit strange, too. So I knew I couldn't get any help there.

I knew we needed it, but I didn't campaign for it because what could I do? I'd lose my position. That opened the door, though. Then I really got interested.

WELL, I DIDN'T THINK of it as sacrificing my career. I was really, in a way, reckless. I never cared for some reason. What did I have to lose? I didn't have a family, which was an advantage. I didn't worry about it.

I DID RESENT PRISON A LITTLE. ESPECIALLY WHEN YOU'RE OLDER. I RESENT THAT.
I LOST EIGHT GOOD YEARS.

But I knew somebody had to go to prison and that it probably was going to be me. I knew that. I didn't like it, because you're not free to do what you want to do, and you can't get what you want to get. But I knew I wasn't a criminal. Therefore, it's easier.

I could have gotten a keyboard in prison. They give you a one-octave keyboard. What can you do with that? If I could have gotten a keyboard for an organ, 41 notes, I would have been happy. Prison would have been a lark. I would have come out a terrific keyboard player.

NO. I CAN'T PLAY ANYMORE. I tried to blow the flute when I got out and I lost my aperture.

I WOULD SAY ACADEMICS were just natural. My two sisters and I were never prodded to do better in school by my parents. They wouldn't even ask what we got on our report cards.

WE'RE ARMENIAN.

MY DAD WAS A STRICT DISCIPLINARIAN, but not brutal. Like most boys, I feared him. And that's good. It kept me alive, because you can see from my behavior as an adult, I'm kind of unpredictable. I could easily have gone off the deep end and become a juvenile delinquent. Who knows?

My father came here and, like most of the other men, he worked in a foundry. And then he branched off and did his own work. I admire what he did.

REALLY, I NEVER LIKED MUSIC then. My older sister could learn popular songs very easily. She taught herself to play piano. My dad knew she liked it. I, at that time, was not musical at all. My father bought an old piano, a used piano. Some of the ivory was missing and it was out of tune. So we got it tuned sufficiently and my sister would play it.

Later, though, the interns' quarters at the university hospital in Ann Arbor had a piano. And I couldn't resist. I said, 'How can anybody play this?' Then I really got interested. My interest was fueled by my love of Bach's music.

I've never been trained in music or art. I practiced to the point where I could play a couple of compositions, simple ones. And I went to the organ then, the pipe organ. That's really Bach's music. You play so much of it, it's almost like you wrote it. So you say, 'I wonder if I could write a couple of tunes?' And that's how I composed a couple pieces.

I have a CD of my work. They did it for me when I got out of prison. When they were making the movie 'You Don't Know Jack,' one fellow had a recording studio in his home, so he made a recording. They hired two professional flutists and a Russian student who was learning keyboard, and they played some of my music. It was really nice. I play it often.

I WAS SKEPTICAL ABOUT THE MOVIE at first. I was against it. I was against the book that was written, too, on which it's based. But they did a heck of a job. It's very, very moving.

I NEVER WANTED TO BE A DOCTOR. I really didn't. I was good at drawing and sketching. I decided to be a civil engineer because I knew the work and I liked it. So I went to college in Ann Arbor for engineering, and I liked it fairly well until I got to analytical geometry. And boy, that killed me. So I decided to switch. I said, 'Well, a lot of my buddies are taking pre-med. Medicine's not bad. It's got prestige. It's a so-called noble profession. You make good income. I'll try that.'

When I applied to medical school it was after the war and there was a real shortage of physicians. All the veterans were coming back. I applied to medical school and there were 2,000 applications for 150 positions.

I don't know what they saw that convinced them. I couldn't believe it when I got accepted. One thing I think that impressed them was that I applied at only one school. Other guys were applying at four or five schools. The second thing was, I had a lot of language. In high school, during the war, they didn't teach German. So I got a book, and I started studying German and Japanese. In the military I kept doing it, and I perfected my Japanese. I think that impressed them. They probably figured, 'This kid must be a character.'

That's it. I went through four years and I decided on pathology, because it's connected to the laboratory with clinical practice. So you've got the whole gamut of medicine.

YES. NOW IT'S LEGAL IN THREE STATES, BUT THEY'RE

NOT DOING IT RIGHT. THEY'RE STILL AFRAID TO DEATH.

THEY'RE WALKING ON TIPTOES. IF A DOCTOR GIVES A PILL TO THE PATIENT, HE'LL GO TO PRISON. THAT'S NOT THE WAY TO DO IT.

I am a little angry over letting the law take away a basic right like that. Not take it away. You don't take away a right. You can't. You're born with every one of them.

WELL, THESE DAYS, it's just make-do things. I enjoy watching 'Judge Judy.' You learn a little law. She takes no nonsense. I like that. The ones who allow a lot of talk and yelling in their courtroom, a lot of joking, to me they're not good judges.

NO, IT DIDN'T HURT ME when they took away my license. I laughed. You knew they were going to take it, so that was a foregone conclusion. I retaliated by burning their injunction against me on the steps of the State House.

I think my trials were all fair except the last one. How can a trial be fair when the defendant is charged with murder and they won't let any witnesses talk for the defendant?

THE 'THANATRON' AND 'MERCITRON' were just highfalutin names. Pieces of junk. I just went to garage sales and antique shops and picked up odds and ends that I thought would work. I didn't have any plans. Today they have 20-sheet blueprints. When it's legal, you watch what they do with it. They'll ruin it.

It's legal now. It's in the Constitution. Is there any law higher than that?

WELL, I JUST STARTED wearing a blue sweater. I don't change clothes very often. I don't change colors or things like that. And I didn't get really dirty. What do I do that's dirty? I don't wear it in an autopsy. I get most of my stuff from the Salvation Army.

No, we auctioned mine off. I have two or three others. This one's tolerable. I don't like the other two that are left. The best one was the one that was auctioned off. I've got a whole closet full of clothes. Some of it's pretty good. But I don't wear them. I don't change clothes very often.

I WENT ON TOO LONG.

My pleasure. ★

MY DAD WAS A LAWYER. I grew up mainly in the Boston-Edison area, Boston Boulevard, near 14th Street. Most of my young life was in the Boston-Edison area.

My father was born in Chicago, but went to law school in Detroit, then continued to live here. My mother was raised in Birmingham and then went to the University of Michigan. So they basically were living either in Detroit or around Detroit when they were young.

I'M A TRAILBLAZER! Central High School. It was a great experience. I had wonderful friends, these are lifelong friends of mine. We still get together frequently. We call it 'The Gang.' My wife also went to Central, three years after I did, and my brother went to Central. So, we're all Centralites.

WELL, I WAS ON STUDENT COUNCIL. I was treasurer of my class, so I was a class officer, but my main extracurriculars were sports with my gang on the playing fields at Central and other neighborhoods in Detroit.

I REMEMBER MY PARENTS would take us down to movies at the Detroit Institute of Arts. Restaurant-wise, my favorite would have been Boesky's on 12th Street. And my favorite movie theater was the Avalon on Davison and Linwood. We used to go to the Avalon on Saturday afternoons. There was always a double feature with cartoons, and I think it was 12 cents for kids.

I'M MOST PROUD OF MY GREAT MARRIAGE, three great kids, three great sons-in-law, six great grandkids. That's what I'm most proud of, is my family. We have a very close family, and I've always felt that that's the most important thing that anybody can do in one's life.

I BECAME INTERESTED IN PUBLIC SERVICE because my dad was interested in public service. He was on the Michigan Corrections Commission, which is a citizens' group that oversees the operations of our prisons. He also was active in supporting President Roosevelt and the New Deal. He was a big fan of Harry Truman. And my mother was a volunteer for a Jewish organization, so she was interested in public service from that perspective. Around the dinner table my dad and mother, my brother Sandy, my sister Hannah, we used to talk politics, about the obligation of people who were lucky enough to live in America to participate in their communities and to take advantage of the extraordinary opportunities that we have in this country.

I was president of the City Council and on the City Council for eight years before I ran for Senate. Since I've been in the Senate, I focus mostly on jobs and anything we can do to promote manufacturing actions to help save the auto industry.

ANYTHING TO DO WITH MANUFACTURING AND JOBS IS
NO. 1 ON MY AGENDA.

And secondly, perhaps, would be the Detroit riverfront, where we've been very active in getting significant funding. We've focused particularly on things like the new dock and a new center where people are going to be able to come into Detroit on boats from the Great Lakes. And we've got funding for the west riverfront now, which will be an expansion to the west of Cobo Hall all the way to the Ambassador Bridge.

FOCUS: HOPE has been important to bring some real hope to that particular part of Detroit. But way beyond that, thousands of people have benefited from being educated at Focus: HOPE and participating in all of their activities. What drew me to it was its idealism. It came out of a riot. It was part of the civil rights movement and it helped bring this city together and its people together. It's a nonprofit institution, a great vision. Its aim is to give people who haven't had an opportunity an opportunity, and doing it in a way that is structured and productive and effective. It's also an organization that is very practical, so the training it gives is practical. It has produced a huge number of machinists and engineers, as well as training and diplomas to people who otherwise would not have been able to complete a high school education.

WELL, I ALWAYS FELT there was a gap in my life because I didn't serve in the military. I wanted to learn more about it. I felt that we had an obligation to understand the military, what its role is, what its capabilities are, and what its limits are. So I joined the Armed Services Committee as soon as I got to the Senate, and I'm chairman because I have the most seniority among the Democrats on that committee.

I opposed the war in Iraq. I felt it was unilateral, and that it was based on a deception that Saddam Hussein, according to the Bush administration, was involved in 9/11. He was not. He was a horrific human being, but he did not attack us on 9/11. He was not connected to Al Qaeda. But the American people were sold that position by the Bush administration, that somehow or other he was part of Al Qaeda and therefore was responsible for the 9/11 attack. I didn't buy the arguments by the Bush administration and voted against it. I felt that going in without the support of the United Nations was a bad mistake, that there would be a big downside with a Western power occupying a Muslim country without international support.

THE LEGACY OF THE WAR? First and foremost are the families that lost loved ones, the holes that are left in so many lives, and the wounded warriors who did survive but now need our full support, care, and understanding.

And I think there's a negative aftermath due to the fact that it was so unilateral and was a Western occupation of a Muslim country. Al Qaeda, who is our enemy, the terrorist group that did attack us, got good propaganda, positive energy for them and their illegitimate cause, because it was a Western occupation of a Muslim country. That's part of the aftermath that we're still paying for. Now we've got to make the best of it and hope that Iraq can become a solid democracy and that some of the violence there can end.

THE FIRST CAR that I smashed up was my dad's Oldsmobile. I ran it into a tree. So that's the most memorable car I ever had. It wasn't totaled, but it had a pretty big dent in the front, and my dad always reminded me of his Olds.

Another memorable car was a Dodge. I worked in auto factories, so I have mixed loyalty on cars. As a kid, I worked in the Big Three factories to help myself through school. So I have a lot of fond memories of cars—not just the ones that I drove, but the ones that were on the assembly line, at least for a few summers, when I helped build them.

I helped build the DeSoto. A few of the old timers will remember the DeSoto. That was the one that I probably remember the best. And I built some Ford trucks in Highland Park. But the DeSoto is the one I remember most fondly, the doors that were being banged on with big rubber hammers as I was inside, tightening the screws.

I WAS ALWAYS GRATEFUL to the UAW. As a matter of fact, I used to carry around my UAW card. I had that for 60 years, and then my wallet was stolen about six months ago. I was a local in Highland Park, as a matter of fact. I would hope that if anybody ever finds my card, that they would please put it on eBay. I'll look for it. ★

JAMES P. HOFFA

GOING TO COOLEY HIGH was absolutely a fabulous experience. I was an all-state football player; I had a great amount of friends. We just had our 50th reunion and everybody showed up. It was a wonderful school to go to, the ideal time in Michigan. Everything was working, there were jobs, and we had a great time.

I graduated in '59. A long time ago. Those were the best times in Michigan and Detroit, right there.

WELL, MY FATHER WAS A LEGEND. He was basically Mr. Teamster in the '30s and '40s. If you see the movie 'Hoffa' with Danny DeVito and Jack Nicholson, it catches it all. It was really quite good. Amazing, how many people have seen that movie. That kind of addresses all of the memories and the legends.

He was a real leader. He was a champion, he was a movie star. People loved him. He was very charismatic, good-looking, gave great speeches, and he was a guy who would go anywhere and do anything. He would get up in the middle of the night and go out on the dock. And that legend lives on today.

YEAH, HE WAS A HERO.

MY FAMILY WOUND UP IN DETROIT due to my father and my grandma. You're going way back. He was born in 1913; he'd be in his late 90s now. They moved here from Brazil, Indiana. When my grandfather died, they had no way to make it in Indiana, so they moved here. At 13, 14 years old, my dad had to go out to try and help support his family. My grandmother took in washing. It was a really hard, Depression-era story. They couldn't make it down in Indiana, so they came to Detroit. And everybody, working together, got it going.

At the time, there were opportunities here with the auto industry. You could always get a job here, and that's why so many people came up from the South, because, in the Depression, the auto companies were still making cars. You'd get $5 a day. Henry Ford had a great saying. He said, 'If I pay my people right, they'll have money to buy my cars.' A lot of people have lost that idea.

FOR ME, JUST GETTING ELECTED was a great story. The Teamsters fell on hard times in the '90s, because they had a guy who got elected who really didn't know how to run the union and the union became divided. It was brother against brother, local against local. I came in and said, 'We've got to pull this thing together.' That was the platform I ran on, and we pulled the union back together when I was elected. I took over in 1999 and I've been there ever since.

Our accomplishments have been amazing, but we've gone through hard times.

These are hard times for unions. But we've kept our membership up, we're organizing, we've unified the union, we've made it stronger, all of our pension plans are operating, and we're taking care of our members.

It's the members that motivate me the most. The best thing you can do is get out of the office. We just led a march of 30,000 people in Los Angeles for better jobs, better hiring, and against the war on workers in Wisconsin and Ohio and Indiana and Michigan. We're battling back against the war on workers, that's our theme. When you go out there it makes you feel good to see the members, how they're excited about what they're doing. That's what gets me up every day.

THE LABOR MOVEMENT IS THE ONLY ORGANIZATION, THE ONLY GROUP, FIGHTING FOR THE WORKING PEOPLE.

If we didn't have unions, who would be fighting for them? The businessmen, the right-wingers, have the Tea Party, they have the Chamber of Commerce. Who would be fighting for the worker? Who would be getting them better wages? Who would make sure they had pensions? Nobody. Organized labor are the only people who do that. We're the ones who set the standards, who are fighting.

YOU SAY, 'WHAT ARE THE CHALLENGES we're facing right now?' It's the economy. Look at Michigan. We're really down. We need jobs. We need to rebuild Michigan. We need to rebuild America. We lost 8 million jobs, just from '08 to now, in America, and those have not come back.

We've got to convince big businesses to invest in this country, to invest in Michigan, and build factories here instead of building them in China or India or Mexico. We've got to turn the tide of the thinking of American business. They've got all of the money, and if they close a plant here in Michigan, and lay off a thousand Michiganders and move it to Mexico, that's a big loss. That's going on right now. We've got to stop that thinking.

THIS IS A GREAT STATE, AND WE'VE GOT TALENTED PEOPLE HERE. WE'VE GOT TO CHANGE THIS CLIMATE, TO
START GETTING JOBS HERE.
JOBS WILL SOLVE EVERYTHING.

Jobs will solve the economy, they'll solve the problem of money and balance sheets in Michigan. It will make Michigan a place where you want to live.

I think, as hard as it was back in my father's day, it's worse now. Because we have everybody lined against us. We're fighting a bad economy, we have new trade bills that have made it legitimate to close down factories here in Michigan and move them to Mexico. That's what's going on. I can list 20 companies that have left Michigan, that were here, with good jobs, families that have been here 30 years, kids going to high school, kids going to college, and all of that came to a crashing end with NAFTA,

CAFTA and the China trade agreement. All of those things ended that and we saw an exodus of jobs from Michigan and from the United States.

That's been one of the worst things that's happened, in addition to the anti-labor feelings in this country going back to Ronald Reagan, George Bush I, and George Bush II.

At the same time, the standard of living for people has gone down in this country. People haven't had a raise in 20 years, people are going down, while the rich are getting richer.

We have class warfare. That's the problem we face. It's harder now than it was during my dad's time. I can honestly tell you that. He did a great job. We had so many people. That was before deregulation. We had maybe half a million people driving trucks. Today, we probably don't have 60,000.

So the Teamsters have had to diversify, go into other areas and organize school bus drivers, auto mechanics, airline mechanics, people who work in airlines. We have nurses; we even have lawyers. We have everything in our union today; we're so diversified. That's one of the reasons why our union has stayed at 1.4 million. I always say, 'We're from airline pilots, A, to zookeepers, Z.' That's why we're so successful.

MY FIRST CAR? I had an old-fashioned Ford station wagon. It was a '52 Ford station wagon with broken doors. It had about 200,000 miles on it. That was the old wagon I used to drive around school. It was a car that had been used in one of the campaigns, and we bought it for nothing, because it was all used up, had a broken seat, broken doors. The guy who owned it before worked for my dad and weighed about 400 pounds. He'd broken the seat. And the doors, I went around the corner and the doors would open up. I thought, 'Uh-oh, somebody's going to fall out.'

I tied the door with my belt; after that, I got some duct tape to try to keep the doors shut. I have a picture of that car. Yeah, '52 Ford station wagon with the appliqué. Remember that? ★

CHRIS HANSEN

I KNEW PRETTY EARLY. I was one of those nerdy kids who decided, when they where about 14, what they wanted to do for a living. And I can remember, vividly, the Jimmy Hoffa kidnapping, which occurred a mile and a half down the road from where my family lived at the time.

I became fascinated with it. I'd ride my bike up and check out the crime scene. And there were FBI agents and local police, and the local reporters, and the network correspondents. I got bit by the bug, and I pursued it from that point on.

THE CHAMBERS BROTHERS STORY really stamped my career in Detroit. I was at Channel 7 Action News at the time. Crack cocaine was a huge story; it had a stranglehold on the city. I had been covering the epidemic and the city's effort to fight it, and the impact it was having on citizens, both users and innocent people who were caught in the crossfire of violence.

So I was following, with my cameraman, the No-Crack Task Force, which was Detroit Police narcotics, the DEA, and other federal agencies. And we were on the raid at a Chambers brothers crack house when we came across these videotapes. It was a treasure trove of video documentation of what goes on inside a major crack-cocaine operation, run by this family. There were tours of the homes, with the 24-karat gold faucets, the cars, videos of them counting the money, joking around about how they were going to give the singles to the poor people, because they didn't need any of that money.

I got my hands on these tapes with the agreement that I wouldn't do anything with them until the undercover investigation was over. We didn't want to put anybody in harm's way by doing anything before then.

So I remember when we broke the story. It was a five-part series, and it was water-cooler talk throughout Detroit. And it made national news. Talk about doing a hidden camera investigation; this was sort of the first one. Even though they weren't our hidden cameras, the videotapes took us inside a world nobody had seen before. It was amazing.

WELL, WDIV WAS JUST A GREAT NEWSROOM. WE HAD GREAT PEOPLE, GREAT PRODUCERS, WE BROKE SOME GREAT STORIES.

I can remember one story in particular where I became aware that the FBI was doing a sting operation targeting Detroit police officers, detectives, including the guy who headed up the mayor's security detail. The allegation was that they were protecting drug and drug money shipments as they came into Detroit City Airport.

I worked and worked on this thing, putting it together, and I knew that arrests were going to go down on a certain day. But if Jimmy Harris, the main person arrested, had agreed to cooperate, they were going to make no announcement about the investigation. They were going to continue to work undercover. If he said no to cooperation, all bets were off, and I was going to break the story.

I remember my wife was pregnant with our first child. It was the day I had taken her for an amniocentesis. I get her home, get settled. Then I made a phone call, and my source says, 'Jimmy ain't talking.' So now I've got to get back downtown. I call the newsroom and say, 'We're breaking it,' because I had the piece pretty much done, I just had to do the opening live tag.

We broke it at the top of the 6 o'clock show, and every other station was caught flatfooted and was scrambling to try to catch up. When you can beat the rest of the city on a story of that magnitude, that's a big deal.

WITH THE DATELINE SPECIAL 'Detroit: City of Heartbreak and Hope,' what surprised me the most—and I know the streets of Detroit pretty well from being a reporter there for 10 years and growing up in the area—was to realize that the amount of vacant and abandoned property and buildings in the city add up to be the size of the city of Buffalo. That was a fact that stunned me.

IT WAS A VERY PERSONAL STORY. WE PROFILED SIX OR SEVEN PEOPLE WHO GO OUT EVERY DAY WITH ONE MISSION: TO HELP FIX THE CITY AND TO HELP THE PEOPLE OF THE CITY.

If that's not inspirational, I don't know what is. We profiled Cordette Grantling, a woman who takes in orphaned children. We featured people who grow crops on vacant land. We spoke to Mayor Dave Bing, who doesn't need this headache, but who, every day, gets up and tries to get this city moving in the right direction amidst all kinds of challenges. And Pam Good, who has a comfortable life in Birmingham, but is so committed to getting these kids in the city reading and writing at a level where they should be.

To see an inner city kid write an essay, flawlessly, about how he wants to be an FBI agent because he doesn't like the crime he sees in his neighborhood, that's pretty inspirational.

We got some criticism because we didn't highlight the Detroit Institute of Arts and the symphony and those things. But that wasn't the story. The story was 'here are the problems in the city; here are the people on the ground, grassroots, front lines, trying to do something about it.' That was not the story that everybody wanted to hear. I think there were some hurt feelings. Some people wanted to be involved with it who weren't. But you can't have a million voices in one hour. That's not how you tell stories. You have to have main characters and a narrative.

Everybody who participated, for the most part, benefited from it. And when those people benefit, the people they help benefit.

'TO CATCH A PREDATOR' started in a conversation with a friend who's a reporter in Detroit. He told me about this group, Perverted Justice, the online watchdog group. I thought that if we could take their ability to be decoys in chat rooms and our ability to use hidden cameras and microphones and wire a house, that the result could be pretty compelling, and that for the first time you could actually get inside this world of online predators.

So I pitched this story and a lot of smart people weighed in with ways to make it better and smarter and we did the first one on Long Island, New York.

I was driving out there, stuck in traffic, and I started daydreaming and thinking, 'Gosh, what if nobody shows up?' And all of a sudden, 45 minutes later, traffic clears and the phone rings and it's my producer saying, 'Where are you? We've got two guys who are about to show up in 45 minutes.'

By the end of the investigation, two and a half days later, 17 men had come to the door looking to have a sexual liaison with a 12-, 13-, or 14-year-old boy or girl, including a New York City firefighter. It was eye-opening.

We did it again in suburban Washington, and we had 24 people show up, including a rabbi, a doctor, a teacher, and a guy who walked in naked. Then we did some 30 hours crisscrossing the country.

It's aired all over the world, and if we did it again tomorrow you'd still get guys showing up. It got to the point where, before I could even say who I was, somebody said, 'Oh, you're Chris Hansen.' I said, 'How did you know that?' He said, 'I never miss an episode. I watch it all the time. I download them from the Internet.' I said, 'Do you understand the trouble you just walked into?'

I think that the takeaway from 'To Catch a Predator,' is that impact journalism, stories well told using enterprising techniques like hidden cameras, really take people inside an issue or problem. And when you understand how the mind of a predator works you can understand how to better protect your child online.

These guys aren't going away. So the only thing you can do is to try to educate people as best you can so that they can avoid falling for it in the first place. ★

BILL BONDS

MY EARLIEST DETROIT memories are of Burlingame, Woodrow Wilson, the Blessed Sacrament Cathedral and Visitation Parish, which is where we went to elementary school, grade school and, for the most part, high school until the '50s. Then we moved to Huntington Woods. We started hanging around in Royal Oak (and) Birmingham. Went to Shrine for a couple of years, went to Catholic Central, Berkley. Then I left for the Air Force.

WE DID ALL THE NORMAL KID STUFF. There were six of us in all, brothers and sisters. We played all the sports, did pretty well in school. School was easy. Fell in love a couple of times. Moved three times, that I remember. We moved from Detroit to Huntington Woods and then to Franklin.

We had a large extended family, a lot of aunts and uncles, most of whom lived around Grosse Pointe. My mother's family was a banking family. Her father and her uncle founded what became Detroit Bank & Trust. And my father's father owned a brewery and sold it in 1927 for a couple million bucks. Then the crash hit.

MY DAD WAS IN ADVERTISING, a very talented guy. My mother was a teacher, had a master's degree. She was a marvelous writer, an excellent teacher, and a great mom.

We were a middle-class American family with college-educated parents, which, at the time, was a little different, back in the '40s.

I remember, in 1943, my best friend and I took a streetcar at Calvert and Woodward to Michigan Avenue, and the 1943 race riot was in full bloom. We saw burning cars, roving gangs, police, burnings. And many years later I reported on the 1967 riots. Those are two things that really jump out at me and, in a sense, maybe define my gut instincts for trying to find the cause of things, why things happen. Why bad things happen, why sad things happen, why good things can happen. I think that's the result of having seen and experienced things that are different than the norm.

I'M NOT REALLY SURE what the hell it all means, except that when you're in an interview like this, you do your best to get in touch with the real you and share it.

I'VE BEEN ASKED several times what was the most important story. And in a 30-year career there is no one thing.

However, certainly,

THE RIOT IN DETROIT DEFINED MY CAREER
AND LAUNCHED A POSITION OF DOMINANCE IN THE NEWS FOR CHANNEL 7.

That was a major, major story. It was the story of an entire community. And maybe it was an American tragedy.

When you look at a career that long, though, names come back. John Kennedy, Robert Kennedy, Martin Luther King, Malcolm X, George Wallace, Medgar Evers, Gerald Ford, Ronald Reagan. Those are all world figures. Those are big American figures. I interviewed all of them. And Walter Reuther, who was the head of the UAW, the most powerful human in the world. I had a station that said, 'If Billy's interview goes 12 minutes, run it.' Nobody else in the country was doing that. I had some marvelous producers and writers who said, 'Damn, this is fun, but it's important!' When you can pump up that kind of enthusiasm, you end up doing some great work as a station.

It probably sounds conceited, but in the Michigan Journalism Hall of Fame, there's only one anchorman who's a member, and that's Bill Bonds. Talk about a compliment.

Yeah, I would go back.

COLEMAN YOUNG? I think it all depends upon who you talk to. And I think a lot depends on what color you are. For a lot of blacks, he was a hero. He made it. He was a brilliant guy, an attractive guy. He was a controversial guy. He didn't create the riot.

I don't think we've ever recovered from the riots. The latest numbers on Detroit are that people are leaving. The school systems don't work. It's a little bit like trying to fix the economy. I don't think there are any easy solutions.

You've got to remember, Detroit was the only American city where federal troops had to be sent in twice in the same century to restore law and order. They had a terrible riot in 1943, maybe even a worse riot in 1967. During the '67 riot I was anchoring. I anchored it for a week. Got nominated for all kinds of prizes. And suddenly Bill Bonds was the anchorman. We had a great news department, and we became the dominant television station, probably the best news operation in the country.

WELL, I CAN TELL YOU, as an Irish Catholic, how thrilled and excited I was when John F. Kennedy was elected president. I had interviewed him. I was a liberal at the time. And how devastated I was when he was murdered. I felt the same way when Martin Luther King was shot.

I think the assassination of Martin Luther King had a greater negative impact on America than the assassination of John F. Kennedy, because I think King had such a gift. He could make the right person listen to what the message was, and care. And suddenly he was gone. You can't keep losing people like that.

I THINK THERE ARE some very, very important issues, and I'm not sure the media is digging hard enough to find out whether there are solutions. I did a commentary the last time I was on the air about trusting your government to tell you the truth. The phones rang off the hook, and it was just an anniversary thing. But not one station called and said, 'Would you like to come in and write a new commentary?' I don't know what to tell you. Everywhere I went, they said, 'Billy, damn it, that's exactly the way I feel.' Not one station called, not even 7. Why not? They're afraid of controversy.

SOME PEOPLE THINK I'm controversial. I don't try to be controversial. I really don't. I think if you honestly pursue the truth, you're going to be OK. And if you're controversial in the process, you know what? Sometimes the truth is controversial. Sometimes the truth upsets people.

THE SECRET TO A GOOD INTERVIEW is listening. Research and listening. I can be very quick, and I can turn phrases quickly. And I can play 'gotcha' in a lot of ways. But I found out that if you're honest with somebody who's a newsmaker, they sense that. Make it a conversation. Don't make it a confrontation. Conversation is more fruitful than confrontation.

I got Bill Clinton to do the first televised town hall meeting in America at Channel 7. I spotted him early and I said to my producers, 'Watch this guy from Arkansas. He's a young governor named Bill Clinton. He's got magic.' So I had him out two or three different times over the course of a year. Then, when he won, I called him. I said, 'Mr. President, this is your old friend Bill Bonds. How would you like to come to Detroit and do a town meeting?' He said, 'You got it.' It didn't happen because I was rich; it didn't happen because I was handsome. It happened because I worked my ass off. I asked tough questions, but fair questions. I was curious. I wanted to be the best there was.

The point is, you don't get there because you're lucky. Bad luck can hurt you, but it can't beat you. If you're good, you keep going and you're going to be all right.

I THINK LIFE IS BASICALLY FAIR. You get what you put into it.

I probably should have been an anchor on the evening news on CBS or ABC or NBC. I was that good. I think I had the appearance, the voice, the style, the charisma. A couple of wrinkles here, a couple bad happenings, but a marvelous career.

RETURN TO ANCHORING? I hope so.

I've got to tell you, it was fun. ★

SHAUN ROBINSON

THE FIRST IMAGE of an African-American woman on television I remember was a local news anchor named Beverly Payne. I stayed at my grandmother's house a lot when I was little because my elementary school, St. Cecilia Catholic school, was close to her house. After I finished watching my afternoon of cartoons, my grandmother would turn on the news and there was Beverly Payne. I recall thinking she was just so beautiful and there was something really special about her. From my eyes, as a little black girl, the fact that she had the same skin color as I did made her special to me.

I LIVED ON A STREET called Linsdale on the West Side until I was 6, when my parents divorced. My mother and my grandmother, brother and I moved to Sherwood Forest, near 8 Mile and Livernois. Then, when my mom got her own house, I lived on a street called Strathmoor, which was around 8 Mile and Hubbell. When my mom remarried, she and I moved in with my stepfather to a street called Cherrylawn. The cool thing was, my dad and my stepmom both moved in just a few blocks down on the same street. It made traveling during the holidays very convenient.

In junior high and high school, one of our most exciting excursions was Bob-Lo Island Amusement Park. We would get on the boat, go across the river and have the best time. We used to be scared out of our wits to ride the Wild Mouse, Nightmare, Falling Star, and Screamer!

CASS TECH WAS THE ONLY HIGH SCHOOL I wanted to go to. Back in the day, it was a really big deal if you were accepted as a student because you had to have a high-enough grade point average to get in. I remember my first day of school, when we had freshman orientation and they assigned us our lockers. You couldn't tell me anything! Oh, I love that school. It's so funny that, even today, people across the country know the name 'Cass Tech.'

I remember our first day of homeroom in ninth grade, our teacher telling us he had someone very famous as a student in his class years ago. Her name was Diana Ross. But, he told us, back then she was called Diane. We were so impressed; we were on the edge of our seats.

The story went like this: One day she was filing her nails in class. He walked up to her and said, 'Miss Ross, aren't you going to do your homework?' And she said, 'I don't have to do my homework because I'm going to be a star!' He laughed, like 'fat chance.' He said, years later, she came back to Cass and had a laugh. We all thought it was hysterical. Years later, I interviewed Diana Ross and told her that story. She laughed, but didn't remember it quite that way.

I BECAME INTERESTED IN A
CAREER IN JOURNALISM
WHEN I WAS IN HIGH SCHOOL.

When I was younger, I really wanted to become an actress because I loved doing theater so much. I started getting roles in plays when I was a kid and belonged to a theater troupe while in junior high. But, eventually, my interests led me to pursuing a career as a reporter and anchor.

I remember when I was in Detroit, at WGPR, *The Detroit News* did a story on me, and they called me Detroit's own Oprah. Well, I haven't gotten anywhere near that, but I'm developing my own show where I want to talk to icons, people who are pioneers in their profession, and discuss what makes them tick, and how we're going to change the world for the better. That's my next step. That's the next chapter of my life. I'm really looking forward to that.

AT 'ACCESS HOLLYWOOD,' one of the highlights of my career was going to South Africa to cover the opening of Oprah Winfrey's Leadership Academy for Girls in Johannesburg. The girls who go to this school are absolutely incredible. A lot of them lived in shantytowns before they were chosen to attend Oprah's school. Many of them came from homes that only had outdoor toilets shared by dozens of families. Many of them walked to their former school with the fear that they would be raped, yet they valued their education so much they never missed a day. And I'm telling you, these girls are brilliant; they're absolutely brilliant. When I left Johannesburg, I thought, 'You should always be thankful for what you have because you could have been born during a much different time and under much different circumstances.'

WHILE I WAS WORKING as a reporter in Milwaukee, I covered the health and medical beat. I got a chance to meet so many people going through the toughest health challenges, and they had stories that I would never forget. There was one man who needed a lung transplant, and his insurance company wasn't paying for it. I did a number of stories on him, and as a result, the insurance company ended up paying for his operation. I also remember doing a story about a teenage boy who needed a heart transplant, but his parents didn't believe in medical intervention because of religious reasons. He ultimately passed away.

MY BOOK is called *Exactly As I Am: Celebrated Women Share Candid Advice With Today's Girls on What it Takes to Believe in Yourself.*

I've had so many girls look to me and say, 'You interview all these amazing celebrities; are they as beautiful in person as they look on TV and in the movies?' More and more, girls are comparing themselves to their favorite star in Hollywood. And I wanted to let girls know that no matter how much money you have, no matter how skinny you are, that does not bring you true happiness. Happiness comes from a much deeper place—knowing that you are wonderful exactly as you are. That's why I called the book *Exactly As I Am.*

I used my access to different celebrities like Oprah, Celine Dion, Alicia Keys, Jennifer Hudson, Kelly Clarkson and Gloria Estefan, and asked them to give girls advice about believing in yourself and dreaming big. And the women talked about their own struggles with self-esteem. It's a book that's for teen girls, but the message is universal. There's no age where we get to the point where we think, 'I'm so secure in myself.' In that sense, this book is for all women.

MY ADVICE? You are not your economic status. You are not your skin color. As Oprah says in my book, 'No matter what somebody says about you, you have a right to be here because you were born.' I think that's important, because a lot of times, girls, when they're born in certain situations, they feel like they're not good enough.

Where you come from is not where you're going. Everybody is the same.

YOU STRIP AWAY ALL THE MONEY, THE GLAMOUR, THE MAKEUP TEAM, AND EVERYBODY IS EXACTLY THE SAME.

What I tell girls who come from challenging circumstances is, the ability to succeed and to better your circumstance comes from within. And yeah, it might be a little bit harder for you than it is for somebody else. But it's all about believing that God has given you a special gift. You're not like anybody else. What you have to contribute to this world comes from that uniqueness and that special thing you were born with. You've just got to keep at it.

I THINK THE SECRET to my success has been perseverance and a great family structure that always told me, 'OK, have a pity party for just a little bit of time—now get off your butt and do something.' That has been my motivator. I think, 'OK, I'm here for a limited amount of time. Let me try to make the best out of it.'

It's also about giving back. I come from a family of really strong women who have been nurturers, and they've always taught me that no matter where you get, always reach back and try to help somebody.

I THINK THE ONE, very fun interview that I love to tell people about is Al Pacino. I don't get starstruck anymore, but he was one guy who really made me nervous. He sat down, we were about to start the interview, and I noticed a crumb on his mouth. So I reached over, because I wanted him to be perfect for the interview, and I'm like, 'Mr. Pacino, let me just—' and my hand got about an inch from his mouth, and I realized it was a mole! I said, 'Oh, Mr. Pacino, I'm sorry, it's a mole!' And he says, 'Just call me mole man! Call me mole man!' He was really good about it. It was very funny.

YOU KNOW ONE PERSON who I would love to interview? The Pope. I was raised Catholic, and that would be really interesting. I would ask him, 'When God speaks to you, what does He say?' ★

DICK PURTAN

MY PARENTS BOUGHT A RADIO. It was a big floor-model radio, and it had an attached microphone. So I would listen to the guys on the radio, and then I would take the microphone and a newspaper, and I'd go in the closet and I'd read the newspaper—the sports, commercials, ads, whatever. My parents said that they thought I had a future. I was only 6 years old, but I knew what I wanted to do, and that's what I did.

FAVORITE HAUNTS? Is that what you said?

Well, when I was a kid, my dad would occasionally bring us on his business trips to Detroit. Although we lived in Buffalo, Detroit was his biggest market in the furniture business. We would eat at the Roma Cafe down at Eastern Market. We'd stay at the Statler Hotel, eat at the Adams Grill, which is no longer there. It was on Adams Street, right at Comerica Park.

I remember Tiger Stadium, too. I loved to go by Tiger Stadium because, being from Buffalo, you could hear some of the Detroit radio stations across Lake Erie. So I grew up with a feeling that I kind of lived in Detroit, even though I lived in Buffalo. And I always wanted to live in Detroit for that reason. When Gail and I got married, we moved to Syracuse, Jacksonville, Cincinnati. But I made an effort to get to Detroit, which I did, and we ended up staying 45 years.

I WOULD SAY I LIKE MOTOWN. It wasn't my favorite music, although I liked it. I thought Marvin Gaye was brilliant. As a matter of fact, I used to have a media hockey team called the Purtan No-Stars. One time Marvin came out and played. He couldn't skate. I couldn't skate either, that's why I played goalie. I had to hang onto the net. But Marvin really couldn't skate. We were at Olympia Stadium, and we were playing before the Red Wings game. I think there were about 16,000 people watching that stupid game. But Marvin came out and he literally was skating on his ankles. It was hysterical. But what a talent. What a great talent.

MY FAVORITE MUSIC IS THE
SINATRA KIND OF MUSIC.
I WAS NEVER MUCH OF A ROCKER.

A lot of the music I played through the years, Top 40 stuff, I wasn't real fond of. But I had to play it, because that was the format of the station.

ONE CAREER HIGHLIGHT would be, I interviewed John F. Kennedy when he was running for president. It was about a month before he was elected back in 1960. This was one of my very first jobs. I was down in Jacksonville. I was a disc jockey on a station there, and I got an exclusive interview with him at the airport when he landed.

And then, another time, we drove to Jacksonville because he was going to give a speech that night. There were about 25,000 people in the park. Kennedy was waving to the crowd, and I noticed he was looking over here and not looking anywhere else. So I turned, and he was staring at my wife. Gail was in press row. I said to her afterwards, 'Was he staring at you?' And she said, 'Yeah, I didn't know what to do.' So I knew then he was admiring a pretty face. He became legendary for that later on, of course.

And probably another highlight would be in 1964, when I brought The Beatles to Cincinnati. I was being courted by a program director of an Indianapolis radio station, and we were in Cincinnati. And he mentioned to me, during the interview, 'Who's got the Beatles for Cincinnati?' Because it had been announced that they were coming to the USA in 1964, their first tour. I said, 'I don't know.' And he said, 'Why don't you look into it?' I said, 'How do you do that?' 'Call New York.' I did. And all I needed to get was a venue of about 14,000 people, and they needed $12,500 down payment. So I called Cincinnati Gardens, and I said, 'Is Aug. 27 open?' They said, 'Yes.' So we booked Cincinnati Gardens. Gail and I only had $2,500 to our name, so I went to four other guys at the station and they opted in. They each kicked in $2,500. Now we had our $12,500. I sent a cashier's check to New York and we had the Beatles. It was as simple as that.

I GOT INVOLVED WITH The Salvation Army because I had a five-year anniversary coming up at a radio station here in town, and we wanted to do something to celebrate. But we wanted to make it meaningful by doing it for charity. So we sat around a table and tried to decide what the good charities were. And unanimously, everybody said The Salvation Army. So I had my producer at the time arrange a radiothon for The Salvation Army.

It was called the Dick Purtan Salvation Army Radiothon. Actually, The Dick Purtan Salvation Army Bed & Bread Club Radiothon. And it ended up where I did 23 of them. It started out very small. We raised $15,000 the first year. And the last year we raised $2.3 million. The audience responded so well. Much to their credit—it's a very giving community, and we had a very giving audience.

Did I think it was going to get as big as it did? It became the biggest one-day, one-radio station radiothon in the country. I never thought we'd get that big. But every year, it just kept getting bigger. I think we totaled more than $24 million over 23 years.

IT'S BEEN ALMOST six months of retirement, and I am absolutely enjoying it. It's hard to believe. Even I have trouble believing it. But I haven't missed it at all. Part of it is, I'm finally getting some sleep. Instead of getting up at 4 in the morning, I'm getting up between 8 and 9. I sleep seven or eight hours. I'm never tired. I work out a lot, which I did then, too. But we stay up 'til midnight. We actually see the end of movies on TV. So it's really been fun.

And the other end of it is that radio has changed a great deal, and I didn't like the changes. Everything had to be done quicker and shorter. And you had to talk about what was on TV the night before—'Dancing With the Stars' and 'American Idol.' That's fine, you can do a little bit of that. But they wanted a lot of it. Well, you know, I didn't always want to talk about pop culture. There were times you wanted to be serious and talk about politics. Occasionally, you had to talk about reality.

So, anyway, it's been refreshing for me. It really has. Gail and I have just had a ball.

YES, MY MOTHER really used Blue Dew. I think it was a whitener, like Downy. Something like that. I was in the studio of Foster Brooks in Buffalo, watching his show with some other kids. I used to do that, watch the disc jockeys quite a bit. I stood there, and I got up right next to his desk. And he started doing this commercial for Blue Dew. And as he was doing the commercial, he kind of grabbed me by my neck, and he said,

'DOES YOUR MOTHER USE BLUE DEW?' AND I SAID, 'YES.'
AND THAT WAS MY FIRST TIME ON THE RADIO. ★

MITCH ALBOM

ABSOLUTELY, I CALL MYSELF A DETROITER. I've lived in Detroit virtually twice as long now as I've lived anywhere else. All of my real adult life has been in Detroit. I got married in Detroit, I married a Detroit girl, all of my extended in-laws and family are in Detroit, and most of my dear friends are in Detroit. So, yeah, I think of myself as a Detroiter, and I'm proud of it.

Sometimes, when you aren't raised in a place, but then you come to appreciate it, you do get a little more defensive about it, because people are always saying, 'What are you doing in Detroit?' People who I grew up with from the East say, 'Why are you still in Detroit?' It's almost like you have to defend your decision, and I do get a little defensive.

A JOB OPPORTUNITY brought me here. I was a young sports writer. I'd only been in the business a few years. I was working in South Florida, and somehow I got on the radar of the papers in Detroit and was offered interviews with both *The Detroit News* and the *Free Press* on the same day. I got a call from one in the morning and one in the afternoon. Then I flew up, and I stayed in the Renaissance Center. I actually checked in one day on the expense account of the *Free Press*, and the next night I checked out and checked back in under *The Detroit News*, just to be fair. I did one interview one day, and one interview another day, and they both offered me the job. Same money. There was something kind of weird about that. Ultimately, I chose the *Free Press*, and I've been here ever since.

The *Free Press* wanted somebody young, and all I really had going for me was that I was young. That was the first time I ever stepped foot in the city, to come and interview for a job. But I knew it was a sports-crazy town, and if you're a sports columnist and you're young, where else do you want to be?

I was in Florida and back then, they only had college and pro football. And here, all of a sudden, was Detroit, which had four sports plus college, so it was very exciting. That was in '85.

I DON'T HAVE A FAVORITE TEAM. I've been here long enough to see great years of every team except the Lions, and they had a pretty good year with Barry Sanders. But I've seen the Pistons win the championship, I've seen the Red Wings win championships multiple times. I've seen the Tigers go to the World Series. I've seen Michigan get a national title and Michigan State have some good years and win the Rose Bowl. To me, whoever has the best story at the time is my favorite team. I don't place one sport over the other.

STEVE YZERMAN stands out. He ended up winning three Stanley Cups and was a captain of the team for a very long time, and he was a pretty damn good player. Joe Dumars was certainly a backbone of his teams, and then became a backbone of the organization. Kirk Gibson was a hell of a baseball player when he was with the Tigers. Alan Trammell was here for a long time. In their respective sports, those are probably the top guys.

I don't measure their greatness just by their talent. To me, it's the whole package of being an admirable person and being part of the Detroit landscape. I think Yzerman embodied a lot of that, and he was here his whole career.

NO, I NEVER ANTICIPATED the kind of success we've had with *Tuesdays With Morrie* at all. I continue to be surprised at how it's now 14 years later and people still are reading that book and teaching that book. *Tuesdays With Morrie* was a labor of love, and I wrote it to pay Morrie's medical bills. So once we paid the medical bills, it had done everything I expected it to do. It's a very small book. We only printed 20,000 copies of it, and that's a long way from how many are out there now. It's crazy.

With the rest of the books, the answer is still no, because after *Tuesdays With Morrie*, everybody said, 'That was your one thing that's going to be successful and reach people like that,' and I probably believed them. But I still tried to do something else, and I've been amazed at the success of some of the other things afterwards.

It's all a surprise to me. It's a big surprise. I go through life constantly surprised and grateful and humbled. And I try to balance it out by using the attention that those things have gained for the good. I don't think you should just sit on a pile of your accomplishments and go, 'Wow, look at me.' If you're lucky enough to have those things happen to you in life—and I do think luck is a big part of it—then I think you almost have to balance the scales with work for other people, or bring attention to other issues.

ALL OF THE PEOPLE I'VE WRITTEN ABOUT, THE REAL PEOPLE LIKE MORRIE, AND HENRY AND RABBI LEWIS OF *HAVE A LITTLE FAITH,* ARE PEOPLE WHO TAUGHT ME.

And that was one of their lessons, to be involved with your community, and give something back. It would be kind of silly to write a book like *Tuesdays With Morrie* or *Have a Little Faith*, and then say, 'I'm not going to help anybody; I just want to show you what these guys said, but, I'm not going to do it.'

THE MOST SATISFYING STUFF I do, honestly, is not writing books anymore. My buddy, who's helping me operate an orphanage in Haiti, just came back. We recently put in a new English program and he said, 'These new kids we admitted, they're speaking English.' I got so excited. Books don't make me that excited, but I can't wait to get down there and see the progress we've made with these kids.

As you get older, you do tend to find more joy in giving stuff away than taking. I don't say that as a cliché. I don't think I would have believed that 10 years ago myself. I would've said, 'Ah, that's corny.' But it's true.

WITH THE PLAY *ERNIE,* Ernie asked me about it about a year before he died. I was up at his house and he asked me if I'd ever considered doing a play or a movie about him and his agent Gary Spicer. I was honored that they would ask me that, but it wasn't the right time, and then Ernie got sick, and it just wasn't a priority.

Then he passed away, and I thought about it, and I said, 'He asked me, and I didn't.' You know, somebody asks you for a favor and you never get around to it. Then you feel like, 'I kind of owe him that.' Ernie was such an inspiring guy, and he was such a good man, and he had a thousand interesting stories about baseball. And I thought, 'It's more than just Ernie; it's a story of Detroit sports and Detroit Tiger baseball from the '60s, '70s, '80s, all the way through.'

I've been amazed at how that play has taken off. We've extended it three times. We have to close it or the actors are going to drop dead. But it's really been successful, and we're talking about bringing it back next year.

I remember the last time, in his home, we had some butter pecan ice cream. He said, 'Lulu, how about some butter pecan ice cream?' He was very sick, but we all sat there, eating our ice cream and just talking about memories.

He was just goodness personified. You didn't want to leave Ernie's presence, because you felt like you were in a glow of a nice light, and you didn't want to get out of that light. I gravitate to people like that. I've been very lucky to have a number of people like that in my life, who I've benefited from, and I've tried to share their stories with other people. ★

ELMORE LEONARD

WE MOVED FROM NEW ORLEANS to Oklahoma City, then Dallas, then back to Oklahoma City, then to Detroit, then to Memphis, then back to Detroit in 1934. My dad, at that time, was looking for dealership locations for General Motors, for Buick, Olds, Pontiac, Chevrolet.

Later he got one, and he lasted six months and died in 1949. He was 56 years old. So I thought, because everyone said I took after him, I would probably not last much longer. But then I finally realized I don't take after my dad, I take after my mother, and she was 92 when she died. So I have a little ways to go.

I DO REMEMBER an ad from the Campell-Ewald days. I went out to Colorado to get Chevrolet truck owners to say something about their truck. I spent two days with this guy; we went drinking together and having a time. And I finally said, 'Look, try and say something colloquial, all right? Like, 'You don't wear this truck out.' ' He says, 'All right, I got it. 'You don't wear this son-of-a-bitch out, you just get tired of looking at it and buy a new one.' ' Well, we left out son-of-a-bitch.

We photographed him with the truck, 100,000 miles on it, and showed it to Chevrolet: 'You don't wear out a Chevy truck, you get tired of looking at it and buy a new one.' But Chevrolet wouldn't run it because they couldn't believe that you'd get tired of looking at it. That was my best ad and it never ran.

YES, I FOLLOWED THE DETROIT POLICE for a story I wrote for *The Detroit News Sunday Magazine* called 'Squad 7–Impressions of Murder.' And it was the best experience I had in preparation for writing crime stories. I spent at least a month with Squad 7 of the Detroit Police homicide section. Squad 7 was the hot squad at that time; they were solving more murders than anybody else.

We got along great. They showed me everything they did. They let me go through their files. And I would sit in the room while they questioned a suspect. The whole thing was so impressionable on me. When it appeared, a gun, a P38 was on the cover of the magazine, with a tag on it. And then the story line, 'Impressions of Murder.' I wrote the whole thing pretty much in dialogue.

WELL, I THINK IT WAS A PENCIL I started writing with, which was 29 cents. But I know the Scripto came in very early. Then I went to the orange pen, which cost $1. It was just a cheap, ballpoint pen, and I used that for several years.

Then I was at a book event where the author would sit at a table, and there were probably 50 of us there. And there was a Montblanc at every place. So I took a couple of them and used a Montblanc for two years, maybe a little longer. Then I switched over to the ballpoint I have now. One of the salesmen for the company sends me all I want.

I DON'T BELIEVE IN WRITER'S BLOCK.
WHAT DOES IT MEAN? YOU'RE STUCK, OR YOU JUST AREN'T IN THE MOOD.

If you're not in the mood, that may be massive writer's block. But if you're just stuck and you don't know what comes next, you're writing the wrong thing. You've developed a scene that doesn't get you anywhere. Scratch it out and start anew.

I THINK MY CAREER HIGHLIGHTS have come in stages, as I sold to the movies. But I think my books are good, and I'm proud of them. And that, to me, is the most successful thing I've done.

To sell to the movies is wonderful if you can make some money off of it. I sold *3:10 to Yuma*, 4,500 words, to a dime western, for $90. And then I got $4,000 for the screen rights in 1953, so that wasn't bad. But I've gotten as much as $2.5 million.

CRIME STORIES? Because it's a genre that sells. Everybody reads mysteries and crime stories, and most of them are very tame. But I don't think they should be, because people who get into crime are bad guys and they do bad things. I'm interested in that.

My criminals are usually kind of dumb. They make mistakes. They'll misread the lead, whoever is after them. It might be a cop. I haven't done more than seven or eight actual cop stories, with a cop looking for somebody.

THE READER ALWAYS KNOWS WHAT'S GOING ON.
THERE'S NO MYSTERY. NONE.
IT'S JUST HOW THESE TWO GUYS FINALLY END UP, WHO WINS.

I HAVE A GOOD TIME DOING IT.

The first 100 pages I'll just introduce everybody. I'll get them going in scenes. And then the second 100 pages I might add another character or so.

The best kind of character is one that you add who doesn't have a name. You think, 'Well, this guy's just going to tell him something, or give him a ride.' Then the guy starts to talk and you think, 'Hey, I'd better give him a name, because he's going to have a place in this book.' So I do. And that character always turns out to be one that I like to write, and I can't wait for him to come along again, and he'll assume a good place in the story.

Most of them are about 350 pages. When I get to about 300, I have to think about the ending—'how should I end this thing?'

That's when I think of an ending. I don't know what's going to happen, so I assume the reader won't either. Some smart readers, or who think they're smart, will say, 'Oh, I knew how it was going to end long before it ended.' Well, there's a certain way it has to end. But I like a little surprise in it.

My new one, *Raylan*, is a little shorter. It's 269 pages. I just went out to get an envelope to mail it back. I finally got an envelope for it. I think the book's going to come out in February, in time for the beginning of the FX show 'Justified,' which is based on that character. 'Justified' said that they will back it. They maintain that my dialogue is what keeps the thing going.

I ALWAYS SAY, 'Be Cool,' 'Get Shorty,' 'Jackie Brown,' and 'Out of Sight' are my favorite movie adaptations. Those were the most recent and they're all good. They were done by good people. I think maybe I like 'Jackie Brown' the best. I was surprised. Tarantino stayed the closest to the material.

I LIKE DETROIT. I've always liked Detroit. I have no reason to move. It's too late to go to San Francisco. It's too late to go anywhere and start anew. We're set up here fine.

Things are going on. As I've said, it's a trombone and whiskey town. I used to say that a long time ago.

I don't know what it means. It just sounds good. It's a shot and a beer town, is what it is. ★

PHILIP LEVINE

WE KNOW THAT MANUFACTURING in Detroit and in the United States in general has practically collapsed. But if you look back at the history of our literature, it's those terrible times that produce all kinds of work. Look at Dickens. A book like *Hard Times*, it's a portrait of the agony of working people. Even earlier, in the 18th century, we have poetry and fiction and essays dealing with the hardships. World War I, for example, produced a body of amazing poetry. I think Wilfred Owen, especially. It's out of this kind of cultural grief that profound art often comes. There's no contradiction.

I've been doing this 60 years, and it's getting more attention because of the collapse of industry and manufacturing, and the jobs that went with them is of national interest now. There's been a steady movement to crush working people and to break their unions by the Republicans and the billionaires. I think this has created a real interest in the kind of thing that I write about.

WELL, CENTRAL HIGH was terrific. Absolutely terrific. My classmates were smart; the teachers were very good. There were always a few turkeys, but for the most part, they were an amazing bunch. They were very patient with us.

I FOUND THAT WHEN I started at Wayne University, for the first two years, I had very little to do because I'd already learned it in high school. The level of teaching at Central High, and the level of the students at Central High was higher than what I encountered at Wayne. I had a terrific time at Central High. It was a hell of a good place to go.

I encountered a teacher there, Mrs. Paperno, who introduced me to modern poetry. This was in the 11th grade. She had us read Wilfred Owen, a great war poet. Now World War II was still on, and I'm 17. I'm thinking, 'I've got one more year, and I'm going to get drafted.' Reading this powerful war poetry and coming to terms with Owen's vision of war, I realized that, in a way, he was authenticating my own attitudes. I did not want to go to war. I did not want to kill people, and I didn't want to get blown to shreds.

Owen died, I think, when he was 25 or 26, right near the end of the war. Suddenly, I'm seeing this young man making it clear that those feelings that I have do not render me a coward or unpatriotic. They're just good, common sense, humanitarian emotions.

I don't know how Mrs. Paperno knew that I would respond to this book. She loaned it to me over the weekend. She said, 'Philip, I want you to read it with white cotton gloves on.' And I said, 'What?' She said, 'Philip, that's a metaphor. I don't want you to spill soup on it.' She was a wonder.

FATHER COUGHLIN? He enraged me. This is an odd thing: I never figured out why members of my family would turn on the radio and listen to that son of a bitch, or why they would listen to Hitler. He'd be speaking at Nuremberg, and you'd get a translation. I'd go, 'What are we listening to these people for? They hate us.'

I found a lot of anti-Semitism in Detroit, and I lost a lot of fights, and I won some. It had a huge influence on me, because at a certain point, I got tired of being beaten up. I found a gym and a boxing instructor who wanted me to lift weights to get stronger, because I was skinny. And, in a way, it sort of influenced my personality. I got this thing: 'Don't give me any shit or I'll give you plenty back.'

It was so petty to have to deal with this crap. I only encountered it once at Wayne, from a teacher. At Central High, I never encountered it. Never. But at Wayne, there was a psychology teacher. He talked about 'Jewish psychology,' and one of the students asked him, 'What do you mean by that?' And he said, 'Well, psychotherapy, where the money is.' Isn't that sweet? That son of a bitch.

YOU CAN'T SEPARATE THE RIOTS FROM VIETNAM. I THINK THERE WAS A GENERAL VISION ON OUR PART: THOSE WHO WERE AGAINST THE VIETNAM WAR, FOR CIVIL RIGHTS, AND ANTI-AMERICAN EMPIRE.

There was a sense that these two wars were akin. It was no accident that there was a racial war in the cities of the United States, and that there was a racial war in Vietnam. We were burning and bombing people over there, and not regarding them as the human beings they were. We were treating them like used Kleenex. Those who lived in the cities must certainly have recognized, 'They're doing to us what we're doing to them.'

I didn't see the riots themselves coming. I'd already lived through one when I was in eighth or ninth grade, during World War II. There was a very serious racial riot. The one in the '60s, though, was almost like a rebellion. Anybody who lived in Detroit at that time knew how incredibly racist the police force was, and how they exercised their authority, without any check, at all times, and that they didn't like black people. They did to them what they wanted and they got away with it.

At a certain point, the citizens said, 'No; enough.' I was completely on that side—of those who rebelled against what was going on. But a very interesting, sad thing happened. After it was over, because I was in California, I went back to Detroit and I walked through the neighborhoods where I'd lived and I realized, 'I am a middle-aged white guy. When they look at me, they see the enemy. They see the honkie, the slave master,' whatever you want to call it. It was a shock. It was a shock to suddenly realize, 'Yeah, that's how I'm seen. And to a degree, that's what I am, because I'm partaking of America.' It was terrible; a terrible time and a terrible feeling.

YEAH, YEAH. EUGENE WATKINS. I remember his name. We were sorting out universal joints. Some could be repaired, some had to be scrapped, and we were throwing the two categories into separate sacks. And one of the sacks said, 'Detroit Municipal Zoo.' Eugene looked at it, and he held it up and said, 'They feed they lion they meal in they sacks.' I thought, 'This guy's a genius; he's just operated on the English language! He's reduced all third-person pronouns to one. He's simplified the language.' And the rhythm of what he said was so engaging; I thought, 'Someday, I'm going to use this. I don't know how, but someday...'

I didn't know how to use it. How old was I then? I don't know, young. I wrote the poem when I was 40, so there's a lot of years passing before I figured out how to use it.

I LOVE DETROIT. I love the city. In spite of the racism, in spite of the anti-Semitism, in spite of the terrible class divisions and the greed of our masters, there were so many interesting people that I met both at school and at various jobs I had. And I like the look of the city, the tree-lined streets. I like the rhythm of it. It was my size.

Detroit was a terrific place. And in a way, it was stolen from me. I had to leave in order to become a decent poet, because I was a big fish in a tiny pond, and I knew there was better stuff being written in America than was being written in Detroit. I wanted to grow as a writer and that was what urged me to go. I'm glad I left.

I didn't have to really see, day by day, the city diminish. When I left, it still had some of its wonderment. I'm sure it still does. ★

JOHN SINCLAIR

ASK ME WHATEVER YOU WANT. Oh, wow.

THE WHITE PANTHER PARTY was formed in Ann Arbor, actually. In Detroit, I was involved with the Detroit Artist's Workshop and Trans-Love Energies. After I moved to Ann Arbor, we started the White Panther Party.

We wanted to support the struggle of the Black Panther Party for survival against the incessant persecution by the police and other authorities, judicial authorities. We thought it was important that our constituency, as we would consider it, of young white people, hippies, needed to be stirred, to understand what the Black Panther Party was, and why they should support them.

We had a rock 'n' roll band called MC5, and we were about to put out our first album, and we wanted to make a statement that was larger than popular music. We wanted to say something about issues beyond the entertainment business. So the MC5, myself, and some of our associates in Ann Arbor formed the White Panther Party to support the Black Panther Party.

I was just chairman of the White Panther Party. But I challenged the marijuana laws in the state of Michigan and went to prison for two and a half years, and ended up overthrowing the law. That was about the biggest thing we did.

Now we've got a black president, and it's a little bit better. Just took so long, 40 more years. That's a long time. But I think it's all paying off now, in some ways. Except they've got two wars now, instead of one. That's twice as bad.

THE MC5? At first, in the late summer of 1966, I was stunned by how great their music was, so I started going to all of their performances that I could.

Then I became friends with the guys in the band, particularly with the lead singer, Rob Tyner. We were very close friends. We exchanged ideas and concepts daily, repeatedly.

We spurred each other on to new heights of imagination and daring.

AFTER ABOUT A YEAR OF THAT, I was influenced by the first visit of the Grateful Dead to Detroit and of their manager, Rock Scully. I observed what he did as the manager of a band that was on Warner Bros. Records, on a national tour, and I thought, 'Geez, I could probably do that for these guys.' I told Tyner and the guys I was willing to try this, because they needed someone to handle their careers. I was with them for two years, from the fall of '67 to the summer of '69.

BOY, YOU'VE GOT SOME TOUGH QUESTIONS TODAY. The Grande Ballroom, at its peak, would be packed to the walls with hippies and long-haired young people, and band members. The bands would be on the stage, raising the temperature and getting everybody excited, and the most exciting of all was the MC5. That was our home base.

YES, OF COURSE, I remember a lot of bands there. From the SRC, The Up, Prime Movers, Jagged Edge, Wilson Mower, The Frost. There were many, many, many. Savage Grace, Alice Cooper, The Stooges. That was our local scene.

THE GREAT DETROIT ARTIST GARY GRIMSHAW DID THE POSTERS. WE WERE MEMBERS OF THE SAME COMMUNE, A COLLECTIVE CALLED TRANS-LOVE ENERGIES.

We managed the MC5, made posters, did the lights of the Grande Ballroom. We had a little Trans-Love store, also at the Grande. We were kind of centered at the Grande.

That was from the fall of '66 to the summer of '69, when I went to prison. I was in prison for two and a half years, until the end of 1971.

IT HAPPENED IN DETROIT.

Yeah. This woman asked me for a joint and I gave her two. She was a police officer, it turned out. A month later, they arrested me under the violation of state narcotics laws and charged me with dispensing marijuana, a crime that carried a mandatory minimum sentence of 20 years in prison and a maximum of life.

I don't know. I mean, when you send an undercover agent in...

YEAH, ABSOLUTELY, IT'S A SETUP, isn't it? She entrapped me into giving her two joints. It was an act of friendship. It was three days before Christmas.

YEAH, RIGHT, EXACTLY. She should've said 'thank you.'

NO, I HEARD THE CONCERT on the radio. It was broadcast live on WABX–FM.

Well, Peter Andrews of Ann Arbor was the producer; my brother David, and my first wife worked very closely with Peter. Peter secured the Crisler Arena at the University of Michigan, and they worked together to attract people to play at this thing, and to speak.

AND ULTIMATELY, OUR FRIEND, JERRY RUBIN, WHO HAD AGREED TO PARTICIPATE, HAD BECOME FRIENDS WITH **JOHN LENNON AND YOKO ONO,** AND HE INVITED THEM AND THEY DECIDED TO DO IT.

OF COURSE, I REMEMBER ALL OF THEM. Stevie Wonder, Bob Seger, Phil Ochs, Commander Cody and His Lost Planet Airmen, Archie Shepp and Roswell Rudd, The Up, Allen Ginsburg, Bobby Seale, and on and on.

I LOVED THE SONG John Lennon wrote for me.

WHY AM I AN ADVOCATE? First off, I'm a habitual user, and as such, I'm subject to harassment by the police and persecution by the state. So I would like to end that, because it's not founded on anything. There's nothing wrong with marijuana. Marijuana never killed a person. It's a medicine; it's good for you. It's an herb. It should never have been declared illegal, so it shouldn't be illegal now.

On top of all of that, I oppose the use of a harmless herb and the people who smoke it, for medicinal or recreational purposes, as the basis of building the police state apparatus they have now. If they ended the war on drugs, they could greatly reduce the police, the prison population, the courts, the jails. They could make all of it that much smaller.

DETROIT WAS A GREAT PLACE. Everything, every day was great. It was a great city. It was a great place to live and to be an artist, a musician, a poet.

THE RIOTS? Sure, I remember the whole thing. I was at Trans-Love Energies' headquarters. We cheered on the rioters.

It lasted a week, until the National Guard and the Army came in and put everything back in the box. It was a rough period, when you look out the window and see tanks coming down the street.

I had my life threatened by the police. That was pretty terrible. They stormed into our apartment with guns at our heads, called us by name. That was the scariest part.

We left Detroit a year later, in May of 1968, after Martin Luther King was assassinated. We thought the city would be under a curfew for the entire summer, and we didn't think we could survive under that, so we moved to Ann Arbor, where they only had 10 police cars.

YEAH. WELL, I DIDN'T START Hash Bash, but I was there, I was part of it.

It's just a time we shared, an April Fools' Day when potheads and other citizens who believe in the legalization of marijuana get together to defy the law and to state their opposition, and to have a good time in the process.

I'M BASED IN AMSTERDAM, but I move around a little bit. I present a moving target. I just came here from Oxford, Mississippi; Little Rock, Arkansas; Fayetteville, Arkansas; New Orleans; Chicago; before that, Barcelona, Madrid, Amsterdam and London. That's in the last three months.

I do radio shows on my Internet radio station. I make CDs, and I write books. I have a book now called *It's All Good: A John Sinclair Reader*. I also edited a book about Sun Ra, *Sun Ra Interviews & Essays*. Then, I make records for a little company here in Detroit called No Cover Records. I've got a new record that's coming out tomorrow called 'Let's Go Get 'Em.' The one before that was with a nine-piece band in Detroit, Viper Madness. And the one before that was 'Detroit Life,' and all of the poems have Detroit in them.

MY ADVICE FOR THIS GENERATION? Turn off your television set. Keep it off. Start from there, and then all kinds of other things could happen. ★

WAYNE KRAMER

WHEN I WAS A BOY, I decided I wanted to be a professional musician. So I tried to join other bands.

I was very young when I started, about 13. And most of the people who were already in established bands were much older than me and played better than I did. So I thought it might be better for me to just start my own band than to try and join someone else's. I looked around at school for other kids that wanted to be in a band, and that's how the MC5 was formed.

Ultimately, it became Fred Smith on guitar, Michael Davis on bass, Rob Tyner singing, and Dennis 'Machine Gun' Thomson on drums.

NO, I GREW UP IN DETROIT. But when I was 12, we moved out to Lincoln Park, so this was at Lincoln Park High School.

THE NAME CAME FROM AUTO PARTS—like a 357 rear end, or two four-barrel carbs. Tyner came up with it.

'GIVE ME A FOUR-BARRELED CARB AND A COUPLE SETS OF SHOCK ABSORBERS AND ONE OF THOSE MC5s,' LIKE IT WAS A SUPER-CHARGER OR SOMETHING.

Later on, we started to imagine what the MC could stand for—Morally Corrupt, Marijuana Cigarette, Mustard and Catsup. It got increasingly absurd the more reefer we smoked. The obvious one was Motor City, but that was only one in a long list. We just liked the initials, because it was like a car part, and it seemed to fit in with being from Detroit. Like a serial number. That's what we were looking for.

I STILL DRIVE A MUSCLE CAR, a Dodge Charger, and I still approach things from an industrial point of view—one that honors work, union, organization. And those are all things I grew up with in Detroit.

I GET THE QUESTION. The MC5's musical identity was a conscious evolution. We talked about it a lot, and we talked about the sound that we were trying to develop, because there was a premium put on originality. I don't think that's the case today, but that was certainly the case in the MC5's era. Every band was looking for its own sound. Today, I think conformity is the rule.

I WAS TRYING TO DO SOMETHING with the electric guitar, to make it sound different. There was a way I could play certain notes with the distortion and the overtones—if you push an amplifier hard enough, you get harmonic overtones. So it didn't sound like a guitar, it sounded like an entire symphony, you could hear the basses and the cellos and the high violins and the brass.

I was deeply influenced by the free jazz movement of the late '60s, the music of Cecil Taylor and Archie Shepp and Albert Ayler and Sun Ra. All of these artists were pushing music into a new sonic dimension. Then there were also the influences of Chuck Berry and the first wave of British bands—The Rolling Stones, The Who. And there were these incredibly hot-shit guitar players like Jeff Beck and Jimmy Page and Pete Townsend. I just idolized them. When I combined that with the free jazz movement, it started to make sense, what the MC5's sound could be—that there didn't have to be any limits on what the MC5 might be able to do. Why put limits on it?

A FAVORITE SONG? That's like picking a favorite kid. It's hard to say. I suppose 'Starship' is one, because it takes what we did as a rock band and shows how we were trying to move it forward, to advance the art into a more pure form. I think art should upset people. It should make them think. And I think that song did, because it started as a rock song, but after a while, it wasn't a rock song anymore. I like that. I think that's a worthwhile thing to do.

WELL, WHEN THE MC5 DISBANDED in 1972, I didn't know it at the time, but it was a great loss for me, because it was everything I had worked on since I was about 13. It was not only my job, but they were also my best friends. It was my community, and everything that I had built and everything that I was part of was gone. It was all gone.

I wasn't prepared for what that meant. I went into a downward spiral, and I started to acquire the maladies of alcoholism and drug addiction. There was great pain involved, and alcohol and drugs are painkillers. Although I didn't know it at the time, I was medicating myself from the grief and loss of my friends, my career, my identity. I started engaging in riskier behaviors and more antisocial behaviors, and started getting in trouble with the police. Ultimately, I was charged with a number of serious federal drug offenses and sentenced to federal prison for four years as a result of all of that.

You've got to remember that this was at the beginning of America's war on drugs. At this point, the federal government was in the business of cultivating drug dealers to arrest to build up their statistics so that they could go back to Congress and say, 'Look, we've locked up this many bad guys, give us more money.' I'm not saying I didn't do wrong—I did. But that's what happened. It happened to me, and now there's more than two and a half million Americans in prison, and half of them are nonviolent drug offenders, just like me. If I had pled guilty to my offense, today I would be doing life in prison.

IT'S CALLED 'JAIL GUITAR DOORS.' I think musicians are generally an incredibly selfish and self-centered group of individuals. It's all about them, all the time. And I've come to believe that for me to be a decent human being, I have to think about somebody else for a change. I've struggled with my time in prison my whole life. For decades, I couldn't think about it. And in the last 10 years, I've been able to look at it and say, 'What happened to me? How did I end up there?'

At one point, I ran into Billy Bragg, and he was telling me about some work he was doing in England, providing instruments for prisoners to use as music rehabilitation—that it was a way to process your problems nonconfrontationally, a way to build self-respect and self-esteem. And he called the organization Jail Guitar Doors. He asked me if I knew the song 'Jail Guitar Doors' by the Clash. I said, 'Yeah, I know it—it's about me.' 'What?' 'The Clash wrote the song about me, Bill.' He didn't realize that the song was about my going to prison, that The Clash had written the song about some of their friends who had trouble with the police, and I was one of those friends. We talked about it and I thought, 'Maybe this is a good opportunity for me to be of service to my fellows, to do something for somebody else for a change.'

We find people who work in prisons, who are willing to use music as rehabilitation, and we go find money. We squeeze money out of people and buy guitars and take them into the prisons, and we leave them there for the people in the prisons to use. The guitars are not gifts. We're not giving people guitars to while away the time. The guitars are a challenge—tools to use for rehabilitation. If playing the guitar can help prisoners to see themselves as more than just a loser or a statistic—if they can see themselves as an artist, a poet—that goes a long way to rebuilding that dignity that the prison experience strips from you.

So if I can be part of that, it makes me feel useful. I want to feel like I'm accomplishing something besides using up perfectly good air.

WHEN I GOT THE SURVIVING MC5 members back together with some special guests, and we toured the world for a couple years, it was big fun. It was terrific to be able to play these songs that we'd written so long ago for a whole new generation of rock fans. The fans knew the songs. They didn't know them back then. And we would be playing at places like Reading, this huge outdoor festival in England, and 30,000 kids would be singing along with MC5 songs. It was pretty exciting.

THE STRATOCASTER? For a guitar player, I can think of nothing greater than having

A SIGNATURE MODEL FENDER STRATOCASTER.
IF I NEVER ACCOMPLISH ANYTHING ELSE, I DID OK, GETTING A GUITAR.

NOT THAT I'M DONE. Long way from it. ★

IGGY POP

THE LONG FORM IS, I saw an iguana on the cover of *Life* magazine when I was a little boy. I was fascinated. There was a piece inside about *Night of the Iguana*, the Tennessee Williams play. So later, when I was in my first band, I suggested we call it the Iguanas. I had an iguana painted on my bass drum. The people got to know me around the area for that, as being the drummer in the Iguanas. And, basically, when I got work with a blues band in the area called the Prime Movers, the name stuck.

So my big chance to get rid of the name was when I started my own band. I started The Stooges, we were The Psychedelic Stooges then, and we went out on our first show. And I hadn't decided what to call myself yet. I was thinking of Jimmy James, actually. But we played and we immediately drew a lot of column inches in *The Michigan Daily*. And they said, 'Iggy Osterberg. Iggy this, area drummer Iggy, Iggy in front of The Stooges.' I'd already been in showbiz; I had my union card three or four years, I knew how hard it is to get attention in this business, so I saw a good thing and I ran with it. I gave up and became Iggy.

POP? I stole that from a friend of The Stooges. A friend of the Asheton brothers and Dave, a kid named Jim Pop. Jim didn't have any eyebrows or hair on his head. He had some sort of weird condition from too much glue-sniffing. And I was fascinated with him, because I thought he had the coolest name I'd ever heard. 'Jim Pop.' Wow. So when I added Iggy, I didn't really like Iggy Osterberg. That sounded a bit too much like I needed to be on a sitcom or something. So I stole his name.

THE GRANDE BALLROOM? I don't remember anything about meeting Russ specifically, but I will tell you that there was a sort of selection process that went on between Russ and I that was kind of, let's say, a private forerunner of the 'American Idol' process. I can't remember if it was before he ever gave us a job or after the first one. I was bidden to hang out at Russ' pad for the afternoon and get to know Russ a little better. He was sort of sizing me up. I remember it was very much like hanging out with the kid who had the baseball. I must have passed, because

we were playing there all the time pretty quickly. I think it was good for everybody. We livened up his bills, and I think we were a particularly good opening act for the Detroit groups, because it made their shows more interesting, like the MC5, the Dukes, SRC.

THE FIRST TIME I STAGE-DIVED
WAS IN DETROIT. IT WAS AT OUR SECOND SHOW AT THE GRANDE. IT WAS ALSO THE FIRST SHOW IN WHICH I FRONTED THE BAND AS A VOCALIST ONLY.

In our first show I was playing guitar, and muttered a couple of vocals. By the second show, I was barefoot with no shirt, and a pair of jeans and white face. It was 72 percent similar to what I still do. We were opening for Frank Zappa and the Mothers of Invention. So we had a very broad spectrum in the crowd, from Saturday Night Special 15-year-old chicks who wanted to smoke a joint and go home with the cutest boy they could find, all the way up to the genuine self-appointed freaks of America, there to check out Zappa. So I wanted to do well. And by about 15 minutes into our 20-minute set, we were doing well enough that—everybody else was seated back about 20 feet from the stage—these two girls came up and plopped themselves down on the floor, right in front of the stage to get a better view, kind of saying, 'Hey, we dig what you're doing.'

They were big girls. Really, really big. And I decided, at the end of the show, I wasn't sure we were getting across to people, so I decided to do what 5-year-olds do when they want to get attention and it's not happening. You know how they'll stiffen themselves up and just pretend to fall forward on the floor? I did that. I did the infantile fall-forward thing, thinking I would land on them. But they separated and I got a pretty good bonk off the floor and chipped off my front tooth, which is visible in any shot of me that has teeth in it until I got them fixed when I became fancier, when I went solo.

There were all sorts of reasons I would do it. Sometimes, depending on my social status, I'd come out on stage with a pen and a piece of paper stuck in my back pocket. I'd stage-dive, and get the number of somebody I fancied. Sometimes I did it just for a visual accent, or a high moment that went with the way I wanted the music to go at that time. I'd put it this way: It was a very early and sort of a primitively physical example of interactive entertainment. I was inviting them to get involved.

WHY DID I DECIDE TO TAKE MY SHIRT OFF? Well, memory is flawed, and mine more than most, because I've had a greater variety of life experiences than a lot of people. But the way that I remember it is that I was sitting in the U of M undergrad library, looking for thematic ideas for the new band that I was in, The Stooges. And I was living in a house on campus with the Ashetons and Dave. I had some Daoist texts and some Egyptian texts spread in front of me on a worktable, and I just kept noticing how the Pharaoh never wore a shirt. There was something clean and riveting about it. Something sort of stripped down, aerodynamic, expressive. I thought, 'Well, my build is about right for that.'

DETROIT? I THINK THERE WAS A FANTASTIC AMOUNT OF OPTIMISM AT THE HEIGHT OF IT. THERE WAS A SUPERCHARGED OPTIMISM.

Which I think had to do with the fact that, geographically, the town was sheltered from the neuroses of the larger urban centers like New York, Chicago, Los Angeles. And yet it was a one-horse town. A great big, one-horse town, and the horse was the auto industry. Because of that doing so well, I don't ever remember,

as a young person, pondering for a moment the idea that I could have a problem getting a job or supporting myself.

There was a nice ignorance that came from the Midwest. We would look at the stuff that came in from Los Angeles, London, and New York, musically, and think, 'I could do that.' Because we weren't troubled with the realization that these people were working from the benefit of high-and-mighty connections. We didn't have that, but we didn't know we didn't have it. So we didn't give a shit. It was a nice, rich and simple time.

Then I think, also, you had time. People had time to imagine, time to dream. The demands of daily life were not that difficult, frankly. It's not like it is now.

There are a lot of things that are good to be ignorant of. We were kind of ignorant, and because of that, when it came to aesthetics, there was no one to please but yourself. You didn't feel like you had to like something because everybody else did.

We're the first town where The Who had a hit in America. Yeah. They couldn't get arrested anywhere in the country. But Detroit got it right away.

ONE OF MY FAVORITE QUOTES—I'm going to steal this from one of the guitar players I've worked with for years—would be, 'Shot from a cannon and still ain't landed.' I stole that from Whitey from The Trolls.

I'D LIKE PEOPLE to remember how good we made them feel. It is showbiz, but I don't feel we're one of those that faked it.

HEY, I GOT TO GO. Did you get it? ★

DON WAS

A HIGHLIGHT? Well, this is pretty good today. I anticipate it will all be downhill from here.

There was a moment, in 1989, when I was in the studio producing Bob Dylan, and he had George Harrison come in to play guitar. He had George play a solo, but he had George play the solo before George had ever heard the song, so he didn't even know what key it was in. He was just messing with George. So George Harrison scrambled to play a solo. And Bob says, 'Yeah, that's great, perfect, thank you.' And George Harrison turns to me and says, 'You can't use that.' And Bob says, 'No, that was great—right Don? What do you think?' Time stopped. And I thought of the Concert for Bangladesh—the two of them standing at the same mic, and how I would have sold my car just to be in the back row. And now, here I was, and they're asking me what I thought! I didn't know what to do. It was like I went into a vacuum and time slowed down. And then, I thought, 'Well, I'll tell him the truth, but I'll be diplomatic.' And I said, 'Well, it was a great solo, but I think you can do better.' And George Harrison said, 'Thank you.' Bob was just playing around, but there was probably an element of test involved.

That's kind of been how I've produced every record subsequently—gentle truth. That was a pretty good moment, though, because I'd been destitute in Detroit four years earlier. Things moved real fast at that point.

I GOT STARTED WHEN MY DAD, in 1958, bought a guitar from a guy who taught a guitar class at the Jewish center. And he brought the guitar, which I still have, home. But my dad just didn't have an affinity for it. So he showed me the couple chords he knew and gave me the guitar. That was it.

I got started playing bass because there were two great keyboard players in my high school and about eight guitar players who were better than me and no bass players. I didn't even know what bass was; I just knew that they needed one.

MOTOWN MUSIC STILL HAS A PROFOUND EFFECT ON ME, TO THIS DAY, AND I CAN'T TELL YOU WHY.

Nor can anybody tell you why. Why does that music get so deeply under everybody's skin? Why are you playing it? You weren't even born when they made those records. There's just something magical in it. For lack of any better explanation, it's magical. It touches some deep, underlying synaptic pathways. I don't understand how it gets in there, but the music goes deep in people. It affects me every time I hear it. It certainly influenced me as a musician.

AS A BASS PLAYER, JAMES JAMERSON is as great as they come. I can play his parts, but I could not have thought them up. I can recreate them. Not as well, but I can play it. But I don't know how he thought of those things. It still mystifies me, the depth of this guy's creativity, to come up with those parts. He's playing the melody, they're lyrical, they've got a great groove going, and he's like a percussionist, all at once. He finds the craziest holes in which to play and it works perfectly. He was a string bass player. He was a classically trained musician, so he had fabulous technique.

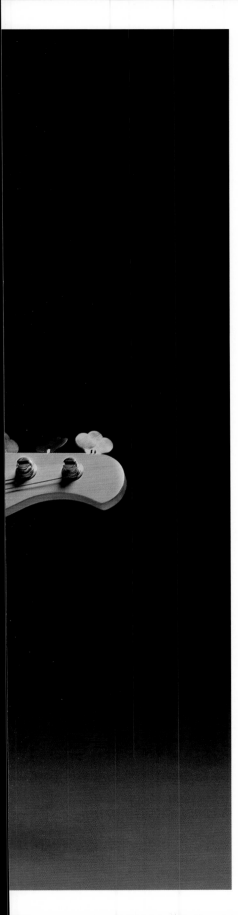

WELL, I'VE WORKED WITH George Clinton, Iggy Pop, Wayne Kramer, Bob Seger, Mitch Rider, Glenn Frey, Marshall Crenshaw... I'm sure there's more. Being from Detroit comes up a lot. The first time I met Stevie Wonder, I was a bandleader, and he was coming in for a TV show. So I went to his dressing room to talk about keys, and his brother said, 'You have two minutes.' But as it turned out, Stevie wouldn't let me go. He said, 'You sound like home; I just like hearing that Detroit accent.' I sat around with him for an hour in his dressing room. You can tell by the way people hit consonants. It's like a little secret fraternity. Hitting hard consonants is the password.

I remember one time going down to the Trans-Love Energies place on Warren and Forest and some of the guys from MC5 were jamming with Pharoah Sanders. That was music you'd never heard before in your life; it was crazy, crazy music—like Sun Ra, just abstract rock 'n' roll that had never been played before.

MY FIRST CAR? Good question. I got it in 1968. It was a 1958 Chevy Impala with big fins. It cost $50. I drove it until the transmission gave out six months later. I just left it wherever the transmission gave out.

The first real memory I have of the car, I was with David Was and another friend. We smoked a bunch of pot and drove on a school playground where it had just snowed. We were in pajamas but pretending they were army uniforms. We weren't 9, by the way; I had a driver's license. We decided to parachute out of the car. So I drove around the snowdrifts, in a circle, and the commander, David, would yell 'Jump!' and you'd have to jump out the door into the snow drifts.

We got arrested, and I lost my license. The crime was driving on a school playground at night with the lights off. If I'd have had my lights on, it was actually legal to do all that. They took us to the Oak Park jail, and I lost my license. I'm lucky they didn't search our pockets; I'd have been in Jackson.

ONE OF MY FONDEST MEMORIES of Detroit is catching the bus at Northland and going down to see shows, like the Dave Clark Five at Cobo Hall. We saw the Rolling Stones there twice. I'd go with my band and we'd pretend we were in 'Hard Day's Night.' We stopped at the Wurlitzer store downtown, Lafayette Coney Island. Those were heady times. It was good.

I THINK ONE OF THE THINGS that makes Detroit unique is that it's not a place where fashion is born. It doesn't come out of New York or L.A. You know the game of 'operator?' Where you whisper something into somebody's ear, and by the time it comes back around the circle the message has been completely distorted and turned into something else? That's kind of what happens to music here. Detroit's provincial enough that by the time whatever's trendy gets here, it's all convoluted, and as a result the stuff that comes out of here ends up sounding very original.

I also think that with the people in Detroit, in general, there's a lack of pretense. You don't drive around and see a bunch of Bentleys on the road, or Rolls-Royces. No one's trying to pretend that they're something else. It's a basic thing, at least when I lived here. You're in a business that's somehow related to or connected to the welfare of the auto industry, and you're just tied into this thing. There's no sense of putting on any airs.

DETROIT IS REFRESHING. DETROITERS ARE GENUINE PEOPLE, AND THEY SPARE YOU THE BULL.

So does the music that comes out of here. It's minimalist by comparison and certainly lacking in gloss. It's not sugarcoated at all. It reflects everything about the city, and people all over the world respond to it. ★

DELLA REESE

I GREW UP on the East Side of Detroit, on Vernor Highway.

BETTE DAVIS, LENA HORNE, AND JOAN CRAWFORD? Well, they had everything that I had ever dreamed of: the fur coats, the round Hollywood beds, the diamonds. I wanted to have all of that. So what I would do was, I would get a line that they said, and I would wear my mother out with it. Bette Davis would have a line, I don't remember what it would be, but no matter what you said to me, I would answer with it. Drove my mom mad.

NO, NO, I NEVER WENT TO CASS TECH. I went to Northeastern. Then I went to Wayne State for a couple of years, until my mother died and I had to come out of college.

Northeastern was kind of different, because my girlfriend and I were the only two black people in the school, and the civil rights situation had not been settled at that time. So a lot of stupid things were done. But we had made up our minds that we were going to finish high school, so we just persevered. There was no help at that time. We talked about it in our homes and things, but we had no legal rights protecting us, so there was nothing we could do. You just had to keep going.

My mother had four daughters and a son, but had never had a child finish high school. And I was determined that I was going to finish high school and go to college because that was something she wanted so bad. So no matter what you said, I would just go forward—if you didn't touch me. If you touched me, we would rumble. But if it was just some snide remark that you said, it didn't bother me, because I wanted to please my mother by finishing school. I wanted to give her that. Unfortunately, she was gone before I could finish college. She died my second year. But she did get a chance to have my diploma from high school, and she did get a chance to see me go to college.

GROWING UP, when my parents weren't working, we just relaxed. We didn't have any money for partying. But one of the things that really sticks in my mind is that we picnicked a lot at Belle Isle. Everything about Belle Isle was fascinating to me. The first exotic birds I ever saw were in Belle Isle. The only animals, other than cats and dogs, I ever saw were in the zoo at Belle Isle. The trees, the flowers—going there was a wonderful experience and it didn't take a lot of money. My mother would pack a lunch and we would get on the bus, and we would go to Belle Isle and spend the whole day there, just running and playing and having a good time. That's something that's still very vivid in my mind.

I WAS A
DREAMER.

On Sunday, we would go to church, and then we would have something to eat. And if you knew anybody who had a car, we would drive through the very rich neighborhoods and we would claim houses. 'That's my house'; 'let's drive around and see my house.' It helped to fortify our dreams. It made us know that these things existed, and it made me know, and other people too, that we could have this, that it was available to us.

So they became dream patterns for us. We would go to Grosse Pointe, we would go to the West Side, we would go where the houses were wonderful, where there were gates and there were flower bushes and marvelous stained glass windows and things of that nature. It was thrilling.

I WENT TO NEW LIBERTY BAPTIST CHURCH. That was my mother's church. And then Church of Our Faith was a church I decided to go to.

At that time, the church was the place for social events. For example, on Wednesdays the teachers taught us after Bible classes. They taught the girls to cook; they taught the young men how to do manual arts. It was a place to go and play with the other children. So it was a very important part in our lives. It was a social center for us.

MAHALIA WAS HER NAME. Mahalia Jackson. See, my mother was a personal friend of God's. And in our house, God had a permanent place. For example, if I wanted to eat, I had to have a Bible verse. It could not be the one I had yesterday. It would have to be one I learned today or else she would say, 'Get up from the table and go learn a Bible verse, and come back and have your dinner or your lunch.'

She was in church all the time, and I loved singing, and that was the place where I had a chance to sing. And one day, Mahalia came to sing at our church, and the lady that was a lyric soprano singing with her discovered that she was pregnant. And the

South being what it was, her husband did not want her to go to the South. Well, I was also a lyric soprano. So the pastors asked my mother if I could go with her. And that's how I happened to become one of her singers.

WELL, I REALLY DIDN'T WORK a lot with local talent. I won a contest and the contest prize was a week at the Flame Show Bar, which was the major entertainment bar in my neighborhood. And I went there to enjoy my week that I won, and the manager ended up keeping me there for 18 weeks. So I was blessed. I opened for Ella Fitzgerald, Nat King Cole; I opened the show for all of the major talents that came to town—Dinah Washington, Sarah Vaughan. I was with these marvelous giants.

MY NAME? I was married at the time. My name is really Delloreese, one word. And I married a man named Taliaferro. My name went across the marquee and down the side! So they ended up just putting up Delloreese, one word. And my manager said, 'We could split this and it would be better for you. A shorter name would always be mentioned in the newspapers and on the marquee.' That's how I became Della Reese.

EVERY MOMENT OF MY CAREER has been a highlight. In the beginning, I didn't know where the next job was coming from, so it was an adventure. It was an excitement, waiting on the next chance to perform.

MY FIRST CAR wasn't an automobile, it was a scoot-mobile! It was a mobile that would take me to jobs. It was good enough to get me around. And then, eventually, I got one of the first four-seated Thunderbirds. I was in heaven, because I could drive anywhere I wanted to drive. Today, if you said, 'Where would you like to go?' I'd say, 'Let's go for a ride.' I like to go for a ride.

IT USED TO BE A TOWN full of magnificent musicians. It used to be a town of family when I was there. Neighbors being close to you. It was a wonderful place to live. I'm glad I was born there.

MY FONDEST MEMORY OF DETROIT IS OF
MY MOTHER AND THE MUSIC.

I'M A PASTOR, and I have a wish for the world: that we will come to recognize who we are and come to know that we are really one, and that if we would just love each other, things would be so much better for all of us. But that's not just for Detroit. I just met you today, and I have that wish for you, too. ★

MITCH RYDER

YES, I GREW UP in Hamtramck. No, the name's not Polish. General Robert E. Lee wasn't Chinese, either.

FOR THE BAND, we had gone through a number of names, among them Michael Rothschild, which was rejected. I can't remember any other names we tossed around... I just remember that when they started getting into 'Michael Rothschild,' I said, 'This is getting silly.' I didn't want 'Billy Lee,' either, because it sounded too much like a hillbilly.

I'm not sure why I felt it was important to change my name. When you're a teenager, which I was when that was all going on, we were pretty much willing to do anything the record companies wanted because we realized that we had a chance to become stars.

YES, GROWING UP, we had music around us all of the time. My mother sang and my father sang professionally. Well, semiprofessionally. He had to give it up because they started popping out babies, and he wasn't established in music.

One day he came home, and my mom had all of his fan mail in the middle of the floor. And when he got home from work she lit the fan mail on fire. She stood over on the side with me and my sister and said, 'You have to make a choice. Which one of these do you want? Do you want me and these kids, or do you want that fan mail?' which was burning in flames on the floor. So she helped him make his choice, and he was forever out of music. I think he resented that. When I became successful, I think he lived vicariously through me.

There were eight of us kids. I wasn't the oldest. I was the oldest boy. My dad was not a practicing Catholic, and she was a Southern Baptist, so I don't get it. They had prophylactics back then. I don't know what the problem was.

Yeah, they're cute, if you can feed them.

WITH THE PEPS, the group was already formed when I ran into them. I met them at a place on Woodward called The Village, which was a launching pad for a lot of rhythm and blues acts. Many of the Motown artists came through there and honed their skills. I was introduced to the band; I was allowed to sing a song with them, and they liked me well enough to invite me to sing more. Then I was assigned background vocal parts. I became harmony, occasionally sharing the lead with some of the other members. It was cool, but I think we would have been limited in how far we could have gone. We were still quite young.

MOTOWN WAS, and is, a factory town. Philadelphia is similar. They're working-class towns. Philadelphia had a lot of records coming out of their city as well, but not to the same degree as Motown.

The problem with Motown was that, in the first decade of their existence, they really didn't sign any white acts. It was frustrating for the kids who wanted to become something. Berry had one white female act and that was it.

SO WE HAD TO GO TO NEW YORK TO DO IT. AND ONCE WE DID IT, THE RECORD COMPANIES SAID, 'OH, THIS IS THE SOUND THAT COMES OUT OF DETROIT.'

So they came in with all of their contracts, and maybe 50 or 60 artists got signed out of Detroit because of the door that we opened.

I think Bob Seger probably would have made it eventually without us opening that door for him. He was trying very hard. But once that door was opened, certainly people were more willing to listen to his music and everybody else that came after him. The list goes on and on all of the way up to today. Eminem, Kid Rock, they just keep coming.

FUN? FOR ME, fun is being onstage. That's the ultimate fun. Other things, they were entertaining in one way or another, but they weren't fun. I'm happiest when I'm onstage. I just am.

I DON'T KNOW HOW TO ANSWER that question. There was no series of concerts that I enjoyed more than others. I used to enjoy the battles of the bands when I was a teenager, before we went to New York. Later, I enjoyed being onstage with Bruce Springsteen doing the medley of my songs, that was fun. I enjoyed opening for Seger at Cobo for seven days. That was fun.

A BATTLE OF THE BANDS? Two bands square off against each other, they do a set, and whoever the audience likes most is the winner. It was pretty serious stuff.

We were lucky because, at the time, most of the bands were copying the British bands. They just played music and sang. We would do the same, but we would also entertain. For example, we would take off our clothes and the bass player would switch with the drummer, the drummer would switch with the guitar player, and the guitar player would sing. It was like a moving circus, and we would be dancing onstage and jumping into each others' arms. There was a lot of athleticism going on, as well as the guitar-playing and singing.

All of the other bands were so focused on their British thing, just standing there and playing, thinking they were cool doing that. We thought there was more to entertainment. We showed them what it was and that was our ticket out, really.

No, I don't remember the other bands. We just referred to them as dust. That's what they are now. Actually, some of them went on to become quite famous, but I'm not going to give them the credit of saying who they are.

I'M NOT SURE HOW WE GOT SO BIG in Germany. But I think the age group that I impacted was impacted because of an anti-authority pose I took on this one European-wide broadcast we did. I started ranting against the conservative government and jumping into the crowd, getting people to sing with me and stuff.

Again, you know, the other artists on the show just stood onstage, and I felt compelled to give more, go further, do more, say more. I think, even though they couldn't understand exactly what I was saying, it was clear to them that this guy is different. He's some kind of rebel, some kind of a weird, freaky guy, and he doesn't like the establishment, and we're teenagers, and neither do we.

That's where my initial base over there came from. They've been very faithful, and they've introduced their children to my music, and they just keep showing up, year after year, for 32 years now. We go over there every year on tour for a couple months at a time. One-nighters. Not an easy schedule. It's a real hard schedule.

I HAD A QUOTE ONCE ON WXYZ; maybe you can use it. I was asked about what made Detroit special and I said,

'IN DETROIT, AS A CULTURE,
WE BEAR WITNESS TO THE NATIONAL BURLESQUE OF MAN'S INTELLECT.'

I think it's true. We're Midwesterners, we're considered stupid, unsophisticated, and yet some of the most horrific things that could go on in the civilized world happen in these sort of cultural iconic cities like New York and L.A. And we get to watch it. We recognize it as being just what it is.

Those are two media centers. And if you happen to be on a football team from there, or a star, they're going to immediately send out national press on you to make you bigger than life. But if you're from Detroit or Chicago or somewhere else, they tend to downplay you, and you have to fight twice as hard to get recognition on the coasts. It's not fair, but it's the way it is because they're looking after their own. But we get to watch them, here in Detroit, when they make their mistakes, and it's cool. It's cool to be able to sit back and say, 'Well, Mr. Class, Mr. Civilized, wealthy guy who knows how to run the world, you just tripped and fell in some shit.'

They hate to have that pointed out to them, but I love it. I think they need to come to a spot where they know that we're all created equal, and they're not worth any more than we are. We're all equal.

WHEN WE WERE TALKING about stars earlier, it's not a big deal. I guess it's kind of a compliment that you would ask me to be in a book of iconic people, but the whole concept of fame is really bizarre. It's really bizarre. To place somebody above you, that's weird shit. It's just the business I chose. ★

TED NUGENT

I'M ON FIRE. Having the time of my life, no matter what anybody says. If you were having as much fun as I am, you'd blow up.

TEXAS, JUST OUTSIDE OF WACO. We moved here about eight years ago. And we have about 0 degrees, and the wind is snorting. Got a little snow and I'm out there playing like I'm some kind of Midwestern motherfucker. I got my big tractor going four-wheel drive, and I'm grinding driveways where I don't even need to grind driveways, but I'm grinding because I like to grind, motherfucker!

And that pretty much sums up my Detroit iconoclastic considerations. So, have a nice day. Write that shit down.

I JUST LOADED UP three giant wild boar and I skinned the fucking back-straps, tenderloins. My hands are still greasy with wild swine fat. Purely organic—which, by the way, I'm the only guy you'll talk to that actually eats free-range anything, and this shit turns me on more at 63 than it ever has, even along the mighty Rouge River at Skunk Hollow, in Redford, near Six Mile and Grand River, motherfucker!

THIS SUMS ME UP. Just write this down. Mrs. Nugent held me in her arms this morning, held me close to her substantial bosom and said, 'Boy, you ain't right.' And that goes all the way back to about 1949. I ain't been right then, and I ain't right now, and it's so beautiful I'm ready to blow myself.

I'M NATURAL. And it all comes from that Motor City spirit, that Detroit Herculean work ethic that my mom and dad didn't just instill in me, but forced in me.

I talked to my sister Kathy and my brother Jeff this morning, and my brother John last night, and we're all glowing, reeking of the American dream, because of the spirit of genuine, rugged individualism, entrepreneurial defiance, the Herculean work ethic that brings you your dreams because you get up earlier and work harder.

A LOT OF BANDS, they didn't practice enough. That's not practice. You would all get stoned. Shut the fuck up.

MOTOWN, HITSVILLE USA, the Funk Brothers, it is inextricably connected to the spirit of what brought us Mitch Ryder in Detroit, what brought us SRC and the MC5 and The Amboy Dukes, what brought us Rare Earth and Grand Funk Railroad, and The Frost, and Bob Seger, and Kid Rock, and Eminem, and Jack White. It is one giant lump. We are not connected, we are one. I know all about Stax. I know all about the Delta, and I know all about the Chicago thing. Fuck you. It's not even close. We're talking apples and grenades.

THERE WAS A VITALITY to how Mitch Ryder showed us how to do it. Now this was before they changed their name. It was Billy Lee out of Walled Lake Casino.

I WAS BORN UNDER THE GLOW OF
LES PAUL'S NEW INVENTION
AND JIMMY MCCARTY SHOWED ME WHAT TO DO WITH IT.

Because I was struggling to do Bo Diddley and Chuck Berry, and Lonnie Mack, and Duane Eddy, and The Ventures, and all that stuff. But Jimmy said, 'No, like this, motherfucker!'

You listen to 'Jenny Take a Ride,' and, I'm sorry, I defy you to find something that is that grinding, between Earl Elliot, Johnny Badanjek, Joe, Jimmy, and Billy Levise. I defy you! It doesn't exist!

And you can hear it, believe it or not—I hope I'm not the only one, but I probably am—you can hear it in Eminem. Eminem, if you go to him and asked him, he'd probably go, 'I don't know what you're talking about.' But, in that geography of southeast Michigan, he couldn't escape it if he wanted to. And Kid Rock. And Jack White.

Kid Rock can pretend all he wants, but I am the bad motherfucker. You can borrow it every night, Kid.

By the way, I'm the only guy you'll ever interview that actually has a bone saw, much less a greasy one. I'd better call my next record 'Greasy Bone Saw.'

I'm a wonderful human being. It ain't right.

MY 6,000TH CONCERT, at the DTE? Stop and think of the statistics involved:

6,000 CONCERTS, 50 YEARS LATER, WITH MY ORIGINAL GUITAR PLAYER,
PLAYING THE SAME SONGS, IN MY HOMETOWN.

Where 'Fred Bear' has become a spiritual anthem. Where 'Stranglehold' is responsible for the Baby Boom.

I'm pretty good with the English language, but I'm helpless to adequately describe the sensation. I just grovel under the firestorm of emotion and spirituality, and giddiness, and erect attitude and erect spirit.

MY FIRST BAND, THE LOURDS, we practiced smart. We listened to Chuck and Bo and Howlin' and Muddy. We listened to James Brown's Famous Flames. We listened to the grind of the Motown soundtrack. All the white guys, their guitars are like, 'sly, sly, sly,' and we went, 'No, man, if you close the high hand up, you get the, ka-ka-ka,' which is where 'Stranglehold' came from.

Then The Amboy Dukes, Dave Palmer on drums, get the fuck out of here. These are all Detroit guys. Greg Arama on bass guitar, who could run right along with Bob Babbitt and James Jamerson, are you fucking me? All our heroes were black. Don't tell Mitch Ryder and his guys that they were white. He might shoot you in the kneecap.

Because I worked so hard on my instrument, The Lourds found me, and they hired me as a guitar player. Wait a minute, I don't think I got paid. But anyhow, I joined that band because I was a bad motherfucker, and bad motherfuckers find bad motherfuckers, and bad motherfuckers play with bad motherfuckers, and people come and see the bad motherfuckers. How simple is that? It works in 2010 perfectly. It will always work, it always has worked.

I think it's important to state that my son Rocco, out in California, struggling to be an actor, accomplished the same forward motion with the same defiant work ethic spirit. He can get a job where no one can get a job because he is willing to do the jobs 'Americans aren't willing to do.' Fuck you. And he gets there earlier and he stays later, and he works hard. And my family's job description is, 'Yes.' 'Yes. Name it, we'll fucking do it. And we'll do it better than anybody else, and I'll get a raise the first night on the job, because I'll blow your fucking mind.'

Listen to 'Stranglehold.' You don't come up with that shit from a stupor.

EVERYBODY I'VE EVER PLAYED and jammed with, everybody references Detroit. If you can make it in Detroit, you're a bad motherfucker. If you can't, you're done.

I LOVE MY ROOTS. I love my birth state of Michigan. I was on the phone with Dick Posthumus and Randy Richardville, speaker of the house, and with the new governor, Rick Snyder. I'm a Texan. I'm teaching them how to talk and barbecue. And my governor shoots coyotes, which is why I live in Texas. But I'm still spiritually embraced and in love with my birth state of Michigan.

MY SHOW? Yeah, just close your eyes and think of a high-speed Japanese train going up your ass. It's unnatural, but in a pleasant way.

When I was forced to move to Chicago in '65, because my dad got transferred out of Michigan, I saw the hottest band in Chicago, which was the Shadows of Knight, and they played like pussies. It took me about eight days to become the No. 1 band in the entire Chicago area, because they'd never seen this before. We just started humping faces. The whole, 'ka-ka-ka,' guitar thing. When we played all these Stones and Beatles and Yardbirds and Who and Chuck Berry and Bo Diddley songs, we didn't play it like the record. We played it faster and harder and louder.

And that's contagious. When the band loves what they're doing, you can't escape. And I loved the Shadows, and they played really good. They're some good musicians. But it wasn't even close. They played like little girls. We came in and just stomped the shit out of them, we ripped their heads off and shit down their neck, trampled the weak, hurdled the dead, twang your ass with Uncle Ted!

Fuck you. Fucking awesome. ★

ALICE COOPER

TO BE PART OF THAT BROTHERHOOD of Detroit music in '68, '69, '70, was amazing, because bands were rooting for other bands. We were fans of Iggy and the Stooges and the MC5 and Ted Nugent, and they were all fans of us.

When we played together, it was truly a fraternity. After every weekend at the Grande or the Eastown, where it would be all of those bands playing, and then a headliner like The Who or Fleetwood Mac with Peter Green, there'd be a party. And every week it was at a different band's house. It would be at The Amboy Dukes' house one week, SRC's the next week, then the MC5's, then ours.

It was a fraternity that I don't think will ever happen again. It was a rock movement, and maybe the most authentic, real, hard rock movement in the United States, that Detroit scene.

IF YOU DIDN'T BRING IT IN DETROIT,
THEY'D KILL YOU.
THE AUDIENCE WAS AS TOUGH AS THE BANDS.

They were blue-collar. They wouldn't go home and put on their black leather jackets and go; that's how they came from work. There was no high society there. Everything was factory. I think that's where the hard rock foundation was from. If you came in and you did folk music, they'd kill you. You had to do it with authority, or they would boo you off the stage.

We felt so at home. That was exactly what we loved, the Detroit scene.

I WAS ACTUALLY BORN in downtown Detroit at Saratoga Hospital, which was called 'the butcher house.' I guess a lot of people died there. Now it's a mental institution. So I was literally born right in downtown Detroit.

MY DAD WAS A USED CAR SALESMAN, and he was an honest used car salesman, which meant we didn't make any money at all. You had to be a very crooked guy to sell a used car. My dad couldn't do it. He was too honest for that and ended up being a pastor.

On Saturday or Sunday, I'd go to work with my dad and sit there in the office and watch the cars. My mom was a waitress at the Coral Gables, which was out in St. Clair Shores. There were two incomes, but we never had any money. We were lower-middle class, but we lived in a nice little house in East Detroit. We never were hungry, but we certainly weren't rich.

It was just my sister and I, and my mom and dad. I remember everything about Detroit, at that time, in the '50s.

OH YEAH. HUDSON'S, Cunningham's, Woolworth's, Kresge's. Cunningham's was the big drugstore then. White Castles; I grew up on White Castles. They were 12 for $1.

My uncle would come over and watch the Friday night fights, and they would drink Stroh's and smoke Lucky Strikes. It was great.

We'd go to Bob-Lo Island. That was such a big deal, going to Bob-Lo, because you went over on a nice little steamboat. That was the greatest day of the year, Bob-Lo Island day.

I DID ALL THINGS DETROIT. I would go to see Gordie Howe play, Al Kaline, Bobby Layne, the real classics. We couldn't always afford those tickets, but when my dad did get them, it was the greatest thing in the world.

I remember, in the winter, there was a lake close to us, by Kantner Elementary School. I went to Kantner. And at night, after dinner, we would go over there and they would have lights on the lake, and there'd be pickup hockey games. You'd put on your skates, and it was like 10-year-old kids and 40-year-old guys, and there were 20 games going on. I remember that so distinctly, playing hockey at night in Detroit.

WITH MUSIC, I was in Arizona at that point, because I had to get out of Detroit. I couldn't take the cold climate, so we went to Arizona.

I was on summer vacation, and I was painting the house with my mom. She made me paint the house, and the radio was on. The radio was Top 40, and they were playing The Four Seasons and The Beach Boys.

All of a sudden this song came on, 'She Loves You,' by the Beatles. I stopped and I went, 'What was that?' It was totally new. I'd never heard anything like that. Then, two hours later, I heard 'Please Please Me.' And within three hours, my whole world, musically, had changed. I said, 'Who are these guys?' And then you saw the picture with the haircuts and the boots and the look. I went, 'This is the greatest thing in the world.'

We got a band together. We were all in the high school letterman's club. I was a four-year letterman in high school, in track and cross-country, and so was Dennis Dunaway, our bass player. We were a bunch of jocks.

For the letterman's club talent show, we decided to do a parody of the Beatles, and we called ourselves the Earwigs. We put on the Beatle wigs and we got up on stage and we sang these songs. And the next day, we went, 'That was really fun. Maybe we could learn.'

Dennis picked up the bass. Over the summer he learned how to play about 10 songs. Glen Buxton was a guitar player already. He knew a guy named John Tatum, who also played guitar. And another guy named John Speer, who was one of our runners, learned how to play drums.

So we got back to school our sophomore year and we could play about 10 songs. And we started playing at parties.

We learned from the very bottom of the barrel. We just kept going. The Beatles and the whole British Invasion is what got us into music.

THE NAME: It was a fact that we were called The Nazz. We'd already moved to L.A. from Arizona and we'd established ourselves as The Nazz. This is before we moved the band to Detroit. So we heard that there was this band from Philadelphia called The Nazz. It was Todd Rundgren's band, and we went, 'Uh-oh, we've got to change the name.' I said, 'Look, we've already got this theatrical image;

we're already on the scary side. We wear the makeup and all of this stuff. Let's not call ourselves something scary. Let's not be 'vampire' this or that. Let's go the other way. Let's get a sweet little old lady's name, or a little girl's name. Alice Cooper. It's just a sweet little girl's name. And then they see us, and there's nobody named Alice in the band. That's just the name of the band, Alice Cooper.' That's where it came from.

It's funny, because the name had a rhythm to it. Baby Jane, Lizzie Borden, Alice Cooper. It had a little bit of a rhythm. And then we really took it far and said, 'Now that we're called Alice Cooper, let's be villains. Let's become this villainous band.' And that's what worked.

THE FIRST EYES were a spider-eye kind of thing. And then, after that, I said, 'I'd like to get more of a demented clown-villain look.' Because there were a lot of rock heroes and no villains. So I was the guy who said,

'OK, ALL THESE PETER PANS AND NO CAPTAIN HOOK. I'LL BE CAPTAIN HOOK. I HAVE NO PROBLEM WITH THAT. I LOVE BEING CAPTAIN HOOK.'

I designed the character to be something that was going to pull you in. And you would have mystery, but at the same time, it would have some amount of black comedy to it.

I DID FIND MY TOP HAT in the garbage can. All of our props were something we found backstage. A mop would be something I could swing around; I could ride on it; it was a girl, because it had hair, so I could dance with it. It was all improv. A sheet, a pillowcase, a pillow, a top hat. It was just a kicked-in, half broken-up top hat. But I put it on and went, 'Oh yeah, that looks good.' It was in the back of the Grande. They must have had some kind of play there or something. We found all kinds of great stuff back there. But the top hat fit, and I went, 'Ooh.' ★

JACK WHITE

THEY'RE POLISH. My mother's side was 100 percent Polish. Her parents were immigrants that came to live in the Polish neighborhood in southwest Detroit. By the time I was born, it was mostly Hispanic. But that's why they were in that neighborhood. St. Hedwig's was a big Polish Catholic church.

So that was that.

Then, down the street was another church called Holy Redeemer, which was like the biggest Catholic church in North America back in the 1920s and '30s.

MY GRANDMOTHER from Poland, her sister had already come over here, so she came to live with her sister. And they worked in a pickle factory on Grand River, which is funny, because the first year I went to Cass Tech, which is on Grand River, there was a teacher who said, 'Yeah, this building used to be a pickle factory.'

I've looked it up and I can't find any evidence of that, but it's so bizarre. Maybe they transformed that building into a high school after my grandmother was there, in the pickle factory. I don't know. We've never been able to figure that out. How many pickle factories on Grand River could there have been? I have no idea.

TO RELAX? I don't think my family's ever relaxed.

YEAH, I'M THE YOUNGEST OF 10.

WHAT DID I DO? I used to hop the fence and sit under the freeway bridges when I was by myself. That's what I would do a lot. I would go to a party store and get a Faygo and some chips, and I'd go hop the fence and sit under there, and just kind of watch the cars.

You weren't allowed to do that, of course, but that was one thing.

It was kind of rough. I spent a lot of time in Clark Park playing baseball. There's still the same thing going on there, street punks and nice kids all mixed together playing this really rugged baseball. We did that a lot, too.

YEAH, MY MOM and my brother-in-law worked at the Masonic. My mom worked a David Bowie concert there, selling concessions. My brother-in-law was an usher. And I worked at a restaurant in the Fox, as a busboy.

I'VE GOT TO BE HONEST. I never grew up with people telling me I had any talent for music. I never heard anyone say that.

In high school I got way more serious about it and was doing a lot of my own recording. I had a lot of ragged gear when I was a teenager. My brothers were in a band and I would get it from them or buy it from their friends. That's how a lot of that started.

I really loved music, beyond anything. But it was sort of a two-sided thing.

I MEAN, I WOULD WAKE UP AT 4 IN THE MORNING AND PLAY MUSIC WITH YOU IF YOU WANTED TO. THAT'S HOW MUCH I WAS OBSESSED.

But at the same time, I had no hopes or dreams about it at all, that I could do something with it, make an album, even.

I always thought that stuff was just not going to happen; that you had to be born in Los Angeles and have an uncle in the business or something like that. I just thought that there was no way, in Detroit, that that was going to happen with me. But I said, 'Whatever I do, when I grow up and have a regular job, I do want to play music with other people. That's my big passion.' So that's all I ever thought about. I never thought, 'I'll go on tour; I'll make an album.' I never thought that was possible.

It was weird.

ARTISTIC CONSTRAINTS make it a lot easier for me to know what to do. Anytime I've gone into a situation where there's too

much opportunity, my brain gets a little bit... whatever would be the reverse of claustrophobia. It's too much opportunity; it's too much access. I have to start narrowing it down.

I just built a studio a couple of years ago. And nowadays, if you're a musician or producer and you build a studio, your goal is to have every possible thing you could want to have there. That was not my goal. My goal was to limit myself. I built a small studio, rather than a large one. I got an eight-track tape recorder rather than a 24-track tape recorder. Just a lot of decisions like that.

The hardest part about art is to know when to stop.

THERE'S SOMETHING PERFECT about the number three. It's the first of many. One is by itself, two is not many, but three is the beginning of many. Three also sort of means infinite to me. Or say a religion, like the Christian religion. If it was just the father and the son, those two ideas... throwing in the third element, of the Holy Ghost or the Holy Spirit, covers all the bases. Now all the bases are covered. Even femininity is covered by that.

From my angle, though, it came from upholstery, when I had my own upholstery shop, Third Man Upholstery. That's where it started with me—three staples, the least amount.

If I had fabric over a table, like a staple here and on each corner, that was the least amount of staples you could use to keep the fabric on the piece. Just on the ends wouldn't do it, you know what I'm saying? Just one in the middle, it would be flapping on the ends.

Then you go back and you put a staple every quarter inch and finish it nice.

I got obsessed with that. I remember: it was a pink couch and it had three staples in it, holding it down temporarily, and I just stared at it for a while, and it became an obsession for the rest of my life.

Whenever I'm creating something, I like to center it around that number, because it is definitely another way of boxing myself in.

THE NAME. Meg had been playing her drums so childishly, and that's what we were sort of feeding off of, the simplicity of that, trying to make it even more simple. 'How simple can we make this and have it still be a song?' 'How little can we do and it's still upholstered?' It's the same mentality. And we were at a drugstore or something and there was a bag of peppermints in the candy aisle. She likes peppermints. I said, 'We should paint that on your bass drum; we should paint a peppermint candy, because you play like a little kid. That would be funny.'

I did paint it on her drum kit, and I said, 'We should name our band after the white stripes of the peppermint candy, because our name is White. Let's be the White Stripes of peppermint candy,' because that also means prisoners' stripes, and being constricted in that way too.

So that's where the name came from.

THE GOLD DOLLAR
WAS THE BEST, THE TOUGHEST, THE NICEST, THE COOLEST...

It was the perfect moment in time for that club to have opened. I thank God that that club was opened. It was just perfect.

It became a positive motivation for a couple of years there, like three years or so, '98 to 2001 or something. It was like our little golden period. And I was going there like four times a week. It only held 120 people or something, but everybody knew each other and it was a golden moment.

I think the last show we played there was for our third album, 'White Blood Cells.' We played it in its entirety at the Gold Dollar. We didn't know anybody at that show, and it was sort of the end. It was the last night. We knew it was over because we didn't know anybody.

Everything has to change. You can't keep Studio 54 or CBGBs going in the same way it is when it has those magic moments, like in the '70s or something like that.

It was great that it lasted that long. That place was perfect. I can't imagine what would have happened had it not existed. There were other great clubs too, like the Magic Stick, which is still there, and a couple other places. But mostly it was the Gold Dollar. ★

JUAN ATKINS

TECHNO IS SHORT FOR TECHNOLOGY.
AND BASICALLY, WHAT TECHNO MEANS AND REPRESENTS IS THE TECHNOLOGICAL REVOLUTION AS IT APPLIES TO MUSIC.

So that was sort of a natural term to place upon music that was being born from technology.

I think techno started here, in Detroit, because of the post-industrial climate in the city. We felt, firsthand, the end of the Industrial Revolution, and a transition into the technological revolution. I don't think there's any other city in America, probably in the world for that matter, that had that same experience. And it was already a city with a rich history for music and innovation, from Motown on up.

I TAKE THE BELLEVILLE THREE to mean me, Derrick May, and Kevin Saunderson. We went to the same high school, which was Belleville High School. So that's where that term started.

I ACTUALLY STARTED THE MOVEMENT. I coined that term, 'techno.' Derrick and Kevin played a role, but they didn't start making records until maybe four or five years after my first records. When they started making music, it started to become popular in Europe. So Derrick and Kevin had a big role in it becoming popular in Europe.

I STARTED PLAYING from around the time I bought my first synthesizer, which was around 1979, my last year in high school. My grandmother bought me a synthesizer. And because I lived in Belleville, there weren't many musicians around who I could play with. So I would have to make up my own tracks using this one synthesizer. I made drum sounds and different sounds with the synthesizer. I came up with whole tracks made up of electronics.

I was in a class in high school called 'Future Studies,' and the reference book that we used was called *Future Shock*, by Alvin Toffler. In that book it talked a lot about the technological revolution and how technology will affect our lives in the near future. Then he wrote another book that came out around '80, '81, called *The Third Wave*, which was about the technological revolution. So a lot of the terms come from his prophecy about technology.

MY FIRST SONG? Well, my first year in community college I met Rick Davis. He was in one of my classes, and he was doing totally electronic recordings as well. He was a lot more advanced; he had sound machines, rhythm computers and things that I hadn't had too much experience with.

So we met up. He heard my demos and thought that we would make a good partnership. We got together and formed a group called Cybotron and released our first record, 'Alleys Of Your Mind,' in '81.

There was a DJ on the radio, Charles Johnson, AKA the Electrifying Mojo. He was on 107.5, WGPR in Detroit. He was on from 10 p.m. to 3 a.m., every night. He didn't have a format. He was very, very popular, probably because of the music mix. He played pop records, rock records, he played James Brown and Jimi Hendrix back-to-back. He played Funkadelic, Prince, Peter Frampton, America, all of that stuff. He used to play 'Horse With No Name.'

It was just a very crazy music mix he had. And he played our record, 'Alleys of Your Mind,' on his show, and it became an instant hit in Detroit. That's how the whole career began.

MODEL 500 was basically a name I used because I wanted to use a number instead of a name, sort of as a repudiation of ethnic designations.

People like to think it was some kind of car, that there must have been some kind of auto reference. But it doesn't have any. Maybe, subconsciously, I may have had that in mind. But no, it doesn't have any direct reference to a car.

THE WAREHOUSE THING didn't really come until the late '80s, when the rave scene happened and people started using the Russell Industrial Center and places like that. That was just an abandoned warehouse that had really good parties.

THE DETROIT ELECTRONIC MUSIC FESTIVAL

IS AMAZING. IT'S A GREAT FEELING, EVERY YEAR, TO BE A PART OF THAT.

You see people come from all over the world, to Detroit, to celebrate our music. It's definitely a good thing to see.

NO. I PLAY A COMBINATION. I use vinyl for my practice setup. I use vinyl controllers so I can switch over and play vinyl as well. I play a combination of digital and vinyl. For me, a lot of the good, classic stuff that I bought years ago, I would rather play the vinyl. Vinyl's more original. There's more of a groovy, warm sound to it. And a lot of the classic stuff you just can't find digitally. So if you still want to play that stuff, you have to be able to play vinyl.

Then, some records, the way that they're put on vinyl, even the newer stuff, has its own character. It's almost like a bottle of wine. Sometimes you just want to see the bottle. Sometimes you don't want to see just the glass, you want to see the bottle, you know what I'm saying?

YES, I STILL RUN Metroplex Records.

When you're doing the type of music I was doing, the style was very innovative, a very new sound, so nobody knew how to really market it or how to present it.

Record company people don't really understand, sometimes, that it's just about what's in the groove. They get way into this almost infinite degree of marketing and hype and promotion, and sometimes they lose sight that the product is the music. But it still boils down to what's in the groove. For me, anyway. ★

EMINEM

NO. ABSOLUTELY NOT. I HOPED. But I certainly never dreamed that it ever would or ever could get to this level.

I ACTUALLY STARTED jotting down and writing things when I was like 12 or 13. I started, almost, mimicking other rappers, just trying to figure out what I wanted to sound like. As years went on I got more serious with it, to the point where I felt like I might be actually good enough to do this.

It's one of the things that I'm definitely the most passionate about. Sometimes it felt like, 'I don't have anything else, so I guess I might as well do this.' Not to say that in a nonchalant way. I really didn't have anything else, or know anything else.

THIS WAS ALL I KNEW, AND THIS WAS THE ONE THING IN MY LIFE I WAS SO PASSIONATE ABOUT.
I JUST LOVED HIP-HOP.

THE MOMENT I REALIZED I had made it? I think there were a couple. They were more like 'holy shit' moments—like, 'Holy shit, my face is on MTV!' I remember seeing the 'My Name Is' video; I was at my manager Paul's apartment. We were waiting for it to come on, because MTV had said they were going to play it, that they liked it or whatever. Just to see myself on something that big was a 'holy shit' moment. And there was another 'holy shit' moment when I did my first sellout show at Tramps. I remember feeling like, 'This is literally, actually happening.'

It still fucks with me to this day, the craziness of it. I don't know if it's something you ever get used to.

THE HIP-HOP SHOP was on 7 Mile and Greenfield. It was a spot Maurice Malone owned; they sold clothes there. I want to say it was a boutique shop. I don't know if that's the right term. So don't quote me on that. And don't judge me either. And don't yell at me either.

It was Maurice Malone's shop. It sold clothes, it sold records, cassettes, CDs. It had a spot for a DJ; DJ Head used to spin records. Sometimes it would be DJ Dez, I want to say HouseShoes; I think he was there, too. There was just a really cool vibe; you'd walk in and beats would be playing, sometimes there would be battles. Every Saturday there would be a thing where they'd kind of pass around the mic, and anybody who wanted to rap would get on the mic.

This was at a point in my life where I had definitely thought about quitting, because nothing really seemed to work. It just seemed like, 'I don't know if this is going to happen.'

At one point Proof called me. We hadn't spoken in like six months because he was out doing his thing and I had a job and was just working. He called me one day and said, 'I've been out making moves; I've been doing shit. You should come down to this spot. I host open mic now at Maurice Malone's, the Hip-Hop Shop.' And I was like, 'Oh, shit; OK.' Proof was like, 'Yo, just come down and rap, we've got an open mic here.'

It would be open mic maybe an hour, two hours, something like that. And Proof told me to come down there when it was getting ready to end so that there wouldn't be that many people there, and if I didn't like it I didn't have to come back. But, you know, to at least give it a chance.

So I went down there and I kind of got a reaction from the few people that were there. There might have been 10 people. But from that point on it was like, 'Holy shit; maybe this could be something.'

I started coming down every Saturday, pretty religiously, and then it started to be, 'Oh shit, they're doing a battle!' Like every five or six months they'd have a battle and you'd put your name in a hat if you wanted to be in it. They'd put the names in a hat and they'd pick two out to see who would battle each other. And it was just a process of elimination.

So the first battle that they had, I won it. Then they had another one and I won that, too. And that was what started giving me the confidence, the self-esteem, to be able to take it elsewhere. I ended up going to Cincinnati, Scribble Jam, things like that.

That was really long. I'm sorry.

ABSOLUTELY, I HAD A LOT OF FUN in Detroit. The most fun thing for me, I think, especially back then, was just the excitement of going to St. Andrews, or going to Alvin's on a Wednesday. Tuesday was Ebony Showcase, Wednesday was Alvin's, Friday would be St. Andrew's Hall, Saturday was the Hip-Hop Shop. There was C-Note, just anywhere there was music, anywhere there was rap, anywhere there was hip-hop, whether it was open mic, people battling, people got together just to network and exchange numbers. 'I make beats.' 'All right, call me.'

You know what I'm saying? Like that, to me, was the most fun shit ever. It was exciting. It was an exciting time. That was pretty much the thing for so many years of my life, religiously.

ABSOLUTELY I MISS IT.

I STILL GO OUT. I go to Wal-Mart and shit like that, hang out.

No, I've been. But, obviously there's a limit to things I can do. It just depends on how much I feel like dealing with certain things, when I do go out. But I do go places, now and again.

MY FIRST CAR? I believe it was a '79 Lincoln.

Yes, it was a beast, and it was a gift from somebody. I won't say who. When I got in it and went to start it, it didn't start. I can't remember exactly what was wrong with it. I'm sure it was a whole slew of things. It just didn't work. But I eventually got it running. It was a boat.

I can't even remember. I want to say 18, maybe. I'm trying to think how I even got my license. I think I just got in the car and drove.

ALL RIGHT. The bonus round.

RAPPERS, BACK THEN, they would do a lot of things with their initials. I think they still do. It was one of those things where it was so obvious. But I always used to not spell it out; it would be just 'M&M,' like the candy.

So I don't remember exactly at what point... I think around the time when I did the 'Infinite' album was when I decided to try to do something a little different with it. I had always been 'M&M'... 'But let me try spelling it out this time...' Then it kind of just stuck with me. That was pretty much it.

I DON'T KNOW IF YOU KNOW the old story of me being on the shitter.

Oh, OK. I told this story many years ago. As graphic as it sounds, some of your best material comes from that, being on the shitter, as you know, I'm sure.

So the name Slim Shady literally just popped in my head. I had been toying with a bunch of names, because Proof had us in his group, D12, the Dirty Dozen. In the beginning it was called the Dirty Dozen and we all had to have aliases. I was thinking Dirty Dozen cowboy shit, like 'Should I call myself Billy The Kid?'

Everybody had different names and all these things. And one day it just hit me. That name just popped in my head and I started thinking about the things that could rhyme with it and thought, 'You know what? I might go with this.' I think probably what I was doing was toying with initials—'M&M,' 'S&S'. Like, 'What could I make out of these letters?' Then, one day, it was just like, 'Hmm, I'm kind of slim... I'm kind of shady...'

I don't know. That's the best story I can come up with right now.

THIS IS THE DOUBLE-BONUS whammy round, isn't it?

I LOVE DETROIT.
IT'S THE CITY THAT I LOVE. IT'S THE CITY THAT I'M USED TO.

You know what I'm saying? I'm very much a creature of habit. I moved around a lot as a kid. I think that once I got somewhere where it was, I don't know how you say it, comfortable enough, once I got comfortable, I was never leaving.

I got used to it. I got used to the people here, just everything about the city. People can say what they want about it, but I love it. ★

BARRY SANDERS

MY FONDEST MEMORY? From being drafted, being a 21-year-old kid, not knowing where I was going to go in the draft, to having a great first year and being Rookie of the Year and being one game away from the Super Bowl in '91, to, later, rushing for 2,000 yards, and having my teammates really pulling for me to be successful and eclipse that 2,000-yard barrier, especially the guys who played on my offensive line, to starting a family here, all of those things are special and unique.

It felt great being drafted. There were a lot of emotions that I experienced. Probably the biggest one was fear, and being overwhelmed at being drafted into the NFL. I didn't know much about the Lions. At that point, we didn't have free agency, so most of the good players tended to stay with the same team. I didn't know if that would happen in my case or not. But it was a bizarre experience, because I was a childhood sports fanatic. So to be drafted into the NFL, for me, was a great feeling.

STAYING IN DETROIT? It just kind of happened that way. I didn't necessarily have any plans. There are so many variables that affect where you end up, and if you're able to stay in a certain place. So I think I realized that you can't expect anything. I didn't know how that part would play out.

DETROIT IS A GREAT FAN HAVEN,
DEFINITELY OF FOOTBALL FANS. THERE ARE A LOT OF MAJOR SPORTS HERE, AND THE FANS EMBRACE ALL OF THE SPORTS.

And there are tons of Lions football fans, loyal fans that have really had to be patient with the team. They're some of the most loyal fans you'll ever find.

I THINK SOMETIMES PLAYERS take on the personality of a city. And if it's a blue-collar area, then the fans may tend to embrace those type of athletes. It goes hand in hand. There's certainly a lot to learn about the people who are here, who make up this area, how they live their life and how they conduct themselves. I think it works both ways, in a lot of cases.

I think what appeals to athletes, as far as Detroit, is that the fans are passionate. You have some great franchises in all of your sports, owners who love the game, and it's a great place for sports because people are really into it. You have amazing teams here. So I think that has a lot to do with it.

WELL, MY FAMILY has kept me in Detroit. Other than that, it's a great place. It's home. I love the four seasons. I still enjoy all of the sports. I enjoy a lot of the activities in the area. It's a great place to raise a family. So I've stayed around for a lot of reasons. It's comfortable, and it certainly has grown on me over time.

MY FIRST CAR was a 1972 Mercury Capri. I bought it from my uncle for $200 in '87 or '88. It was a stick shift and it was mostly blue, but it had some other color to it. That was one of my proudest days, when I took possession of my own car.

I'm not sure who the first person I gave a ride to was. I have a lot of brothers and sisters. But when I think about it, I don't remember having many people in that car. It was my prized possession, so you had to be really special. It was probably my mom. It didn't last very long, unfortunately. It had a lot of miles on it when I bought it. I think it may have lasted a year or two. I was in college in Oklahoma. But it definitely served its purpose. ★

NICKLAS LIDSTRÖM

I STARTED WHEN I WAS 7 YEARS OLD, just playing street hockey and then pond hockey, and then eventually real hockey, ice hockey. From the moment I first stepped on the ice, I fell in love with it. When you have your friends there, your buddies—we all loved it.

In my neighborhood we had a community ice. There were no boards; it was just a sheet of ice. You could grab your skates after school and head over there.

ACTUALLY, I DIDN'T KNOW if I was going to be drafted and have a chance to play in the NHL. And I didn't know anything about the Red Wings at all. I knew Gordie Howe played there for a long time; I knew about Steve Yzerman being a leader and captain. Besides that, I didn't know a whole lot about the organization. But I'm very happy that I was selected by the Wings, and I've been fortunate enough to play with the same team for a long time

When I first came over here in the spring of '91 to sign a contract, I'd never been to the U.S. before. So I didn't know what to expect. The first thing I noticed was just the big city, the distance anywhere you wanted to go. It took you half an hour to drive out to the suburbs. I thought it was a nice downtown, with all of the tall buildings, how the arena was right downtown. I thought it was a neat little city.

I've been fortunate not to be traded or to have to go play for another team. I was never sitting around waiting for July, for the first day of free agency, to get a chance to go play somewhere else. I always signed a contract before that day because I wanted to stay with the organization.

MR. AND MRS. ILITCH have been committed owners. They want to win, they want the best product on the ice. And for that reason alone, I didn't want to go play elsewhere.

It's the place that I consider home now, and that's another reason why I didn't want to go and play somewhere else. I fell in love with the area. The people are friendly here, and we have a chance to win every year.

THE OCTOPUS? I didn't know about that tradition. I didn't know what it meant or why people were doing it. But some people explained it to me and I got to know it. I think it's great, to get the fans fired up, especially here at home. The fans get really into it and it gives the team a boost.

I think they smuggle them in. If you throw one on the ice you're supposed to get kicked out. I don't know if that happens at home, but I've heard it happens on the road when fans do it.

IT'S FLATTERING, and it makes you proud, that the fans want to wear your jersey with your name on it. It's a great feeling.

I TRY TO BE IN THE RIGHT POSITION. To be in the right position you have to read the play and sense where the puck is going to go, or how the play is going to develop. I've learned that over the years. Reading the play helps me a lot, especially as I get older. With the new rules that we've had in effect since 2005-2006, it's harder to play defense than it was in the past. You have to be able to move really well, you have to be mobile and you have to be able to read the play.

READING THE PLAY
IS ONE OF THE REASONS I'VE BEEN INJURY-FREE. MY STYLE OF PLAY, TOO: I'M NOT AN OVERLY PHYSICAL DEFENSEMAN; I'M NOT TRYING TO RUN PEOPLE OVER.

I try to be in the right spot and read plays instead. I take care of myself in the offseason. I work out hard and I stay in shape, so I'm able to play a long year with 82 games, plus playoffs. Staying healthy is a combination of those things.

WE'RE SUCCESSFUL due to all of the above—the coaching, the players, the dynamics. I think we have, from the top, committed ownership and great management. Ken Holland and his scouting

staff are able to find players in the later rounds of the draft. You have players that want to come here, they want to play for the Red Wings, and that helps us find new talent. We have a great winning tradition here that attracts a lot of people.

I've been very close friends with Tomas Holmström since he came to the team back in '96. He's from Sweden as well, and we hang out a lot together on the road. We go down to the Joe together on practice days and game days. Steve Yzerman is a player I admired before I came here. I knew a lot about him as a player but not as a person. I admired him a lot for what he did for the team and for the state all the years he played here.

THE STANLEY CUP WAS THE HIGHEST ACHIEVEMENT,
WINNING THE CUP AND SEEING WHAT IT MEANT TO THE CITY WHEN WE FIRST WON IT IN '97. THAT WAS THE FIRST TIME IN 40 YEARS.

Seeing the fans come out, more than a million people at the parade. But the Cups are all special in their own ways.

They're like your children. They're all a little bit different, but you love them all. I mentioned that the first one was very special. Being able to repeat in '98—Konstantinov had his limo accident in '97 and it felt like the team played for him to win another Cup. 2002 was special because I won the Conn Smythe and Norris Trophies that season. And '08 was special because I was the captain. So they all mean something to me in different ways.

I HAVEN'T MISSED MANY GAMES throughout my career. That's one of the things I'm most proud of. Winning the Norris Trophies, too. I'm very proud of being the first European to win that award.

BEING NAMED CAPTAIN? I was very excited, very honored. And I saw it as a challenge, especially following Stevie's footsteps and seeing what he's done for the team for so many years. I looked at it as something honorable and challenging.

You have to really love the game, because you have to play for a lot of years and still have the motivation to go through your offseason workouts and all of the practice. And you want to win again. Those go hand in hand. You want to finish on top; you want to win another Stanley Cup.

YES, THE DETROIT CROWDS are hard. But I think they've been a little bit spoiled over the years. And we expect to win, too.

WHEN I'M NOT ON THE ICE? I love going to other sporting events. I love watching the Tigers. I'm a big football fan, so I try to go to some of the Lions games. I love concerts. I've seen Kid Rock play a bunch of times; I'm a big fan. My kids get a little spoiled by getting good seats and getting a chance to get close. Those are some of the things we like to do.

My wife cooks. She's a great cook, but we also have Ikea in town. They have a good restaurant. They've got good Swedish meatballs over there; its one of the things I can recommend. And lingonberries. They're good, too. It's the real deal.

MY FIRST CAR here in town was a Pontiac. My first car in Sweden was actually a Swedish car, a Saab.

Used. Very much used. It was an old one. ★

WILLIE HORTON

I GREW UP IN THE JEFFERIES PROJECTS. That's about 15 minutes from Comerica Park, where I work today. We played baseball, football, basketball, boxed. You tried everything. You had a lot of activity going on when you were a kid back then.

I was raised up near Tiger Stadium. Rocky Colavito was my hero as a ballplayer, as a kid. Because me and my buddy used to slip in the ballpark, and we got caught one day. Rocky said, 'Let us have those kids.' He was with Cleveland; I thought he was a policeman. But he got us part-time jobs down there. Later on, he came to play with the Tigers. And when I signed with the Tigers, he kind of passed left field down to me. He's always been there for me.

REALLY, I NEVER HAD A DREAM of being a baseball player. I was very fortunate. I had people in my life as a young man like Judge Damon Keith. He was a lawyer then. My mom got him to be my legal advisor, to show me the way. Him and my little league coach, Mr. Ron Thompson. I just had the right people around me who knew I could become a Major League player. Myself, I wanted to be a fireman. I used to run behind fire trucks when I was a kid. Something about fire trucks just fascinated me.

My dad never pushed me; nobody pushed me. They just let me go out and play.

MY BIG SECRET AS A HITTER? I was fortunate to have people around me to help bring out my God-given ability. And that was also my way when I started coaching after I retired. Each individual is different.

I talk to the guys, I tell the coach, 'We've got to bring out his ability, let him grow, so he can create a good foundation and have good decision-making skills.' That's the secret. I was just very fortunate to have Ron Thompson, and the coaches I had in professional baseball, help me continue to grow my foundation. Some of that is missing nowadays.

It's part of getting back to when you played as a kid in high school. Yes, somebody's got to win—but just go out there and have fun.

YOU'VE GOT TO GET BACK TO PLAYING BASEBALL WITH YOUR DAD IN THE BACKYARD. YOU'VE GOT TO KEEP THAT LITTLE BOY IN YOU. AND HAVE FUN.

Once you lose that little boy and you say, 'I have to do these things,' it cuts off your learning. Keep that little boy going.

ONE OF MY FONDEST baseball memories is, when I first came up with the Tigers, I hit a pinch-hit home run off Robin Roberts, who was a great, Hall of Fame pitcher. I hit it up there where my dad used to sit with me in the bleachers. He was sitting up there that day, and he and a guy got into it, because the guy didn't believe I was his son.

So after the game, we kept waiting on Dad. I didn't know they had a little cell down there to keep people in. They used to keep people until everyone left, then they let them go home. I was so happy; I'd hit a home run that helped win the game. We're waiting, all the lights are cutting off, and I asked Mom, 'When's Papa coming? Everybody's gone.' Later, here he comes. Back then, you didn't dare ask your dad where he'd been. He said, 'Let's go,' and that's all he said. But I found out a day or two after, through the ground crew, what happened.

I'll never forget that. That's the hardest thing I ever had with the Tigers organization—getting my dad centerfield bleachers tickets. He would never sit down with the family by the dugout.

He saw me play up to the time he and mother were killed in a car accident, on New Year's, '65. But he saw me play, and he got to sit up in the centerfield bleachers.

ALL-TIME FAVORITE? Frank Robinson. I played against him. But there are so many—Willie Mays, Mickey Mantle, Roberto Clemente. Pound for pound, I would say Roberto Clemente is the best. But Frank Robinson was my favorite.

NO, I DIDN'T HAVE the same batting helmet my whole career. I had two. Charlie Dressen gave me one in spring training, in '63, '64. Then I gave my agent one of them. I've still got the other one.

YES, THAT'S TRUE. I always took care of my equipment. That's something I always did. I never threw my helmet, never got mad. People would strike out and throw their helmet, swing their bat. I never did that. I kind of kept it off to the side and protected it. Doing that, I learned to respect players, and I learned to respect pitchers. It's not the bat and helmet that made me strike out.

I THINK WE'RE STILL CELEBRATING the '68 Series. It's something I'm part of and it's part of my life. There are a lot of great ball players, Hall of Famers, who haven't been in a World Series or have a World Series ring.

THE HIGHLIGHT OF MY CAREER?
THROWING LOU BROCK OUT.
THAT WAS THE FIFTH GAME OF THE SERIES AND THE TURNING POINT, WHEN WE CAME BACK AND WON. THAT HAS TO BE THE HIGHLIGHT.

THE OUTREACH STARTED IN '67. I was very blessed. I was involved in, I guess you could say, helping to heal the city. HBO had a special out, 'A City on Fire,' and I'm part of that.

WHEN THE RIOTS STARTED, they came in and told us to go home for security purposes, but I ended up leaving the ballpark in my uniform, going out onto 12th Street, and trying to talk to people while I was standing on top of my car. From that day on, I got involved in the community and became a person who tried to bridge the gap for relationships in the community.

I can shut my eyes and see myself right now standing on top of the car. And one thing that's amazing is that the people I was trying to talk to were very concerned about Willie Horton not getting hurt. They said, 'Go home, Willie.' I'll never forget the words they said that evening, as I was trying to talk to them.

I DO LIKE MY STATUE. I get nervous every time I go out there with people now, because I'm alive to see that. Most people who have statues made of them are deceased. When they were making it, I kept thinking about when I was in school—how you read in the history books about presidents, their statues. I don't even have the words to express my feelings about it. It's about the people. I think that statue represents what Willie Horton is about. My whole career was through the fans. That's a promise I made to my dad when I first signed. He said, 'Don't sign that contract unless you make a commitment that your life belongs to the fans and to your job.'

MY WIFE'S NAME IS GLORIA. We have seven children. Nineteen grandkids and eight great-grandkids. So we're very busy, spend a lot of time with the grandkids.

I'm very fortunate to be with the Tigers. It gives me the opportunity to be at spring training, and we've got grandkids and great-grandkids in Lakeland, Florida.

MY FIRST CAR? Well, me and my buddies, we made a car when we were kids. You could see the ground when you'd drive. We were in high school.

The first car that I had owned, though, when I first signed, the Tigers gave me a brand-new Bonneville. I was a kid. I didn't keep it that long. I had a little accident with it, and my dad got it fixed. I thought he was going to let me drive it, but he got it fixed and sold it. He said, 'You'll get another car. You'll have your own name on it. You'll be 21.'

They used to give you cars, years ago. And, later, I was going to buy the car that the Ford Motor Company gave Al Kaline. I'd always had it on my mind, though, what my dad said: 'You've got to be 21 before you own a car.' I was in the big leagues, and I was still scared to take the car home. But I finally took the car home.

That was one of the best times of my life. ★

AL KALINE

I THINK EVERY PLAYER would want to spend their whole career in one city. Sometimes they don't have control over that, and sometimes they do. Of course, after a player gets established, the most important thing for him is to be on a winning team and get a chance to play in the playoffs and in the World Series. But I think everybody would love to spend their whole career in one city, because their families put roots down and it's much easier. It helps if a player stays in one town. The fans get to know him.

Fans are resilient, though. They pull for their team. Players leave and then new players come in and they gravitate to them. They respect them and they continue to be fans. No matter who comes and goes, they stay loyal fans.

I STARTED PLAYING BASEBALL at an older age than most kids because I was born right in the middle of Baltimore, and I didn't start playing until I was about 12, 13 years old. We had to play softball, because if we played baseball in the middle of the streets we'd break windows. So we had to play softball in the streets. I remember being on a team when I was 13 years old and a local drugstore gave all of us a T-shirt. That was one of our proudest moments. We finally had some kind of a uniform to put on. And we wore jeans and shorts or whatever, but we all had the same jersey, the same T-shirt. That was my first recollection of being on a baseball team.

I think where I learned how to play baseball at a very competitive level was when I was 15, 16 years old, playing against former professional players who had been signed and then came back home, being released. I really got great experience playing with older people, and learned a lot from them.

THE FIRST TIME I put on a Major League uniform, being 18 years old and all of a sudden playing in a Major League ballpark, it was awesome, just sitting on a bench and watching the game. And the first time I had a chance to come into Tiger Stadium and play in front of the home fans, that was a big thing. It was called Briggs Stadium instead of Tiger Stadium, way back.

The first time I went into Briggs Stadium was about 2, 3 in the morning, coming off a trip. We'd travel by train in those days. We got off the train at the station, got our luggage, got in a bus, and we came down Michigan Avenue. I was sitting next to my great friend Johnny Pesky. And he says, 'Al, look out the window here. That's going to be your home for the next couple years.' That was Briggs Stadium. It was night, and I couldn't see a lot of it, but it looked like an old battleship. I couldn't wait to get up the next day and walk to the ballpark and see exactly where my home was going to be for the next couple of years.

I WAS VERY, VERY EXCITED TO PLAY IN THE '68 SERIES. I WAS A LITTLE BIT NERVOUS. BUT I WAS ALSO CONFIDENT THAT I WAS GOING TO BE ABLE TO CONCENTRATE AND PLAY TO THE BEST OF MY ABILITY.

Sometimes you do good, and sometimes you do bad. Fortunately, I was on a pretty good streak and things went well for me.

I WAS NEVER AFRAID TO FAIL. I just wanted an opportunity. I always wanted to challenge myself against the very best. I looked forward to playing in big games and playing against the best competition. You fail many, many more times than you succeed, but all you want is the opportunity. And I was able to be successful a few times.

I was a senior member of the ball club, as far as years with the team, and to get a chance to play in the World Series, with all my friends and teammates, and then finally become world champions—well, it's what every ball player dreams about when he's growing up. It was a tremendous year. And for that final out to be caught by the great Bill Freehan, Mickey Lolich pitching an unbelievable game, I'll never forget that.

HOW DID WE CELEBRATE? Well, we had a few cocktails. Quite honestly, the next couple of days I was completely mentally exhausted. I just wanted to rest and get back to normal. But people in the neighborhood and friends wouldn't let you do that. It was great. It was great to be able to bring a world championship back to Detroit.

THERE WERE SO MANY GREAT THINGS. To get a chance to play in the World Series certainly is the highlight.

Winning the batting title was a tremendous honor. The team wasn't very good that year and we didn't do very well. But as far as an individual thing, it was great to become a batting champion in the Major Leagues, and also to become the youngest player ever to win a batting title. It was huge. But the World Series is a bigger highlight for me.

I ONLY HAVE ONE GOLD GLOVE in my house. My family and my sons and my grandkids have the other ones. I don't display a lot of things in my house, but I do have the one Gold Glove.

YOU HAVE TO REALIZE, ERNIE HARWELL was a great friend of mine, and we had known each other for many years. And yes, he made the comment that I was the best player to wear a Tiger uniform. But I think what he really meant to say was that I was the best player he saw play. You can't forget about Ty Cobb, Charlie Gehringer, Harry Heilmann, way before me. I think he might have meant I was the best player he saw play.

I remember he and his wife, Lulu, and my wife, Louise, and I taking a cruise together, and we had a chance to spend dinner every night together. And to be able to sit one-on-one and just listen to his great stories about what he had done growing up, in the military, his broadcasting career, it was fantastic to sit and listen to all the stories he had. He was a great storyteller.

I THINK
WHAT I LOVE ABOUT DETROIT
MORE THAN ANYTHING ELSE IS THE FANS.

They're very loyal. All they ask for is somebody to do the best they can, whether they're successful or they fail. But they can recognize when somebody is really giving 100 percent. And I think we all appreciated the fact that we were lucky enough to be professional baseball players, and we were going to try to do the best we could for them. I think that's what stands out to me more than anything else, are the fans here in Detroit. ★

JAMES TONEY

I HAD A VERY INTERESTING CHOICE. I was a quarterback and defensive back, and I could have gone to the University of Michigan as a defensive back, or Western Michigan as a quarterback. But in high school, you know how it is, peer pressure and all that, I wasn't concentrating on my grades. I didn't pass the SATs. So I went back to boxing; that was my backup sport.

I MET JACKIE KALLEN when she had a fight with Bobby Hitz, and we were training at the same gym in Livonia. One day, she saw me down there, sparring, beating up everybody like I always do. The next thing you know, she started asking about me. And the rest is history.

There were a lot of misconceptions with Jackie and I. First, they thought we were lovers. And then, after we split up, they thought I was trying to kill her. There were so many things about me and Jackie being said, nobody ever knew the truth coming from me or from her. Everything was just assumptions. But all in all, I think we had a great career together.

It was great working with her. Her family is great. I wish her the best.

THE HARDEST SPARRING SESSION I ever had at the Kronk was against Gerald McClellan. God bless him, he's paralyzed now. He was tough. I think if you're not a fighter from Detroit, it's hard to understand what we go through, and why I'm so great, why Tommy Hearns is so great, Hilmer Kenty, Milton McCrory, Joe Louis, Ray Robinson.

THE BEST FIGHTERS AND THE
GREATEST FIGHTERS IN THE WORLD, PERIOD,
ARE BORN AND RAISED IN THE CITY OF DETROIT.

THAT'S TRUE. When I was living in Redford, somebody threatened to burn a cross in my yard. Yeah, it was the next-door neighbor. He didn't tell me that, but he told one of my sparring partners. He was a racist. Redford's like an all-white town, and we, the fighters, were the only black people in like a five-mile radius. It kind of got crazy, but after a while, they calmed him down, and he ended up becoming a friend to one of the other fighters.

MAN, FIGHTERS TODAY lack everything. They lack character, they lack heart, they lack dedication. They want it now. They don't want to work hard for it. And I'm an old-school fighter. I was taught how to fight old-school by Bill Miller. He's one of the greatest trainers of all time. And I learned from him, I watched tapes of old fighters like Ezzard Charles, J.J. Walcott, Joe Louis, Rocky Marciano, and learned from that.

MY FAVORITE BOXING memory from Detroit is Aug. 2, 1980, Joe Louis Arena, when Tommy Hearns won his first world title, when he knocked out Pipino Cuevas in the second round. That had to be the greatest. I was proud, because Tommy did it, the city of Detroit was put back on the map after years of being like we are now, dormant. It was a great, beautiful feeling. It was like I did it.

FONDEST MEMORY OF DETROIT? No. 1, when the Pistons won the title for the first time in a long time. And definitely, the birth of my girl. She was born in Royal Oak.

OH, MY GOODNESS! You had to bring that up? Good thing my wife's upstairs. She'd laugh at this one. My first car was a Granada. Do you know what that is? You're too young. It was a 1977 Ford Granada. I was 16. I took my mom for a drive. We went around the block. It was a rust-bucket, too. It was powder blue, with rusty holes on each side of the fenders.

A QUOTE? How about, 'Motor City, can't get enough of it.'

OH, MY NAME. Well, one day, right before my pro debut, my manager, Greg Owens—God bless him, he's my man right there, I love him—we were driving down the highway, coming from the gym before my first pro fight. He said, 'We need a nickname for you.' I said, 'How about Too Sweet?' He laughed. I laughed too; it was kind of foolish. I said, 'How about Ice T?' He said, 'All right, Ice T.' But I guess one day he was listening to a rock 'n' roll song by somebody that said, 'Boom, out go the lights,' and he said, 'Lights Out!' I said, 'Lights Out? Are you kidding me?' 'Yeah, Lights Out.' I fought it for a while, but the next thing you know, it stuck. And when I went and I started fighting, everywhere I went, everybody said, 'What's up, Lights Out?' 'How you doing, Lights Out?' It just stuck.

I'VE GOT MORE TO PROVE. I've won the heavyweight title three times; now I want to win the unified heavyweight title. Now I want to win all the belts and be the oldest unified heavyweight champion ever. I believe in myself. I know I can do it. ★

JACKIE KALLEN

I WAS A NEWSPAPER WRITER, a journalist. I was working for *The Oakland Press*. I started out doing entertainment. I covered the Academy Awards, the Grammys, the Emmys, and I traveled quite a bit, going to press junkets for movies.

I'd already met pretty much all of the people, like Sinatra, Elvis, who I wanted to meet. So I segued over to sports in the mid-'70s, and there were very few females doing sports writing. One of the first assignments I got was to cover a Tommy Hearns fight. He was a young four-round fighter. I was fascinated by him, by the sport, by Emanuel Steward, the whole world that I had put a toe in.

I started writing more and more about boxing, and then I evolved into a publicist for the boxing industry, then a manager, then a promoter, and I kind of jumped all the way in. I went to work for Emanuel as a publicist, and I worked for him for many, many years, and there developed two of the strongest friendships I have, with Emanuel Steward and Thomas Hearns.

WORKING WITH TOMMY HEARNS was amazing, because I got to work with him from when he was a 19-year-old four-round fighter all the way up through six world championships. So I really got to experience the whole boxing world: starting out as an amateur, turning pro, working your way up the ranks, fighting for a championship, winning the title, defending it and then getting more belts and more belts and more belts!

I STARTED MANAGING FIGHTERS IN 1988. That was 10 years after I first began going to the gym all the time and watching how Emanuel maneuvered his fighters up the ladder towards title shots. I thought if I found a young fighter who Emanuel wasn't managing, who didn't have a manager, maybe I could kind of learn and develop together with him. I was very lucky because I found some really good ones. James Toney, of course, was my star pupil. He became my first world champion.

The first time I saw James I was at a gym with another fighter who I was working with. James was just an angry guy. He'd gotten mad at something that someone said, or he didn't like the way he sparred that day, and he was kicking the spit bucket and punching the lockers. I was very taken by his spirit; he was really passionate about everything. He was a wild man and I thought, 'Wow, if we can take that energy, that fire in him, and direct it properly, he could be a world champion.' Fortunately he needed a manager at that same time, so our paths crossed and the rest is history.

JAMES WON HIS FIRST TITLE in Davenport, Iowa, in 1991. So I paid my dues. I put in a lot of years before I reached that point. When James won his title, it was in the other guy's backyard. He fought the champion, Michael Nunn. Nunn was very well respected. Both fighters were undefeated. Somebody had to lose. We fought him in his hometown, which is a very big disadvantage. But James knocked him out. It was a wonderful night, a historical night. He had a woman manager, which was very unusual, and he beat the champ in his own house, so to speak. It put us both on the map.

Watching James win his first belt was almost as good as having my first child.

IT WAS LIKE GIVING BIRTH, IN A SENSE, BECAUSE I KNEW I HAD GIVEN BIRTH TO ONE OF THE ALL-TIME-GREAT BOXERS.

That's been the greatest moment of my boxing career so far, James Toney beating Michael Nunn, May 10, 1991.

BEING A WOMAN? To be honest with you, I never once thought of it as a negative or a liability. I always thought of it as an asset because I felt like I could get into the heads of people a little bit better than the guys could. Women have that nurturing, maternal instinct, and I think that I was able to take the feminine side of my personality and mesh it with the male strengths I was born with. I think it made me almost an androgynous person. I don't think people looked at me as a woman, they just looked at me as someone who knew boxing, who's good at what I do.

'FIRST LADY OF BOXING'?
THAT WAS GIVEN TO ME BY ONE OF THE MAGAZINES BACK IN THE EARLY '80S.

They did an article and they called it 'The First Lady of Boxing,' and it stuck. Nobody has come along to challenge that, so here I am, 34 years later, still the First Lady of Boxing, and there's nobody closing in on that who I can see.

WELL, HAVING MEG RYAN play me in the movie, 'Against the Ropes,' was interesting. It wouldn't have been my first choice but, obviously, she's one of the top names in the world of motion pictures, so it was an honor to have her portray me. But I'm not sure anybody can ever portray you better than you. Not that I wanted to. I'm not an actress. I would just say it was an honor.

I'M OPENING A GYM in the old Masonic Temple, the Galaxy Boxing Gym. I had a gym here for years in the '90s, then I moved to California. I came back to recapture the glory that we had with James Toney, Bronco McKart, some of the wonderful kids who came through the door. I want to build a really solid amateur program of young kids who have dreams of being a fighter. I want to give them a place to train and learn. And I want to have some volunteer teachers there, so after the fighters get through training they can do their homework. Some of them don't have degrees; we can get them their GEDs. I'm starting a program for executive boxers—doctors, lawyers, businessmen who want to get in shape. I'm going to do a fantasy camp where they come in for 10 weeks and work out with real fighters and then, at the end of the 10 weeks, they'll be able to fight. We'll do a charity event with these guys fighting each other. I'm starting a program for women as well. Not just to box, but for the workout. I hope it's a well-rounded gym with a lot of different age groups, different ethnic groups, different interest groups.

I JUST LOVED GROWING UP in the '60s, period. I think I would have loved it in any city. I love the music, the sports. The world in general was so happy in the early '60s. Then, of course, there was Vietnam, and things changed. But the late '50s, early '60s, growing up in Detroit were the glory days. It was such a wonderful city and so vibrant, and the downtown was so alive. Then, parts of Detroit were like living out in the country.

Everybody kept their doors open and we all knew each other and everybody hung out on the streets together and sang on the street corners. It was really a wonderful time. Detroit had a lot of heart. That was the best era. Not just because it's my era, because I've lived through all the generations since then, but we didn't know anything about drugs. Nobody we knew did drugs, smoked pot, got in trouble. The worst anyone did was maybe have a kegger, drink some beer and go to one of the parks and hang out. It was 'Happy Days,' just like the show. It really was 'Happy Days.'

MY FAVORITE THING TO DO? That's easy, because in Detroit, during my era, we had Bob-Lo. You took a boat over to the island. There was an amusement park there, and that was always the most fun thing you could do, was go to Bob-Lo in the summer. And we'd go to Belle Isle. They had horseback riding, they had canoeing, and they had the Belle Isle Casino, where music groups came.

It was a beautiful, beautiful city. It was a very happy time. The country was prewar and postwar, because we were between World War II, the Korean War and Vietnam. So it was that peaceful Baby Boom era. Lots of young kids and happy times. ★

EMANUEL STEWARD

I CAME TO DETROIT on a Saturday night. My mother put me and my two sisters on a train with her on a Friday night; it was a 24-hour trip. It rained the entire trip, and I was crying all night. I was the oldest. I was 11. And my sisters, Diane was 5 and Laverne was 3. So I was the oldest one and the only boy.

I didn't want to leave West Virginia. I didn't understand what was going on. I didn't understand that my parents were going through a divorce.

We moved to the East Side. I lived in an area close to McClellan and Mack, and I went to Pingree Elementary School. It must have been in the fall, late September or October, when we came.

My experiences were for the most part good, but I got in a fight. On Sunday, I was on the porch before everyone had gotten up in the house, and a little boy came along and we started talking, and he laughed at me because I had a West Virginia hillbilly accent, and I called 'going across the street' 'going across the road.' So we got into a little fight right there, in the bushes in front, and my aunt came out and told my mother that in three or four months we were going to have to move.

It was a very nice neighborhood, though. It wasn't like the stories; it wasn't the ghetto. But I was in trouble a lot. So my mother gave me an ultimatum. Right away, I had to start going to the supermarkets, taking peoples' groceries home and trying to hustle, because my mother was working at a restaurant, and we were living on her tips and whatever I could rustle up doing odd jobs.

So by the time I was 12, I was selling hot tamales and sausages with a cart in Detroit at night. I would walk five miles, selling hot tamales along the way. We would start at Vernor and Chene. By the time it was 1 a.m., I would be at this one particular bar. The people would come out, so I would sell all of the Polish sausage and hot tamales that were left, then make the trip back home. And that's what really started me out learning how to hustle in the streets of Detroit.

When I was 14, I got in trouble for street fighting again. And this time they were going to put me away. My mother told them that I used to box when I was in West Virginia, though, and I was not a bad boy. So as a result, they cut a deal, that if I would go to a recreation center, and not get in any trouble for a year, they would not put me away. I did that. I had to go to a place called Brewster, which was one of the most famous recreation centers in the world. Brewster was a place where all of the blacks in Detroit came to. All the blacks, for the most part, lived on the lower East Side back then.

LATER, THE HAPPIEST TIME IN MY LIFE WAS
WHEN I WON THE NATIONAL GOLDEN GLOVES.

I came home and the mayor had me down; I was taking pictures and signing autographs. And just 48 months before, they were about to put me away; I was a disgrace to the city.

To be down there and to be honored, that was the biggest thing in my life, even with the Hall of Fame, the awards, my HBO broadcasts—nothing ever will exceed being honored here at home when I was 18. That was the biggest thing ever.

RECENTLY, I've been spending a lot more time in Detroit because of my job with HBO and the fighters I'm managing. I'm working with Wladimir Klitschko and Andy Lee.

I'm rebuilding the amateur program and working with the pros here. This is the first time in many years I'm spending more time in Detroit. Before, I was working with big superstar fighters and I had to spend 10 to 12 weeks in Germany, or I would have to go to Australia, like with Jeff Fenech. I would be gone two or three months, then back to Norway with another fighter I had, Ole Klemetsen. I was traveling so much and seldom even knew what was going on here with the gym. And as a result, it died.

Fortunately for me, my nephew, Javan Hill, one day he says, 'Emanuel, since you're traveling so much, maybe I can go down and start training some of the boxers.' This was about '93. And as a result, the amateur program developed all over again. He's been the catalyst for that.

Now we have more trainers coming in, kids coming in from all over. The gym has really changed. In the '70s and '80s, outside of about five white kids, all the fighters were black. Now, the Bonas brothers, Jacob and Joseph, are Romanians. We have Andy Lee, who's from Ireland. We have Erick DeLeon, who's Mexican. And there are a lot of Arabic kids training here. So the Kronk Gym has a different, totally international flavor compared to what it was originally. It's really amazing.

It's so much different from the little neighborhood gym it used to be. I would go out in the parking lot, like in '74 or '75, and there would be no cars except mine. Thomas Hearns and his brother, John, they would catch two buses to come from the East Side. Mickey Goodwin came from Mevindale. Milton and Steven McCrory and Jimmy Paul and Duane Thomas were coming from the far, far northeast. We had the bus schedules on the wall so everybody knew what time to run out the door to go catch their bus.

Then, around '85, I'd look out in the parking lot, and we had about three guys who were world champions, and we had Rolls-Royces, Cadillacs, all kinds. And sometimes, when Tommy would come to the gym, he might have a limousine.

It's amazing that all of this came from just a bunch of guys who came to a gym.

KRONK WAS MORE THAN JUST A BOXING GYM.
IT WAS A WAY OF LIFE.

And that's the relationship the kids have kept throughout the years, too. They all get together, they all come by the house a lot, and we laugh and joke. We're all still very close.

TOMMY HEARNS was not at the very top in the beginning, but he was the most disciplined and dedicated. Tommy would get on the bus and come every day, never complained about who he boxed or nothing. And all of a sudden, by the time he was 16, he'd started to blossom. He was not one of the most naturally talented, but he was the most disciplined and dedicated.

In 1984 we had six gold medal winners training in our program with us, which was unbelievable. Mark Breland, Tyrell Biggs, Frank Tate, Steve McCrory, Pernell Whitaker, and Jerry Page all won gold medals in the '84 Olympics.

I became much in demand with big-name fighters. Julio César Chávez, after his first loss, asked me to help him get his title back. De La Hoya asked if I would help get him back on track. Lennox Lewis was knocked out, so they asked if I would help him to get back on track. Then Evander Holyfield came.

I became much in demand. And at one time, in the '90s, I was thought of as the hired gun to be brought in when there were problems with major fighters. They all came to me. And fortunately, I have never lost one of those fights.

MY SECRET? I teach basic boxing. Everybody else is getting into so much advanced stuff. All I teach is balance and a good, solid jab, and how to think in the ring. I teach balance and footwork, and that's really all I do.

When I work with any of the top fighters in the world, the first thing I do is, I start training them as if they're beginning kids. They laugh. But it makes everything work easier. ★

THOMAS HEARNS

THE GREATEST KNOCKOUT of my career was against Pipino Cuevas. It changed my life. Winning my first world title was just outstanding. It was a change that I was expecting, but I never knew when it was going to come. All of a sudden, like a snap of a finger, everything changed. Everything got brighter. The future was more comfortable. I'd already accomplished a goal, so I was looking forward to bigger and better things. I was 18.

I didn't do any wheeling and dealing to make the fight, but my trainer Emanuel Steward did. Not just to get the fight, but to bring it to Detroit. That was the problem. There had to be some extra money in the pot.

I performed better in Detroit. It made me eager to go out there and get the job done even quicker.

We said, 'OK, we'll do it at this much money, but only if you come to Detroit.' He felt like he was the better fighter because he had such a great record and his knockout record was even better than mine.

So he came to Detroit, where all the fans were acting crazy whenever I fought. But he didn't know that until he got here. When we were introduced that night a lot of fans were for him, but for me the crowd was even crazier. Hearing the audience, he was shocked. I said, 'Man, where'd all these people come from?' I mean, we had about 13,000 or 15,000 people in the arena. And I was like, 'All these people came just to see me. I've got to put on a great show. If I don't, they'll be disappointed.'

I went out there and I put on a show like they'd never seen before. And they were very, very thrilled and happy about it. And that made me even happier. I was so happy because I won the fight, but I was even more thrilled because of the people. I gave the people what they wanted to see. They went home and were talking about it for weeks, for months. Any place I'd go, people were talking about the Pipino Cuevas fight. It went on for years, people talking about that fight.

MY POWER? I guess it's half my mother. My mother is a very sure woman. I think I got my power from my mother. But learning how to develop that power is something I was taught to do by my trainer, Emanuel Steward.

I met Emanuel about 1972, 1973. I met him at the Kronk Gym. My other gym had closed so I went to the Kronk. And I found out that it was where I wanted to be. That's why I stayed. I was about 13 then.

What made Emanuel and I such an effective team is that we spent a lot of time with each other. Each and every day we were together, three to five hours a day, learning how to deal with each other. Sometimes Emanuel would say something to me I didn't like, and sometimes I'd say something to Emanuel that he didn't like. We had to accept that. We weren't saying it to hurt each other, we were just saying it because that was a way of getting our anxiety out.

THE ROBERTO DURAN FIGHT was one of my greatest victories because I beat a legend. He was there for a long time. He was destroying people.

WHEN I WAS ABLE TO
DEFEAT ROBERTO DURAN, MAN—I WAS GOING PLACES.
I WAS MOVING. THINGS IN MY LIFE STARTED TO CHANGE, AND I HAD A BIGGER PIECE OF THE PIE.

I felt, deep inside, that it was a part of God's will that things were happening for me. I beat Pipino Cuevas, then I came out and beat Roberto Duran. I couldn't believe what was happening, but it was happening, right before my eyes.

I APPRECIATE THAT, but I know that I'm not the greatest. Men have come before me like Muhammad Ali, Joe Louis, 'Sugar' Ray Robinson. Those are the guys I look at and say were some of the greatest fighters. Rocky Marciano.

That was before me. But now, in my time, I left something behind that people can look at. Younger people can make comparisons. Muhammad Ali was a boxer, a straight-out boxer. Thomas Hearns is a boxer-puncher. That's the difference. I can box when I have to; I can punch when I want to.

I don't voice my opinion about opponents like Ali did. I'm not good at that. I'm more of a quiet person. But don't say too much. If you do, I'm going to go in there and get the job done fire-quick.

I used to love watching 'Friday Night Fights' on TV, 'Wide World of Sports,' watching Ali. He fought everybody. He didn't duck no one. Ali took them all on. I said, 'I want to be like that guy—but I don't think I'm going to have the mouth he has.' I do not have a gift for gab like Ali did, but I learned how to box like him. That was my goal. 'Float like a butterfly, sting like a bee.' 'Rumble, kid, rumble.' I tried to rumble. I tried to float a little bit, too. I know I stung a lot of people. Floating and all that stuff, I don't think I did too much of that. But I stung a lot of people.

WHEN HE DIED, MY GRANDFATHER was 110 years old, and he had a huge hand. He used to knock out animals. My grandfather knocked out a horse. I was down south, my grandpa was in front of the horse, and the horse bit at my grandfather. My grandfather—swack, thump! I couldn't believe it. I was about 5 or 6 years old. And the horse fell, and I said, 'Grandpa, you knocked a horse out!' He said, 'That's OK, son. He's going to be all right. Don't worry about it.' And the horse got up and shook it off. He looked at my grandpa, my grandpa looked at him, and the horse just got up and walked around.

I'VE GOT A WBO super middleweight title, a WBA welterweight title, the WBC middleweight title, the WBA light heavyweight title. I have others, too.

I have about 12 different belts at my house, and all of them are very important to me. 'I fought for this title, and it took a lot from me.' It took a lot of hard work for me to attain a title, and I'm very fond of all of them. I fought for them; I got them now.

RIGHT NOW, I'M HAVING TOO MUCH FUN. I'm having fun against opponents and showing them that, even today, at 52 years old, you can't touch me. And a lot of these guys, they get upset because I say that, but it's true. I've been around too long. I learned too much. I have too much ability. Every guy wants to be able to say, 'I boxed Tommy; I did good.' I'm not going to give you an opportunity to say that. I'm not going to have that.

MY FIRST CAR? A 1963 or 1964 Rambler station wagon, that was made by... who made it? American Motors. I loved that car. It was a three-speed. I was gone. I was a speed demon in that car. That was fun. It was old. It wasn't new at all.

THE FIRST PEOPLE I took for a ride? Probably my friends on my block. I was young, having just got my license. Not too many people would ride with a guy like that: a young man who just got his license and was going out and trying to have a good time. I enjoyed it.

I'M VERY MUCH looking forward to getting out there and doing a commercial for a major company. I'd like to do a major ad for some designer clothes, because clothes are one of my passions—knowing how to put things together and look good in them. Clothes don't just highlight me, I highlight the clothes as well.

Shoes are a very important piece of your wardrobe. If you don't have the right shoes, if they don't look the part, it'll mess your whole outfit up.

I like to look good from head to toe. ★

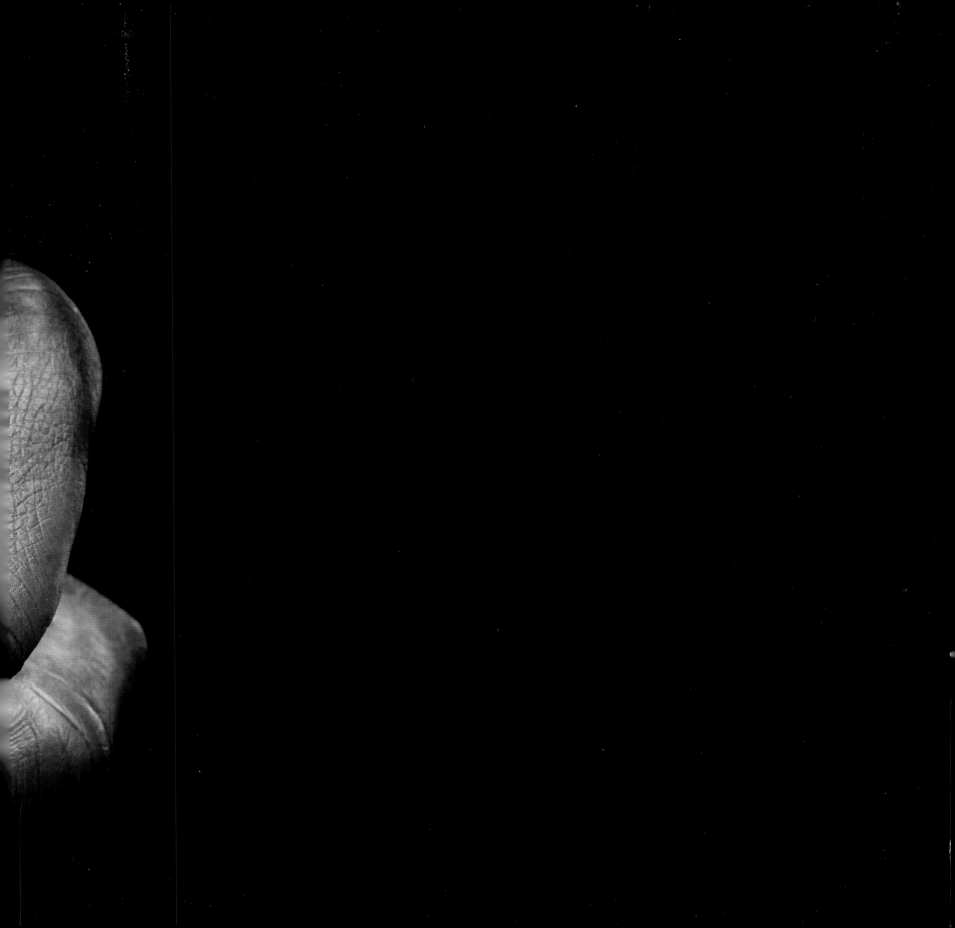

DETROIT IS ONE OF THE

TOUGHEST

CITIES IN AMERICA.

WE ARE ONE OF THE MOST

INSPIRING

CITIES IN AMERICA.

WE ARE A CITY OF
COLD REALITIES AND GLITTERING DREAMS.

AFTERWORD

OUR DREAMERS, LIKE HENRY FORD AND BERRY GORDY, created things, inspired by our city, that changed the way the world lives. Detroit is a town that's defined by industry, creativity and invention. We are the Motor City. Cars set the common man free to travel distances that from the dawn of humanity most people could never have imagined they would ever cross. *Heart Soul Detroit* is filled with Detroiters who followed in Ford's footsteps to transform our lives for the better.

Detroit will forever be Motown. The music born in that era helped close the cultural gap caused by racism and helped to heal the wounds of the Civil Rights movement. The sound of our city is driven by the twin turbines of deep-rooted soul music and the blue-collar rock 'n' roll that gave us another nickname, 'Detroit Rock City.' We're the home of Mary Wilson, Mitch Ryder, Martha Reeves, and Eminem. We rock on down the road, and the world rolls with us—we're the birthplace of techno, thanks to Juan Atkins, as well as the birthplace of the White Stripes.

Detroit is my city. I was made there. I was born and raised there. It taught me the value of hard work and a hard-earned dollar. As a kid I witnessed the twilight of our town as a workingman's paradise. Anybody from anywhere could find as much work as they wanted. My father and his peers went from sharecroppers to homeowners, and saw their children through college, within a generation. Hard times have worn some of our streets ragged and made our spirit to survive and thrive.

Despite our struggles, though, the elegant spirit of Detroit still shines through. The architecture of downtown and historical neighborhoods like Indian Village showcase the best work of architects such as Daniel Burnham, Albert Kahn, and Louis Kamper. Our public art rivals that of the world's major cities. Murals painted by the great Diego Rivera cover the walls of the Detroit Institute of Arts. Famed sculptor Isamu Noguchi's fountain pumps the lifeblood of the Detroit River through his fountain in Hart Plaza. Only steps away, in the shadow of the Cobo Center, Robert Graham's statue of Joe Louis' mighty fist stands as a monument to the fight that's in the heart of every Detroiter.

Growing up, I loved to study the workings inside factories like the Better Made Potato Chips and Vernors ginger ale plants. These were the precursors to today's Apple stores, the icons of our current retail landscape, where structural transparency is the most highly prized luxury. My city instilled in me the sense that people could build anything—that they could transform an idea into a business that could employ people, and help them on to a better life.

Detroiters have pride in all we do and who we are. In our darkest hours we are all always proud to be Detroiters. Detroit is a phoenix; it's in our city lore and motto. It's a new day again in Detroit. We make the perfect backdrop for movies; we're so varied that all of America can be found within our city limits. Artists have gathered to turn chaos into inspiration with endeavors like the Heidelberg Project. Where buildings have fallen to rubble the neighbors have dug in and raised crops. In this book you can meet the people who make our town amazing. We are a city of survivors—resourceful people who know the value of a hard-earned dollar and the invaluable asset of investing in an impossible dream.

— VERONICA WEBB

BIOGRAPHIES

MITCH ALBOM

To say Mitch Albom has a golden touch would be a massive understatement. Joining *The Detroit Free Press* as a sports columnist in 1985, he began writing a non-sports column in 1989. He would go on to be named the best sports writer in the country by the Associated Press Sports Editors a record 13 times, that organization's best feature writer seven times and the recipient of its Red Smith Award for Lifetime Achievement in sports writing in 2010. While Albom began publishing books with collections of his columns in the '80s, it was in 1997 that he released his breakthrough work, *Tuesdays With Morrie*, which spent four years on *The New York Times* best-seller list, has sold more than 14 million copies and is the best-selling memoir of all time. Albom followed up with *The Five People You Meet in Heaven*, *For One More Day*, and *Have a Little Faith*, all hugely successful and, like *Morrie*, adapted into films. He is also a playwright, radio host, and songwriter. These days, he devotes much of his energy to the seven philanthropic organizations he has founded, including, most recently, the Have Faith Haiti Mission, an orphanage that his A Hole in the Roof Foundation began operating following that country's devastating earthquake in 2010.

TIM ALLEN

Launching his career at Mark Ridley's Comedy Castle in 1979 on a dare, Tim Allen would go on to become one of Hollywood's most successful comedians and actors. He struck gold in 1991 when, already enjoying a burgeoning stand-up career, he collaborated with Disney to develop his stand-up act into a sitcom, 'Home Improvement.' With Allen starring as hapless husband, father, and home-repair show host Tim Taylor, 'Home Improvement' was an immediate hit. By the 1993-1994 season it was the No. 1 TV show in the country; it would remain one of the most watched shows on TV until its final episode on May 25, 1999. Allen has enjoyed similar success in films, starring in the hugely popular 'The Santa Clause' and 'Toy Story' series. In November 1994, 'The Santa Clause' was the No. 1 movie in the country, 'Home Improvement' was the No. 1 TV show, and *Don't Stand Too Close to a Naked Man*, which Allen penned, was the No. 1 book. He currently stars on and executive-produces the NBC show 'Last Man Standing.'

JUAN ATKINS

Widely regarded as the father of techno music, Juan Atkins first gained widespread recognition with fellow electronic music pioneer Rick Davis under the banner of Cybotron. The duo's break occurred in 1981 when Detroit DJ Charles Johnson, AKA the Electrifying Mojo, put their 100 percent electronic dance single 'Alleys of Your Mind' on heavy rotation. After releasing several other records with Cybotron, including the highly influential single 'Clear,' Atkins embarked on a solo career in 1985. Recording and performing under the names Model 500, Infiniti, Channel One (with musician Doug Craig) and his given name, often for his own label, Metroplex, he would go on to create the tracks that many credit with laying the foundation for techno, including 'No UFOs,' 'Night Drive,' 'Technicolor,' and 'It's Channel One.'

SELMA BLAIR

Before finding Hollywood fame, actress Selma Blair spent her school days at Cranbrook juggling her passions for writing, photography, and theater. After graduating magna cum laude with a degree in photography from the University of Michigan, the Southfield native finally decided to hone in on acting and made the jump to L.A. Equally comfortable in dramatic and comedic roles, she won rave reviews and popular acclaim as naïve high school student Cecile Caldwell in 1999's 'Cruel Intentions,' a reimagining of 'Dangerous Liaisons.' Blair would secure her place in Hollywood's pantheon of leading ladies with films such as 'Legally Blonde,' 'The Sweetest Thing,' and Guillermo del Toro's 'Hellboy' series, as well as dozens of independent features. Most recently she was cast as the female lead opposite Charlie Sheen in the FX show 'Anger Management.'

BILL BONDS

Bill Bonds was the anchor for the nightly news at WXYZ for more than 25 years. During that time he won more Emmys than any other anchor in the country. Initially rising to prominence with his coverage of the 1967 Detroit riots, Bonds soon propelled Channel 7 to No. 1 in Detroit. During the course of his career he also launched several successful interview programs, including 'Up Front' and 'Bonds On.' He has interviewed such luminaries as President John F. Kennedy, Robert F. Kennedy, Malcolm X, Martin Luther King, George Wallace, Medgar Evers, President Gerald Ford, and President Ronald Reagan. In 1991 he anchored the first nationally televised town hall meeting for Democratic Party presidential candidates, including a young Bill Clinton. He was inducted into the Michigan Journalism Hall of Fame in 2010, the only news anchor to be so honored.

JERRY BRUCKHEIMER

Jerry Bruckheimer is among the most successful film producers of all time. After first rising to prominence in the world of advertising, Bruckheimer transitioned to films, where he initially hit it big with 1980's 'American Gigolo' and 1983's 'Flashdance.' A seemingly unending stream of hits followed, including 'Beverly Hills Cop,' 'Top Gun,' 'Armageddon,' 'Bad Boys,' 'Con Air,' 'Black Hawk Down,' and 'National Treasure.' In 2003 Bruckheimer released the first chapter of what would come to be his signature work, the enormously successful 'The Pirates of the Caribbean' franchise. The second, third, and fourth 'Pirates' films are all among the top 10 highest-grossing movies in Hollywood history. As a television producer Bruckheimer has worked similar magic, notably with the 'CSI' franchise. Like Eddie Murphy's character Axel Foley in 'Beverly Hills Cop,' he is a graduate of Mumford High.

GEORGE CLINTON

The funkiest man in the universe, George Clinton has wowed audiences, critics, and fellow musicians alike with his inimitably creative sounds for more than five decades. A pioneer who's both the originator and master of his genre, Clinton is one of the most sampled artists ever, and hailed as an influence by musicians across the spectrum of music, from rock 'n' roll to hip-hop. A onetime Motown songwriter, Clinton continues to get audiences around the globe moving with his ever-expanding, rotating, and evolving funk collective. While he's best known for classics like 'Atomic Dog' and 'Flash Light,' he's had more than 40 hit singles on the R&B charts, including three No. 1 songs. Along with 16 members of Parliament-Funkadelic he was inducted into the Rock and Roll Hall of Fame in 1997.

CONGRESSMAN JOHN CONYERS JR.

United States Congressman John Conyers Jr. is the second-most-senior member in the House of Representatives.

First elected in 1965, he is a founding member of the Congressional Black Caucus. Conyers, a longtime champion of Civil Rights, was the driving force behind the Martin Luther King Holiday Act of 1983—for which he fought 15 years to have passed. Other legislation he has been instrumental in passing includes: the Violence Against Women Act of 1994, the Motor Voter Bill of 1993, the Alcohol Warning Label Act of 1988, the Jazz Preservation Act of 1987, and the Help America Vote Act of 2002. Conyers employed Civil Rights icon Rosa Parks as his office manager from 1965 until her retirement in 1988. He was elected to his 24th term in 2010.

ALICE COOPER

The father of shock-rock, Alice Cooper has sold more than 50 million records. Born Vincent Damon Furnier at Saratoga Hospital in Detroit in 1948, his hits with the band Alice Cooper, which he formed in 1964, include such rock classics as 'Eighteen,' 'Under My Wheels,' 'School's Out,' 'Be My Lover,' 'Elected,' 'No More Mr. Nice Guy,' and 'Billion Dollar Babies.' Since embarking on an eponymous solo career in 1975 he's topped charts with 'Only Women Bleed,' 'I Never Cry,' 'You and Me,' and 'Poison.' He was inducted, with his original band, into the Rock and Roll Hall of Fame in 2011.

EMINEM

One of the most successful artists of all time, Eminem has sold more than 90 million albums. Born Marshall Bruce Mathers III, he first rocketed to national attention with 1999's 'The Slim Shady LP,' which, largely on the strength of the single 'My Name Is,' was certified quadruple platinum, and won the Grammy for Best Rap Album. He followed up with 2000's 'The Marshall Mathers LP,' which sold 1.76 million copies in its first week, making it the fastest-selling solo album in U.S. history. 'The Marshall Mathers LP' went on to sell more than 20 million copies—as did 2002's 'The Eminem Show.' Success continued with 2004's 'Encore' before Eminem took a sabbatical from music from 2005 to 2008. He returned in 2009 with 'Relapse' and, in 2010, 'Recovery,' which was his sixth consecutive No. 1 album in the United States, the best-selling digital album in history, and the best-selling album in the world for 2010. Eminem has also had success with Detroit super-group D12, with which he had two No. 1 records, and Bad Meets Evil, a project with Detroit rapper Royce da 5'9", with whom he had one No. 1 record. He is the best-selling artist of the 2000s.

MEL FARR

It's difficult to say what Mel Farr is best known for in Detroit. He first gained fame as a stellar running back with the Detroit Lions, winning Rookie of the Year honors in 1967 and being named to the Pro Bowl in 1967 and 1970. Retiring from football in 1973, he committed himself to entrepreneurship and opened up his first Ford dealership, at 10 Mile and Greenfield in Oak Park, in 1975. Farr was even better at selling cars than he was at football: By 1998 The Mel

Farr Automotive Group was the most successful African-American-owned business in the country. But to every Detroiter who had a TV set in the '80s, Farr is probably best remembered for his unforgettable commercials in which he, billed as 'The Superstar Dealer,' could be seen flying through outer space in a red cape, 'fighting high prices to bring you a Farr better deal!' It was largely due to his marketing savvy, coupled with his ability to offer credit to many previously overlooked buyers, that he achieved success. Through a twist of fate, he can also be heard singing backup on pal Marvin Gaye's 1971 classic 'What's Going On,' widely considered one of the greatest songs ever recorded.

BILL FORD JR.

Bill Ford Jr. is the executive chairman of the Ford Motor Company. The great-grandson of Henry Ford, he joined the company in 1979 as a product-planning analyst. He has since held positions at Ford in manufacturing, sales, marketing, product development, and finance. He served as the company's chief executive officer from 2001 to 2006, taking it from a $5.5 billion loss in 2001 to three consecutive years of profitability. A committed environmentalist, he established Ford's first wildlife habitat, led the world's largest brownfield reclamation project at the Ford Rouge Center, and championed the Ford Escape Hybrid, the world's first hybrid-electric SUV. He is the vice chairman of the Detroit Lions and led efforts to build Ford Field.

SUTTON FOSTER

A triple threat of talent in singing, dancing, and acting if there ever was one, Sutton Foster spent her adolescence performing in productions at Troy High School, in local dance troupes, and at theaters around metro Detroit. Fate struck when, at 17, she was cast in director Tommy Tune's national tour of 'The Will Rogers Follies.' But Foster's true breakthrough role came in 2002 when she, as a relative unknown, won the lead role in the Broadway show 'Thoroughly Modern Millie.' Wowing audiences, she received a Tony for Best Lead Actress in a Musical, among other awards. Foster would go on to be recognized as one of Broadway's brightest lights, earning praise for her roles in productions of 'Little Women,' 'The Drowsy Chaperone,' 'Young Frankenstein,' 'Shrek the Musical,' and, notably, 'Anything Goes,' for which she won another Tony Award for Outstanding Actress in a Musical in 2011. She will soon be seen on the ABC Family series 'Bunheads.'

BERRY GORDY

As the founder of Motown Records, Berry Gordy is responsible for developing some of the world's most beloved musical acts. Originally operating out of a small record studio at 2648 W. Grand Blvd., Motown was home to such legendary groups as The Supremes, The Temptations, The Four Tops, Smokey Robinson and the Miracles, Stevie Wonder, Gladys Knight & the Pips, The Jackson 5, and Martha Reeves and

the Vandellas. From 1961 to 1971 the label produced 110 hit singles, many of which are now regarded as highlights of American music, including 'The Tracks of My Tears' and 'The Tears of a Clown' by Smokey Robinson and the Miracles; 'Where Did Our Love Go?' and 'Stop! In the Name of Love' by The Supremes; 'My Girl' and 'The Way You Do the Things You Do' by The Temptations; 'I Heard it Through the Grapevine,' 'What's Going On?,' and 'Let's Get It On' by Marvin Gaye; and 'Dancing in the Street' and '(Love is Like a) Heatwave' by Martha Reeves and the Vandellas. Through it all, Gordy was the driving force, playing a central role in all aspects of the label, from conceptualizing groups to songwriting to production to promotion. By 1966, 75 percent of Motown's releases were making the national charts, and the label was well on its way to becoming the most successful African-American-owned business in the country. He was inducted into the Rock and Roll Hall of Fame in 1988.

TYREE GUYTON

Artist Tyree Guyton is responsible for the conceptualization, creation, and maintenance of one of Detroit's most unique attractions, the Heidelberg Project. A native of Heidelberg Street, Guyton worked as a firefighter and an autoworker before eventually following his passion for art and enrolling at the College for Creative Studies. In 1986, with his grandfather Sam Mackey and then-wife Karen, he began work on the Heidelberg Project—an outdoor art initiative that saw Guyton, in response to the blight of the neighborhood largely brought on by the riots, lavishly decorating nearby abandoned houses, often with brightly colored polka dots. Throughout its more than 25 years of existence the Heidelberg Project has met with sporadic resistance from the city, and was partially demolished twice, once by Mayor Coleman Young and again by Mayor Dennis Archer. Both times Guyton pressed on and, increasingly, was recognized both within and outside of the city for his work. He has received awards from the State of Michigan, the Detroit City Council, Governor John Engler, and Wayne State University, among others. He was the subject of the 1999 HBO documentary 'Come Unto Me: The Faces of Tyree Guyton.' In 2009 he was awarded an honorary Doctorate of Fine Arts from the College for Creative Studies.

CHRIS HANSEN

'Dateline NBC' correspondent Chris Hansen was initially inspired to become a journalist by the Jimmy Hoffa kidnapping, which occurred near his house in Bloomfield Hills, at age 14. After beginning his career at WILX in Lansing, Hansen soon returned to Detroit, where he worked as a reporter for both WXYZ and, from 1988 to '93, WDIV. During his time in the city he covered such stories as the raid on the infamous Chambers brothers' crack cocaine ring and a 1991 FBI sting on a group of Detroit police officers alleged to have been involved in a drug-smuggling ring. Hansen joined NBC in 1993 and, in 2004, launched his now-famous investigative series 'To Catch a Predator.' In 2010 he hosted the 'Dateline' special report 'Detroit: City of Heartbreak and Hope.' Hansen has received seven Emmys for his investigative reporting.

THOMAS HEARNS

One of the greatest boxers ever to lace up the gloves, Tommy Hearns began his pro career in 1977 under his longtime amateur trainer Emanuel Steward. Fighting out of the Kronk Gym, 'The Hitman' knocked out his first 17 opponents. In 1980, boxing at the Joe Louis Arena, Hearns won his first championship by knocking out Pipino Cuevas in the second round, ending the fight with a crushing right hand—a punch that would soon be recognized as one of the most lethal weapons in the annals of boxing. In 1981 he brought his undefeated record of 32-0 into a super-match with 'Sugar' Ray Leonard. Winning the fight on the cards, Hearns was knocked out by a resurgent Leonard in the 14th round. For the match the fighters made a combined $17 million, the largest purse in sports history at the time. In 1982 Hearns moved up to light middleweight, where he won yet another belt by beating Wilfred Benetiz, before, in 1984, challenging another all-time great, Roberto Duran, whom he knocked out in two rounds. In 1985 Hearns once again rose in weight, this time to middleweight, to challenge 'Marvelous' Marvin Hagler. In what is generally considered the greatest three rounds in boxing history, the two fighters exchanged bombs for more than eight minutes before Hearns finally succumbed to Hagler's onslaught in the third. In 1991 Hearns became the first boxer ever to win titles in four weight classes. He continued to fight successfully into the mid-2000s, and his record stands at 61-5-1, with 48 KOs.

JAMES P. HOFFA

James P. Hoffa is the general president of the International Brotherhood of Teamsters. Elected in 1998, Hoffa was subsequently reelected to five-year terms in 2001, 2006 and 2011. Under his leadership the Teamsters have diversified their membership, maintained a union of 1.4 million workers, and kept their pension programs operating. Hoffa is known for his outspoken criticism of government trade policies and 'anti-worker corporate agendas.' The son of legendary Teamsters President James R. Hoffa, he is a graduate of Cooley High School, Michigan State University, and The University of Michigan Law School.

HOLLAND-DOZIER-HOLLAND

Holland-Dozier-Holland is the writing team behind many of Motown's most beloved songs. Composers Lamont Dozier and Brian Holland and lyricist Eddie Holland began working with Motown and Berry Gordy in the early '60s. From 1962 to 1968 they wrote more than 50 of the songs Motown would come to be most identified with, including '(Love is Like a) Heat Wave' for Martha Reeves and the Vandellas; 'How Sweet it is (to be Loved by You)' for Marvin Gaye and

'Baby I Need Your Loving,' 'I Can't Help Myself (Sugar Pie, Honey Bunch),' and 'It's the Same Old Song' for The Four Tops. Staring in 1964 they wrote six consecutive No. 1 hits for The Supremes, including 'Where Did Our Love Go,' 'Baby Love,' 'Come See About Me,' and 'Stop! In the Name of Love.' Holland-Dozier-Holland was inducted into the Songwriters Hall of Fame in 1988 and the Rock and Roll Hall of Fame in 1990.

WILLIE HORTON

One of only six Tigers to have his number retired and to be honored with a statue at Comerica Park, Willie Horton is one of the top sluggers ever to wear the Old English 'D.' A star player at Detroit's Northwestern High School, Horton signed with the team in 1961. Over his next 15 seasons as a Tiger, 'Willie the Wonder' was named an All-Star four times and hit 262 home runs. He had the biggest play of his career in game five of the 1968 World Series, not with a hit, however, but a pivotal throw, to catcher Bill Freehan, who tagged St. Louis Cardinal Lou Brock out at home plate. The Tigers came back to win the game and the Series. Horton's appeal in Detroit went far beyond the field. During the 1967 riots he famously took to 12th Street in his uniform and, standing on top of his car, attempted to facilitate peace. Today he works with the Tigers as a special advisor.

LEE IACOCCA

Lee Iacocca is one of the most iconic CEOs of his era. Beginning his career as an engineer at Ford in 1946, he soon found his true calling in sales and marketing. Quickly moving up the ranks, Iacocca was responsible for the development of several key Ford models, including the Lincoln Continental Mark II, the Escort, and the revival of the Mercury brand. But in 1964 he unveiled the car he would forever be identified with—the Ford Mustang. Ford sold 417,000 Mustangs in its first year, demolishing sales goals. Following that success, in 1970 he was named president of Ford, a position he held until 1978. Joining Chrysler as president in 1979, Iacocca did what many thought impossible, transforming the struggling company into a powerhouse. By 1984, under his leadership, it was posting record annual profits of $2.4 billion. It was also at Chrysler where he acquired the Jeep brand and introduced the minivan, which led U.S. automotive sales for 25 years. In 1982 he was handpicked by President Ronald Reagan to lead the restoration of the Statute of Liberty and Ellis Island, the largest restoration project of its kind in American history. In 1986 he published his autobiography, *Iacocca*, which sold almost 7 million copies. Profits from the book went to his Iacocca Family Foundation, dedicated to diabetes research in memory of his late wife, Mary Iacocca.

AL KALINE

Known as 'Mr. Tiger,' Al Kaline spent his entire 22-year career as a right fielder for the Detroit Tigers. In the eyes of many he is the greatest Tiger of them all: Kaline is a 15-time

All-Star, 10-time Gold Glove winner and, in 1955 at age 20, became the youngest player in the American League ever to win the batting title. Still, he is often remembered for one hit—a single that drove two runs in and propelled the Tigers to victory in pivotal game five of the 1968 World Series. In 1980 Kaline was the first Tiger to have his number retired and, the same year, was inducted into the National Baseball Hall of Fame—only the 10th player to be admitted in his first year of eligibility. Today he is a special assistant on the Tigers. He has been with the team for more than 60 years.

JACKIE KALLEN

Starting her career as an entertainment journalist, Jackie Kallen was drawn into boxing following a fateful 1977 interview with a rising young star, Tommy Hearns. Kallen, a Mumford grad, spent the next 10 years learning the ropes of the business as a publicist for Hearns and the Kronk Gym—including working Hearns' two mega-fights with 'Sugar' Ray Leonard. In 1988 she struck out on her own as one of the few female mangers in the sport, guiding the career of James 'Lights Out' Toney. Under Kallen's management Toney defeated Michael Nunn for the IBF middleweight belt in 1991, an event that was fictionalized in the 2004 film 'Against the Ropes,' in which Kallen was portrayed by Meg Ryan. She is the author of the book *Hit Me With Your Best Shot* and continues to manage fighters.

DR. JACK KEVORKIAN

The hugely controversial Dr. Jack Kevorkian rose to international fame in the 1990s for openly practicing physician-assisted euthanasia. Kevorkian claimed, from 1990 to 1998, to have assisted in 130 such suicides, despite having his medical license revoked in 1991. In his fifth and final trial in 1999, representing himself for the first time, the Pontiac native was convicted of second-degree murder and subsequently sent to prison. He was paroled in 2007. The son of Armenian immigrants, the University of Michigan-trained Kevorkian was also a skilled painter and musician, particularly fond of Bach. He passed away from complications arising from kidney and respiratory problems on June 3, 2011, shortly after being photographed and interviewed for this book. His tombstone bears the inscription: 'He sacrificed himself for everyone's rights.'

WAYNE KRAMER

As one of the original guitarists for Detroit rock band MC5, Wayne Kramer casts one of the longest shadows in all of rock 'n' roll. Founded by Kramer, fellow guitarist Fred 'Sonic' Smith, singer Rob Tyner, bassist Michael Davis, and drummer Dennis Thompson, MC5 would, in their brief original incarnation, release three of the most influential records of its era: 1969's 'Kick Out the Jams,' recorded live at their home base of the Grande Ballroom, 1970's 'Back in the USA,' and 1971's 'High Time.' Combining expansive musicianship that included elements of psychedelic rock and free jazz into one high-octane cocktail, MC5 was, along with fellow Detroit rockers The Stooges, among the originators of the punk-rock sound. Though MC5 fell apart due to internal pressures in the early '70s, after Tyner passed away in 1991 the surviving members came together for a tribute for his family. Beginning in 2003 they would occasionally tour with guest vocalists, though Davis passed away in 2012. Kramer kept a relatively low profile from the time of MC5's disbandment until the '90s, when he began releasing a string of critically acclaimed solo albums, as well as writing scores for many films and television shows.

ELMORE LEONARD
One of America's most celebrated writers, Elmore Leonard is the author of 45 novels. Beginning his career writing Westerns, he transitioned to thrillers as the Western market dried up, subsequently enjoying success with such classics as *Glitz*, *Bandits*, *Touch*, *Freaky Deaky*, *Killshot*, *Get Shorty*, *Rum Punch*, and *Out of Sight*. The many film and television adaptations of his work have been equally well-received; popular favorites include '3:10 to Yuma,' 'Get Shorty,' 'Jackie Brown,' 'Be Cool,' 'Out of Sight,' and the current FX series 'Justified.' Three of Leonard's books have been nominated for the Edgar Allan Poe Award by the Mystery Writers of America, and he was presented with the Mystery Writers Grand Master Award in 1992. His most recent book is 2012's *Raylan*.

SENATOR CARL LEVIN
Carl Levin is the longest-serving senator in Michigan history. Elected to the Senate in 1979, he won re-election for the sixth time in 2008. A Democrat, he is chairman of the Senate Armed Services Committee and chairman of the Senate Permanent Subcommittee on Investigations. A champion of the manufacturing sector, Levin is also known for his support of environmental causes, his opposition to the 2003 invasion of Iraq, his legislation against abusive credit card practices, and leading the Senate investigation into the 2008 financial crisis. In 2006 he was named by *Time* magazine as one of America's top 10 senators.

PHILIP LEVINE
Perhaps the artist most identified with illuminating the struggles of factory life in 20th century Detroit, poet Philip Levine was the Poet Laureate of the United States from 2011 to 2012. Born in 1928, he was educated at Central High School, then Wayne University. He would soon head West for educational and teaching opportunities, but it was the experiences of his youth in Detroit and his time spent working in factories that would inform his most celebrated work. A teacher at California State University, Fresno, for more than 30 years before retiring from teaching in 1992, he now divides his time between Fresno and Brooklyn. In 1991 he received the National Book Award For Poetry for his collection *What Work Is*, and, in 1995, won the Pulitzer Prize for Poetry for *The Simple Truth*.

NICKLAS LIDSTRÖM
In his 20-year career with the Detroit Red Wings, Nicklas Lidström won four Stanley Cups, seven James Norris Memorial Trophies for best defensive player in the NHL, and was voted into 11 All Star Games. The captain of the Red Wings from 2006 through his retirement in 2012, he is in the opinion of many experts the greatest defenseman of his generation. Lidström was with Detroit his entire NHL career and played more games as a Red Wing than any player except Gordie Howe. A native of Västerås, Sweden, he is the first European-born and trained NHL captain ever to win the Stanley Cup. He was named 'Player of the Decade' by both *The Sporting News* and *Sports Illustrated* magazines in 2009.

SYD MEAD
Syd Mead is a leading futurist designer. After graduating from the Art Center School in 1959, Mead was hired at Ford's Advanced Styling Center, where he worked on concept cars. He left Ford after two years to take on independent projects for companies such as U.S. Steel, Celanese, and Atlas Cement. In 1970 he launched Syd Mead Inc., in Detroit, where he worked with clients such as Philips of Holland. Beginning in the late '70s, Hollywood came calling, enlisting Mead's help in dreaming up futuristic landscapes for science fiction movies such as 'Blade Runner,' 'Tron,' '2010,' 'Short Circuit,' 'Aliens,' 'Time Cop,' 'Johnny Mnemonic,' and, most recently, 'Mission: Impossible III.' His love for transportation design never faded, though, and Mead continues to envision designs for such vehicles as solar-powered unicycles, cars, luxury yachts, cruise ships and jet interiors—including a 727 for the Sultan of Brunei, a 747 for King Fahd of Saudi Arabia, and a 747 for the Sheik of Oman.

TED NUGENT
The Motor City Mad Man, Uncle Ted, The Nuge—whatever one calls him, Ted Nugent is one of the great gonzo guitar heroes. First breaking through with his band The Amboy Dukes and their psychedelic hit 'Journey to the Center of the Mind' in 1968, Nugent would go on to become one of the biggest stadium rock acts of the '70s. Frequently named among the most skilled guitar players in rock history for his virtuoso, hard-edged playing style, his concerts became known for epic performances of anthems like 'Stranglehold,' 'Cat Scratch Fever,' and 'Dog Eat Dog.' He was the top-grossing tour act in the world in 1977, 1978, and 1979. Nugent's success continued in the '80s and '90s with super-group Damned Yankees, particularly with the 1990 hit 'High Enough' and, in 1995, as a solo artist with hunting paean 'Fred Bear.' All told, Nugent sold more than 40 million albums from 1967 to 2009. An avid outdoorsman and hunter, he has also hosted a number of radio and television shows centered around the great outdoors. On July 4, 2008, he celebrated his 6,000th live performance at the DTE Energy Theater.

IGGY POP
'The godfather of punk,' Iggy Pop first rose to fame with iconic Detroit rock band The Stooges. Fast, raw, and with a wholly original sound, the band's first three albums, 1969's 'The Stooges,' 1970's 'Fun House,' and 1973's 'Raw Power' are considered to be among rock's most influential recordings. Together with fellow Detroit rockers MC5, The Stooges are often credited with laying the foundation for punk rock. Born James Osterberg in 1947, Pop is known for delivering one of the most energetic live performances in music. He has also enjoyed a successful career as a solo artist; post-Stooges hits include 'Real Wild Child,' 'Candy,' 'Lust for Life,' and 'China Girl,' the latter two the results of a longtime collaboration with David Bowie. Pop re-formed The Stooges with original members Ron and Scott Asheton in 2003, also releasing a new record, 'The Weirdness.' While Ron Asheton passed away in 2009, the group continues to tour, with original guitarist James Williamson recently rejoining the lineup. The Stooges were inducted into the Rock and Roll Hall of Fame in 2010.

DICK PURTAN
A favorite Detroit on-air morning personality for more than 45 years, Dick Purtan has routinely been named the city's top DJ by nearly every local publication. Known for his comedic commentary, wit and the 'Purtan's People' cast of characters, he is also the driving force behind one of the city's most successful charity fundraisers, The Dick Purtan Salvation Army Bed & Bread Club Radiothon. In its more than 23 years the annual radiothon has raised $24 million for the Salvation Army's Bed & Bread program. Purtan has received numerous local and national awards for his work, including the industry's top honor, The National Association of Broadcaster's MARCONI Award in 1993. He retired from the airwaves in 2010.

DELLA REESE
Born Delloreese Patricia Early, Della Reese is a singer, actress and minister. First gaining attention at the age of 13 touring with gospel artist Mahalia Jackson, Reese later won a weeklong engagement at Detroit's Flame Show Bar. Due to her popularity, the manager ended up retaining her for 18 weeks. She subsequently signed her first recording contract with Jubilee Records in 1953. A steady stream of hits with Jubilee, then RCA, came over the following decades, including 'And That Reminds Me,' 'Don't You Know?,' 'Not One Minute More,' and 'Someday (You'll Want Me to Want You).' Concurrently pursuing acting, Reese appeared in films such as 'Harlem Nights' and, in 1994, was cast in the leading role of Tess in CBS' 'Touched By An Angel,' in which she appeared until 2003. Reese is the founder of the Understanding Principles for Better Living Church in Los Angeles.

MARTHA REEVES

Discovered by a Motown producer while performing at Detroit's Twenty Grand club in 1961, Martha Reeves would go on to become one of Motown's biggest acts. With her group The Vandellas, Reeves rose to international stardom in 1963 with '(Love is Like a) Heatwave.' The following year, Martha and the Vandellas released what came to be their signature song, 'Dancing in the Street,' which went to No. 2 on the Billboard Hot 100. In 2004, Martha and the Vandellas were named to *Rolling Stone* magazine's list of 'The 100 Greatest Artists of All Time,' and, in 2011, both 'Dancing in the Street' and 1965's 'Nowhere to Run' were named to the '500 Greatest Songs of All Time' in *Rolling Stone*. From 1963 to 1972 the Vandellas had 26 hits. They were inducted into the Rock and Roll Hall of Fame in 1995. A lifelong Detroiter, Reeves served on the Detroit City Council from 2005 to 2009.

CLAUDETTE ROBINSON

Named 'The First Lady of Motown' by Berry Gordy, Claudette Rogers Robinson was a member of The Miracles from 1957 to 1972, and the first woman signed to a Motown-affiliated label. Originally joining the group to replace her brother, Emerson Rogers, at Smokey Robinson's request after Rogers went into the Army, she sang with The Miracles on Motown's first million-selling record, 'Shop Around,' as well as classic hits like 'You've Really Got a Hold On Me,' 'Ooo Baby Baby,' 'The Tracks of My Tears,' 'The Tears of a Clown,' 'Going to a Go-Go,' and 'I Second That Emotion,' to name a few. One could say it was a family affair: Her cousin is fellow Miracle Bobby Rogers and, from 1959-1986, she was married to Smokey Robinson, who penned 'My Girl' for her. Claudette and Smokey have two children together, Berry William Borope Robinson and Tamla Claudette Robinson. She continues to tour, record and occasionally perform with The Miracles. She was inducted with The Miracles into the Rock and Roll Hall of Fame in 2012.

SHAUN ROBINSON

As a weekend co-anchor and correspondent for entertainment news show 'Access Hollywood,' Emmy Award-winning journalist Shaun Robinson can regularly be seen interviewing Hollywood's biggest stars. A graduate of Cass Tech and Spelman College in Atlanta, Robinson began her on-air career at Detroit's WGPR-62 before moving on to markets in Milwaukee, Austin, and Miami. As an actress Robinson has appeared in such films as 'Bruce Almighty' and 'America's Sweethearts,' as well as on television shows such as 'Law & Order.' She is the author of the 2009 book *Exactly As I Am: Celebrated Women Share Candid Advice with Today's Girls on What it Takes to Believe in Yourself*.

SMOKEY ROBINSON

Smokey Robinson is one of the 20th century's most celebrated artists. A driving force behind the success of Motown as a performer, songwriter and executive, he first began collaborating with Berry Gordy in 1958. As the lead singer and primary songwriter for The Miracles, which he founded in 1955, Robinson's high tenor became one of America's most distinctive instruments. Beginning in 1960 The Miracles recorded classic after classic with Robinson-penned tunes such as 'Shop Around,' 'You've Really Got a Hold On Me,' 'Ooo Baby Baby,' 'The Tracks of My Tears,' 'Going to a Go-Go,' 'The Tears of a Clown,' which he wrote with Stevie Wonder, and 'I Second That Emotion.' Robinson also wrote many hits for other Motown acts, including 'The Way You Do the Things You Do,' 'My Girl,' and 'Get Ready' for The Temptations; 'Ain't That Peculiar' for Marvin Gaye; and 'My Guy' for Mary Wells. Heavily involved in the recruitment of talent and production since Motown's inception, he served as its vice president from 1961 until 1988 when it was sold to MCA. After retiring from The Miracles in 1972 Robinson enjoyed solo success with hits like 'Just to See Her,' 'Cruisin',' 'Baby That's Backatcha,' and 'Being With You.' He has received the Grammy Living Legend Award, the NARAS Lifetime Achievement Award, Kennedy Center Honors, and the National Medal of Arts Award. He was inducted into the Rock and Roll Hall of Fame in 1987.

MITCH RYDER

Mitch Ryder and the Detroit Wheels came screaming out of the gates in the mid-'60s with a 100-mph live show and a grinding, hard-edged take on classics like 'Jenny Take a Ride!,' 'Devil With a Blue Dress On,' and 'Good Golly Miss Molly.' Ryder, born William Levise Jr. in Hamtramck in 1945, formed The Wheels in 1964 after singing in a series of other bands, and was barely out of his teens when The Wheels hit it big. Signed to DynoVoice Records, their success was responsible for creating national interest in Detroit rock bands and the subsequent signing of what would come to be many of the city's most successful groups. Their real legacy, though, is their tough, inimitably Detroit sound, responsible for influencing legions of Detroit rock acts to come. A solo artist since the late '60s, Ryder released his most recent album, 'The Promise,' in 2012.

BARRY SANDERS

Barry Sanders is one of the greatest running backs of all time. After winning the Heisman Trophy his junior year of college at Oklahoma State, Sanders was drafted by the Detroit Lions with the third overall pick in 1989. That season he rushed for 1,470 yards and was named the 1989 NFL AP Offensive Rookie of the Year. In a 10-year career with the Lions, Sanders rushed for more than 1,000 yards every year, was named to the All-Pro team every year, was a four-time NFL rushing champion, a two-time AP NFL Offensive

Player of the Year, and was named to the 1990s NFL All-Decade Team. His banner year came in 1997 when he rushed for 2,053 yards and gained another 305 yards on 33 catches for 2,358 combined yards gained, and was named the league's Most Valuable Player. By the time Sanders retired in 1998 he held nearly every Lions' rushing record and numerous all-time NFL records. He was inducted into the Pro Football Hall of Fame in 2004.

JOHN SINCLAIR

John Sinclair is a poet, musician, writer, founding member of the White Panther Party, marijuana advocate, and one-time manger of Detroit rock band the MC5. In 1969 Sinclair was arrested in Detroit for giving two joints to an undercover policewoman. His subsequent 10-year prison sentence sparked national outrage, resulting in the John Sinclair Freedom Rally at Ann Arbor's Crisler Arena in 1971—a benefit that featured performances from a number of artists, including John Lennon, who also wrote a song titled 'John Sinclair,' Yoko Ono, Stevie Wonder, Archie Shepp, and Pete Seeger, while speakers included Allen Ginsberg, Abbie Hoffman, and Bobby Seale. Sinclair was released from prison three days later, when the Michigan Supreme Court ruled the state's marijuana laws unconstitutional. Today he is based in Amsterdam, where he broadcasts his Internet radio station radiofreeamsterdam.com.

EMANUEL STEWARD

Among the greatest trainers in the history of boxing, Emanuel Steward, who passed away shortly after the completion of this book, coached more than 30 world champions. A winner of the 1963 National Golden Gloves amateur tournament, Steward was employed as an electrician at Detroit Edison in the early '70s when he began training kids at the Kronk Recreation Center in southwest Detroit. He soon transformed the unknown rec center into one of the world's most famous boxing gyms, and a veritable championship factory: Detroit kids trained by Steward from scratch to world champions include Tommy Hearns, Hilmer Kinty, Milton McCrory, Steve McCrory, Duane Thomas, and Jimmy Paul. His talents increasingly in demand as the years went on, he was recruited by such fighters as Oscar de la Hoya, Julio César Chávez, Lennox Lewis, Naseem Hamed, Evander Holyfield, and Wladimir Klitschko to help perfect their game. As a longtime commentator on HBO Boxing, Steward was a familiar face to millions of Americans. He was inducted into the International Boxing Hall of Fame in 1996.

ANNA SUI

Known for her hip, feminine looks, Anna Sui is one of America's most renowned fashion designers. A native of West Bloomfield, she studied at Parsons The New School For Design. After graduating, Sui worked for several labels before striking out on her own in the early '80s. Encouraged by friends such as photographer Steven Meisel, she had her first runway show in 1991. The show was extremely well received, garnering a great deal of international press, and a deal with Japanese distributor Isetan followed. Soon, her clothes were available at department stores and freestanding Anna Sui boutiques around the world. Today, her line also includes shoes, cosmetics, fragrances, and accessories. In 2009 she received the industry's highest honor, the Council of Fashion Designers of America Geoffrey Beene Lifetime Achievement Award.

LILY TOMLIN
Raised on the corner of Byron and Hazelwood at the D'Elce apartment building, Lily Tomlin is one of the great comedians of her era. Honing her skills on the stand-up circuit after graduating from Cass Tech and studying at Wayne State, Tomlin's big breakthrough came when she joined the cast of 'Laugh-In' in 1969. It was on that show that America fell in love with many of her characters, including telephone operator Ernestine, philosophical 5-and-a-half-year-old Edith Ann, prudish Mrs. Judith Beasley, Susie the Sorority Girl, and The Consumer Advocate Lady. Tomlin's 1971 comedy album 'This is a Recording,' featuring the recorded calls of Ernestine, is the highest-charting album ever made by a female comedian, and won that year's Grammy for Best Comedy Recording. As an actress she has starred in such films as 'Nashville,' 'Nine to Five,' 'All of Me,' 'Short Cuts,' and 'A Prairie Home Companion,' as well as on TV shows such as 'Murphy Brown,' 'The West Wing' and 'Desperate Housewives.' Tomlin was featured on the cover of *Time* magazine for her 1977 one-woman show 'Appearing Nitely,' for which she won a Lifetime Achievement Tony Award, and in 1986 won another Tony, for Best Actress in a Play, for her show 'The Search For Signs of Intelligent Life in the Universe.'

JAMES TONEY
Employing an old-school style he credits to late Detroit trainer Bill Miller, James Toney is one of the greatest pound-for-pound boxers of his generation. A three-time world champion, he holds wins over such notable fighters as Michael Nunn, Mike McCallum, Iran Barkley, Vassily Jirov and Evander Holyfield. His relationship with manager Jackie Kallen, who is also featured in this book, was dramatized in the 2004 film 'Against the Ropes.' Toney has twice been named *Ring* magazine's Fighter of the Year and is considered a shoo-in for induction into the International Boxing Hall of Fame upon eligibility.

JOHN VARVATOS
Largely inspired by the aesthetic of Detroit bands like The Stooges and MC5, menswear designer John Varvatos launched his eponymous line in 2000. The Allen Park native's elegant, masculine looks were an immediate hit and soon picked up by the country's top department stores and boutiques. Varvatos has twice been awarded the Council of Fashion Designers of America Menswear Designer of the Year Award, in 2001 and 2005. Today, his line has expanded to include accessories, footwear, eyewear, watches, and fragrances. Bringing his garage rock roots full circle, in 2008 he established a John Varvatos boutique in the space where legendary punk club CBGB was once located. There he often showcases the country's top rock acts for live performances. He currently hosts the show 'Fashion Star' on NBC.

DON WAS
Born Don Fagenson in 1952, Don Was first came to prominence in the 1980s as part of experimental pop group Was (Not Was) with David Was, aka David Weiss. Known for their eclectic, funky sound, the group enjoyed success with hits like 'Walk the Dinosaur' and 'Spy in the House of Love.' In 1989 Was enjoyed a major breakthrough as a producer for other artists with the multi-platinum Bonnie Raitt classic 'Nick of Time.' He's since gone on to produce commercially and critically successful records for many of the world's great artists, including Bob Dylan, The Rolling Stones, Ringo Starr, Elton John, Stevie Nicks, Brian Wilson, and Bob Seger. Was won the Grammy Award for Producer of the Year in 1995.

VERONICA WEBB
Veronica Webb was the first African-American model to receive a major cosmetic contract, becoming a spokesperson for Revlon in 1992. Webb graduated from the Waldorf School in Indian Village before moving to New York to study at Parsons The New School For Design. She was quickly discovered while working as a cashier at a store in SoHo. Appearing in editorials for such magazines as *Elle*, *Vogue*, *Glamour*, and *Details*, she was instrumental in breaking down doors in the fashion industry in the '90s, advancing the cause of equal pay and opportunity for models of all ethnic backgrounds. Webb did some of her most memorable work with such giants of fashion as Steven Meisel, Bruce Weber, Azzedine Alaïa, and Isaac Mizrahi. As an actress she has appeared in such movies as 'Jungle Fever,' 'Malcolm X,' and 'For Love or Money,' and as a presenter co-hosted the first season of Bravo's 'Tim Gunn's Guide to Style.'

JACK WHITE
One of the great musical visionaries of his generation, Jack White was the driving force behind iconic rock band the White Stripes. White was raised in southwest Detroit and attended Cass Tech. In 1997 he formed the White Stripes with drummer Meg White. Developing a heavily blues-influenced, stripped-down sound, the White Stripes would go on to release some of the era's most memorable rock albums, including their self titled debut, 'De Stijl,' 'White Blood Cells,' 'Elephant,' 'Get Behind Me Satan,' and 'Icky Thump.' Outside of the White Stripes, White has enjoyed success performing with old friends Brendan Benson, Jack Lawrence, and Patrick Keeler as the Raconteurs, as well as with Alison Mosshart, Dean Fertita, and Jack Lawrence in the Dead Weather. In 2009 he founded Third Man Records, a label that has quickly gained a reputation as a leader in vinyl. He's produced more than 120 records in less than three years, working with artists as varied as Jerry Lee Lewis, the Smoke Fairies, Wanda Jackson, Black Milk, and Stephen Colbert. To date White has won nine Grammys in seven different categories. In April 2012 he released his debut solo album, 'Blunderbuss.'

ALLEE WILLIS
A genre-hopping phenom, songwriter Allee Willis has sold more than 50 million records. Her hits include 'September' and 'Boogie Wonderland,' both performed by Earth, Wind & Fire; 'What Have I Done to Deserve This?' performed by The Pet Shop Boys; 'Lead Me On,' performed by Maxine Nightingale; and 'I'll Be There For You,' perhaps better known as the theme from the TV show 'Friends,' performed by The Rembrandts. In 1985 Willis received a Grammy for Best Soundtrack for 'The Neutron Dance,' performed by The Pointer Sisters and featured in 'Beverly Hills Cop.' Like that film's producer, Jerry Bruckheimer, who is also featured in this book, Willis is a graduate of Mumford High, though the two didn't know each other as students. Most recently she co-wrote the music to the Broadway show 'The Color Purple.'

MARY WILSON
Mary Wilson is a founding member of The Supremes, and the only member of the group to remain in the lineup through its entire two-decade existence. Jokingly dubbed 'the no-hit Supremes' by their Motown contemporaries after the relatively tepid reception of their first record, 1962's 'Meet the Supremes,' beginning in 1964 the trio of Mary Wilson, Diana Ross, and Florence Ballard went on a chart-topping streak matched only in the history of popular music by The Beatles, scoring five consecutive national No. 1 hits: 'Where Did Our Love Go,' 'Baby Love,' 'Come See About Me,' 'Stop! In the Name of Love,' and 'Back in My Arms Again.' The most successful Motown act of all, The Supremes scored 33 Top 40 hits between 1964 and 1976, including 12 national No. 1 singles. Wilson continued to perform and record with the group, with a rotating lineup of singers, long after Ross and Ballard were gone, delivering The Supremes' final performance at London's Theatre Royal on June 12, 1977. She is the author of two best-selling books, 1986's *Dreamgirl: My Life as a Supreme*, and 1990's *Supreme Faith*. The two were combined into a single volume, *Dreamgirl & Supreme Faith: My Life as a Supreme*, in 2000. In 1988 she accepted a Lifetime Achievement Award on behalf of The Supremes upon their induction into the Rock and Roll Hall of Fame. Wilson continues to tour and record as a solo artist, and is involved in a wide variety of humanitarian causes.